D0205752

History,
Historians,
and the
Dynamics of Change

WILLIAM A. GREEN

HISTORY,
HISTORIANS,
AND THE
DYNAMICS OF CHANGE

PRAEGER

Westport, Connecticut
London

Library of Congress Cataloging-in-Publication Data

Green, William A., 1935-
   History, historians, and the dynamics of change / William A.
Green.
     p. cm.
   ISBN 0-275-93901-4. — ISBN 0-275-93902-2 (pbk.)
   1. History—Methodology. 2. Social change. I. Title.
D16.G78   1993
902—dc20   92-26023

British Library Cataloguing in Publication Data is available.

Library of Congress Catalog Card Number: 92-26023
ISBN: 0-275-93901-4
     0-275-93902-2 (pbk.)

First published in 1993

Praeger Publishers, 88 Post Road West, Westport, CT 06881
An imprint of Greenwood Publishing Group, Inc.

Printed in the United States of America

The paper used in this book complies with the
Permanent Paper Standard issued by the National
Information Standards Organization (Z39.48-1984).

10 9 8 7 6 5 4 3 2 1

To my parents

Contents

Introduction

This is a book about history and about some of the great historians of our century. It was undertaken to relieve a void in my own historical training. The book is presented in hope that it will illuminate aspects of the historian's enterprise for others. It is addressed to reasonably sophisticated undergraduate and graduate students as well as others who seek insight into the structure of historical knowledge and the theoretical formulations upon which contemporary historians base their work. It is hoped that the book will have value for history faculty at various academic levels—for people like myself who emerged from years of formal university education with little training in the structure of history, the history of historical writing, or the philosophy of history.

The book emerged by way of diversion. I was engaged in preliminary reading on a project involving the economic integration of the Atlantic world in the early modern period. To my distress, I discovered that I was operating without any well-formulated understanding about how change occurred at the macrohistorical level, and I was chagrined to find that many of the historians I was reading were no better informed than I. My research focused on the "transitional" period between what we have defined as the Middle Ages and early modern times. If the Western world was in transition, then there had to be some extraordinary dynamic at work in European civilization. But what was it? Different historians had entirely different opinions on the topic, and all too many demonstrated no consistency in their analyses, offering one type of causal explanation for one set of changes and a second for others without ever attempting to integrate those explanations into an over-arching model for change. My confusion led to frustration; with some reluctance, I set aside my main project—ever so briefly, of course—in order to inform myself, as best I could, about the prevailing theories of change that should, or could, guide a historian studying the period between the Middle Ages and the Industrial

Revolution. In time, this diversion became a passion, and the original project came to rest in a file drawer.

The book is divided into three main parts, plus a summary. The first introduces readers to the many pitfalls of historical writing and to questions about what we can and should learn from the past. While it emphasizes the limitations of our discipline, it attempts to alert readers to the importance of sound theory. One of the most important and least debated aspects of historical theory is periodization. Chapter 2 discusses the importance of periodization and the historical evolution of our current mode of periodization. It raises the question, which is revived in the final chapter, whether the prevailing mode should be overhauled.

Part II of the book addresses the chief theories that historians in this century have used to explain the process of change in European history. Part III extends the range of theoretical concern to world history. Part IV draws together many threads that emerge throughout the work and offers recommendations on specific theoretical issues. The book consistently draws its examples and seeks reference points from the period between the eleventh and eighteenth centuries, chiefly in Europe.

I am grateful to the Rockefeller Foundation and to the American Philosophical Society for support of my research. Holy Cross College, once again, has provided me time and resources to pursue serious study and writing. I am very grateful to my wife, Karin, for her continuing encouragement and understanding. Two outstanding students, Kathleen Hamel and Richard Wareing, offered me vital help on Marxist historiography and the demographic school of historians, respectively. My special thanks are owed to Ellyn McNeil, who has generously given many hours on the word processor and provided invaluable assistance in the compilation of bibliography.

In hope that this book conveys a sense of the pleasure as well as the mystery of learning, that it offers some wisdom, some stimulation, and some good judgment, I dedicate it to my parents, whose wisdom, stimulation, judgment, and love have been among the abiding treasures of my life.

Part I
History and the Historian

1

History: The Elusive Quarry

Those who cannot remember the past are condemned to repeat it.
George Santayana

This maxim from the pen of George Santayana boasts an ancient pedigree. The greatest of the classical Greek historians, Thucydides, considered history a guide to conduct, a medium by which thoughtful men could acquire wisdom through example. For Christian writers of the Middle Ages, history revealed God's truths. Voltaire, the eighteenth-century philosopher-historian, contended that knowledge of the past enabled the living to escape the errors of the dead. More recently, England's leading military historian asserted that history "shows us what to *avoid*" even if it cannot teach us what to do.[1] For all such thinkers, history is profoundly useful. It provides a rational ordering of human experience. It satisfies humankind's insatiable need to know whence we have come. For the deeply initiated, it affords the capacity for intelligent prediction.

Such optimism, though comforting, requires qualification. What happens in history, happens once. Each historical event involves a vast array of human and physical factors that cannot be reproduced in the same combination a second time. No historian can account for the totality of forces that have influenced past events, nor are historians able to test hypotheses in the way that physical scientists can endlessly re-run the same laboratory experiment under controlled conditions. Since historians cannot verify their private interpretations of past events, their work is always subject to attack by other scholars possessing contrary evidence, additional evidence, or a different range of vision.

In view of the kaleidoscopic diversity of educated historical opinion, one must be cautious about Santayana's maxim. Historians perpetually engage in the search for truth, but what they seek is an endlessly elusive quarry. Different people perceive the "logic" of history in different ways, and different perceptions occasion different conclusions concerning what constitutes appropriate human conduct. In spite of these uncertainties, historians continue to encounter the past with a driving will to reduce it to manageable order, to harness its spirit, and to reconstruct relationships—in effect, to wrench order from chaos and afford meaning to the human experience. The purpose of this first chapter is to examine major problems in the structure of historical studies and to identify the most notorious pitfalls that all serious students must encounter in reading and writing about the past.

SUBJECTIVITY

Every historian is a prisoner of his or her own time, language, and culture. "It is impossible," wrote Gerhard Benecke, "for anyone living today to hear early music with the ears of those who first heard it, and it is idle to pretend otherwise."[2] When we examine earlier forms of agriculture or industry or early social institutions, we advance upon them with an elaborate body of preconceptions derived from our contemporary understanding of these things. This breeds *anachronism* in history, the imposition of ideas or conditions upon past peoples who could neither have shared those ideas nor recognized such conditions. Because we live in a highly complex and diverse economic society, we are inclined to foist modern economic incentives on earlier peoples. We often assume, for example, that medieval traders possessed a degree of economic sophistication that, in reality, was beyond their understanding and inconsistent with their collective mindset, as indeed we presume that such traders had options and choices of which they were certainly ignorant. It is only with the greatest of effort that twentieth-century students can comprehend a pre-industrial value system that allowed hospitals to be adorned with valuable pieces of art while they suffered chronic shortages of beds. The time warp is inescapable. However we try, we cannot cross the barriers of value and perception that separate us from our distant progenitors.

The values we share in our own time will be reflected in the type of history we write. During the nineteenth century, a time of ardent nationalism in Europe, diplomatic and military history enjoyed wide acclaim. In the late twentieth century, social history commands center stage. Traditional military history with its emphasis on human valor and the nobility of arms has virtually slipped from sight. Diplomats and statesmen of the last century who meticulously preserved their personal papers and correspondence in the certain knowledge that historians would one day comb them for every nuance would be appalled to discover that many of today's scholars are at least as interested in scattered scraps of information bearing witness to the lives of uneducated handloom weavers or rebellious peasants.

When historians view the past from the underside of society, the history they write may bear little resemblance to that of historians who take an elitist perspective. Until recently, intellectual history involved the study of great thinkers, but in response to the remarkable achievements of cultural anthropologists and in keeping with our growing collectivist mentality, intellectual historians have begun to concentrate on the study of mass movements and of the myths and symbols that have provided unity and coherence to popular culture. In the past, histories of the Italian Renaissance, like those of modern European empires, have concentrated on elite populations, their problems and their creative endeavors. The very concept of "the Renaissance" might not have occurred to historians had they persistently viewed the culture of Italy in the fifteenth and sixteenth centuries from the democratic perspective of the masses.

Subjectivity is most evident in our use, or abuse, of language. Governments come and go; economies experience episodes of prosperity and depression. In perceiving these changes, we commonly ascribe biological properties to them. Civilizations "decay" and "die." Nations become "sick" and "degenerate." Yet, argues the sociologist Robert Nisbet, "No one has ever seen a civilization die."[3] Such expressions are metaphorical.[4] They are also imprecise and misleading. Hayden White, an eminent philosopher of history, contends that historical writing is "an essentially *poetic* act."[5] History, he declares, is a product of philosophy—of the historian's own personal mindset, not of objective reality. It is created by historians who give expression to their poetic presuppositions through strategically chosen literary devices.

The idea that history is the mythological creation of historians is a central theme of modern structuralist thought. From their beginnings in

France in the 1960s, structuralist thinkers have extended their intellectual influence throughout the West. They challenge the very premises upon which historians presume to draw conclusions from so-called objective facts, denying the possibility that the real life of the past is capable of being comprehended or described. The past is but an "infinite regress of distorted representations," they argue, and historians must face up to the "artifices they employ" to give shape and substance to their work.[6]

Most historians reject the extreme implications of structuralist assertions. If history is to survive as an academic discipline, historians cannot abandon their empirical tradition. But, as the structuralists correctly observe, neither can historians escape the subjectivity of language. In order to communicate ideas above the most primitive level, historians must employ abstract generalizations. Expressions like feudalism, mercantilism, capitalism, bourgeoisie, the Scientific Revolution, the Renaissance, the Enlightenment, and the Middle Ages are grandiose abstractions created by scholars to provide common denominators for understanding. For all their utility, however, such terms offer wide latitude for misinterpretation. Social patterns in different periods and in different countries—even in separate sections of the same country—have been so varied that we can only employ the same general words for them at the risk of misapprehending reality.[7] This situation intensifies as historians gather distance either in time or cultural context from the object of their investigation. Occidental scholars writing on the Orient commonly impose conceptual patterns embedded in the abstract language of the West upon cultural patterns in which those patterns fit awkwardly or not at all. The problem is similar, if not so grave, for scholars who translate the life of eleventh-century Europe into the idiom of the twentieth century.

Even if we could agree on terminology, our problems would not be resolved. Many of the most common generalizations in history have assumed heavy ideological overtones. Marxist historians not only impart different meanings to the words "feudalism" and "capitalism" than non-Marxists, but the words themselves, like terms such as "bourgeoisie" and "proletariat," have become ideologically charged. When historians approach the past with personal lexicons of socially weighted terms, they carry a theory of history concealed in their vocabularies.

THEORY IN HISTORY

All historical theory is rife with subjectivity, but history as a study of society cannot proceed without theory. The raw material of the historian remains an atomized mass of assorted facts until it is screened and organized for the purpose of testing a hypothesis. Any hypothesis, however weakly formulated, represents some over-arching idea, some theory. It is theory that gives shape to history, just as it is the historian with his biased intellectual baggage and his particular orientation to the past who gives shape to theory. Only the most naive writers can still claim, as did the leading French medievalist of the late nineteenth century, "Tis not I who speaks, but History, which speaks through me."[8]

No large body of scholars has been more immune to the theoretical properties of their discipline than historians.[9] The main reason for this is the historian's preoccupation with unique phenomena. As a conscious practice, most historians work inductively—that is, they reason from the specific to the general. Having identified a subject for investigation, they plunge into the archives, turn over immense quantities of data in response to their hypotheses (which are often vaguely formulated), and then presume to draw conclusions based on this evidence. Because they concentrate on the singularity of each historical experience, they have no reason to develop elaborate methodological strategies for identifying uniformities in human behavior that might transcend the time and place of their particular studies.

This practice contrasts rather sharply with the approach of economists, sociologists, or political scientists. Such social scientists might agree that every event is unique, but they would probably add that no event is unique in all ways. Human beings are essentially what they have been for centuries, and it is reasonable, therefore, to suppose that similar stimuli operating upon people of similar disposition under similar conditions will, in all probability, generate similar forms of conduct. In daily life, this type of reasoning lends wisdom to the ordinary citizen. But in academic life, it has been the province of social scientists, not historians, to seek out regularities in human conduct as a basis for establishing laws of behavior that facilitate prediction. Of late, sociologists, anthropologists, and economists have invaded the historians' domain in increasing numbers, bringing with them a rich theoretical tradition and a diverse assortment of research methods initially designed to study contemporary society. Although such methods do not lend themselves to all, or even to most, historical questions, the emphasis that social scientists place on theory and their concurrent criticism of the theoretical confusion exhibited by traditional historians has, at long last, awakened the latter to the theoretical implications of their own work.

MODELLING

The most important contribution of social science to history is the analytical model. Models are explicit theoretical representations of the structure and function of social phenomena. As abstract mental constructs, they serve the student of society in the way that physical models serve engineers and architects. Just as urban architects build balsa wood models to represent networks of buildings, avenues, and subways, social scientists create conceptual models to aid them in explaining the structural relationships that give coherence to a social system, to its specific elements, or to whole congeries of social systems. The very term "social system" is an abstract concept. It presumes the existence of regularity and order over a particular body of people inhabiting a specific geographic space. A model of a social system attempts to delineate the complex nature of that social order, to comprehend its hierarchies, to identify linkages between critical elements, and to explain how the system experiences change. A famous example of this is Karl Marx's model of the nineteenth-century capitalist system. Marx defined the functional relationships of that system and identified the means by which it underwent change. But no model, whether the Marxian model or any other, provides a mirror image of reality. All models are approximations. All are born in the intuitive intelligence of their creators. None can possibly incorporate all the facts of history that bear upon social structure. But they can assist us in identifying categories, comprehending relationships, and perceiving historical processes with greater clarity.

Some historical work is particularly suited to modelling. Models are used most frequently and successfully in treating well-defined, fairly circumscribed problems where the data base is strong, but they are also useful in macrohistorical studies that examine the process of change across broad fronts. Not every historian will choose to create or choose to use explicit theoretical models. Nor should they. Humanist historians who prize the artistic qualities of their discipline and view the writing of history as the gradual unfolding of a story would consider the explicit declaration of theory and method associated with model building an intolerable intrusion upon good historical literature. This does not relieve such historians from considerations of social theory. Wherever the guiding theory of a work of history is not stated explicitly, it will manifest itself implicitly. Only by being alert to the theoretical implications of their scholarship can historians avoid the embarrassment of unwittingly incorporating several antagonistic theoretical positions in a single work.

If a concern for theory is essential to the historian, so too is an awareness of the limits of theory. Theory in history is derived both *deductively* and *inductively*. The deductive process involves reasoning from the general to the specific in that one draws conclusions concerning specific phenomena from general propositions. Inductive reasoning operates in reverse, drawing general conclusions from specific information. Deductive historical theory is most evident among philosophers of history in the tradition of Vico, Croce, Spengler, and Toynbee.[10] These thinkers have purported to explain the course of human history in sweeping cyclical or other terms although, by and large, their works often exhibit little basis in empirical research and no important bearing on historical reality. In contrast to such deductive theorists, most practicing historians perceive themselves as inductive scholars who closely examine their evidence before attempting to refine their theories. Nevertheless, *inductive reasoning cannot function independently of deduction*. Every historian approaches his or her evidence with an assortment of prejudices or presuppositions already intact. These presuppositions can be considered proto-theories, vague orientations consciously or unconsciously held, that await refinement and confirmation through the research process. At some point in that process, induction blends imperceptibly with deduction. Precepts are affirmed, and they serve as organizing principles for the assembly and sorting of additional data. Karl Marx performed a prodigious amount of detailed empirical research on his model of the capitalist economy, but it is impossible to determine from his work where induction ends and deduction begins. Elias Tuma claims that Marx's grand theory of history was essentially formulated *before* he pursued his extensive research and that his empirical studies merely brought "his model closer to reality than if he kept it an abstract theory."[11]

If Tuma is correct, Marx was operating in a manner not unlike that of modern social scientists. As a rule, they propound a general theory, draw a working hypothesis from the theory, then test the hypothesis through empirical research (the theory-hypothesis-data method). The risks of such a method are obvious. The existence of a firm guiding theory, deductively derived, will dispose the researcher, consciously or not, to select evidence that confirms his hypothesis. At the same time, he may be prone to overlook, perhaps even conceal, evidence that contradicts his theoretical position. For social scientists who focus on contemporary problems, the perils of manipulating or ignoring data are relatively great as a result of the public nature of much of their evidence, not to mention their need to achieve a certain level of predictability. For historians, research data is usually more private. They deal with events already passed for which no public test of predictability is possible. Most historians would agree that an unscrupulous or dogmatic researcher can find some evidence to support any theoretical proposition, however bizarre.

The noted Cambridge historian and historiographer, Geoffrey Elton, believes that the theory-hypothesis-data method when employed by historians merely reduces history to "a repository of examples selected or distorted to buttress [a theoretical] scheme."[12] Elton's criticism belies his preference for the inductive approach; but as we have observed, there can be no purely inductive process. The historian cannot approach his evidence without some underlying hypothesis, however vague, or without some personal values that will govern his analysis of data. Whether explicitly declared or implicitly held, deductive reasoning is an inextricable element of all historical analysis. The differences in orientation between Elton and the social scientists are differences of degree. Does the open, social-scientific declaration of theoretical premises produce a more or a less prejudicial approach to empirical research in history than an implicitly theoretical, more clearly inductive process?

Certainly Elton is justified in his claim that historians who engage in modelling are prone to *reify* their abstractions. Reification is the mental process by which abstract concepts are given the property of reality. One might contend, for example, that people's advocacy of the "rights of man" during the French Revolution was a product of the Enlightenment. Yet the Enlightenment had no power of production, no ability to give or to take. The Enlightenment is an organizing principle, an intellectual abstraction that seeks to encompass within a single term a congeries of eighteenth-century orientations and ideas. Abstractions are not realities. The writings of Thomas Paine or of Jean-Jacques Rousseau may have stimulated advocacy of the rights of man, but to give that power to the Enlightenment is to reify an abstraction.

Theoretical models should be seen as analytical tools. They should be tested against the facts and reshaped and revised to meet the demands of conflicting evidence. Since no model can accommodate all the contradictory facts of history, there is a limit to which anyone can revise his theory without undermining its logical integrity. When that point is reached, scholars are often tempted to advance from declaring their models merely "the best reasonable means" of explaining an aspect of human behavior to identifying their models with reality itself.

TELEOLOGY

The most troublesome pitfall for historians, particularly those engaged in formal modelling, is the teleological trap. A teleological explanation is one that assigns meaning to historical events in terms of the implications they might have for other events that follow them in chronological time. Stated differently, teleological explanations attribute significance to persons, institutions, or events in terms of some destiny toward which the historian believes history has moved or is moving. Again, we can take our example from Marx. The orthodox Marxian concept of history declares that human society must pass in stages from one level of development to another en route to a classless communist society. A common criticism of Marxist historiography, precisely the one expressed by Elton, is that Marxists are prone to judge the significance of all historical events exclusively in terms of the bearing they might have upon this preconceived evolutionary process.

Most teleological explanations are not occasioned by grand theory but by methodological strategies or by the methodological blunders that historians are often unaware they are committing. Because we know that the French Revolution erupted in 1789, we are prone to examine all events during the preceding era in terms of the effect they might have had upon the outbreak of the revolt. Clearly, in treating eighteenth-century France, our approach to the collection and classification of evidence as well as our analysis of the evidence we collect has been of a different order from what it would have been had we remained ignorant of 1789. Because we know what happened, we scrutinize with special care those developments that appear to have had bearing upon the revolution while neglecting those that did not. It is important to keep in mind, however, that the people who lived in France in 1780 and 1785 could not have known that a revolution would occur at the end of the decade. They thought their thoughts, made their choices, and took their actions in utter innocence of the impending event. As historians, should we weigh their motives and actions in terms of their own perceptions of the world they lived in, or should we shape their history in terms of the cataclysm that ultimately befell them?

We should do neither exclusively. A reasonable balance must be struck, but even those scholars who are genuinely committed to achieving such balance slip unawares into teleological traps, ascribing motives to the actions of human beings in light of historical knowledge that we possess but that the actors themselves could not have had. The creators of historical models, knowing how history has evolved, are particularly prone to weave taut teleological webs of causal interaction. It is all too easy to start at the end and work history backwards to the beginning, subordinating all things to the acknowledged end. In reality, people live their history from the beginning in perfect ignorance of the ends toward which they are moving.

FREE WILL VERSUS DETERMINISM

Because theoretical models emphasize social forces and regularities in human behavior, they tend to sublimate the free will of individuals. This is particularly true of macrohistorical models in which the role of individuals is swallowed up and rendered insignificant by the tidal flow of vast historical forces. The importance of individuals in shaping events lies at the heart of much of the antagonism between humanistic history and social science. Have figures like Luther or Columbus made a difference in the grand march of human affairs? Would their exploits, however notable, have been performed by someone else had they never seen the light of day? Before Luther, the unity of the Christian Church had been repeatedly threatened but never shattered.[13] Is it the case, then, that Luther's particular personality and genius were critical in determining when and how the ultimate fissure in Christianity occurred? Had Columbus not landed in the West Indies in 1492, others would shortly have discovered the New World. But would they have claimed it for Spain? And without the alluvial wealth of America, could Spain have sustained its position as Europe's greatest power in the second half of the sixteenth century? In similar fashion, it is reasonable to question whether German unification under the monarchical principle would have been conceivable as early as 1871 without Bismarck. Could the Nazi Party have gained and sustained power in Germany without Hitler? Could a successful revolution by the Bolsheviks in Russian have occurred without Lenin?

These questions are impossible to answer, but our sensibilities tell us that the will of specific individuals has made an important difference in history. How much difference? Perfect free will does not exist. The exercise of freedom is always qualified by the contextual conditions in which one has his being—the value system one embraces, the countervailing wills of people with whom one engages, and the particular circumstances in which one's life takes place.[14] Do individuals influence the course of history only in the short run, hastening or retarding processes that must inevitably come to pass? All historians grapple with this problem, and the conclusions they reach will influence the way they write history. But the scale of the problem itself obliges sober scholars to mediate cautiously between the role of individual actors and the power of the social forces that enveloped them.

Historians acknowledge the importance of individual will to the extent that they allow for *contingency*. Except for confirmed determinists, historians generally presume that what has happened in history (in the short term, at least) need not have happened, at least it need not have happened in the way that it did or at the time that it did. The importance of contingency in history is manifestly evident in controversies such as the one that probes the origins of World War I. Provoked by the war guilt clause of the Versailles treaty, which attributed all responsibility for the outbreak of the "Great War" to Germany and its allies, historians of many nations have repeatedly re-examined the causes of the war and the relative responsibility of the participating great powers. Their numerous efforts generally pivot on the assumption that this universal catastrophe—one that shredded the world order, facilitated the Bolshevik Revolution, and set the stage for a second, more costly world conflict—might have been avoided, localized, or moderated by the action of individuals. With few exceptions, studies of the origins of the war have focused on political and diplomatic figures.[15] It is the abiding characteristic of diplomatic history to view the past in terms of the contingencies confronted by statesmen. Every phase of the prewar drama is examined in light of the options available to the chief actors, and the assumption underlying this mode of analysis is that wiser or different individuals might have pursued a different course and thereby altered the destiny of humankind.[16]

Do we, at the end of the twentieth century, possess the power to preserve this planet, or are we led by inexorable forces to contaminate our living space through multiple forms of pollution or, even worse, to terminate history in nuclear holocaust? How much can the will of individuals affect these ultimate questions? We may never know with certainty, but there is reason to believe that groups of people as well as individual leaders consistently take rational actions on the basis of perceived dangers or discomforts, adjusting their behavior to avoid the impact of negative forces. Such adjustments usually befuddle the predictions of social scientists and occasion public rebuke of their work.[17]

The repeated inexactitude of social scientific predictions tempts humanistic historians to condemn the theoretical and methodological pretensions of their social science colleagues. But the shortcomings of social science should have only the most sobering implications for historians. Most social scientists work in broad daylight. The utility of their theories and the relevance of their calculations are perpetually being tested by contemporary behavior. Yet, despite their easy access to vast amounts of relatively reliable data and their intimate acquaintance with contemporary individuals and institutions, social scientists have great difficulty determining the laws of motion that govern contemporary society. How, then, can historians, who are frequently oblivious to theoretical and methodological principles and who write history by the seats of their pants, presume to unravel the more complex and difficult problems of the past with any degree of accuracy? Willard Quine has written of the natural sciences, "all is tentative, all admits to revision."[18] His point is doubly true for history. There is good history and bad history, good theory and bad theory. But there is no history without theory, and good history depends upon good theory.[19]

NOTES

1. B. H. Liddell Hart, *Why Don't We Learn from History?* (New York, 1971), p. 15.

2. Foreword to Hermann Kellenbenz, *The Rise of the European Economy* (New York, 1976), ix.

3. Robert A. Nisbet, *Social Change and History: Aspects of the Western Theory of Development* (New York, 1969), p. 3. For the most part, Nisbet is correct. However, in the case of American Indians, one might argue that within a single lifetime it was possible to witness the decay and virtual disappearance of a distinct culture.

4. Nisbet's point is well taken, although there are some cases, like North American Indian civilization, for which such language would not be wildly metaphorical.

5. Hayden White, *Metahistory: The Historical Imagination in Nineteenth-century Europe* (Baltimore and London, 1973), x.

6. In a highly controversial structuralist-Marxist analysis of pre-capitalist economic patterns, two British authors have resisted any involvement with empirical data in their attempt to evaluate Marxist concepts. See Barry Hindess and Paul Q. Hirst, *Pre-Capitalist Modes of Production* (London, 1975). Succinct statements on the impact of structuralist thinking in history appear in a symposium published in *History Workshop*, vols. 5–8 (1978–1979): see articles by Richard Johnson, Gavin Williams, Keith McClelland, Simon Clarke, and the editors themselves. Quoted phrases in the text of this book are taken from vol. 6 (1978): 2. For a stinging counterattack against the structuralist critique of empiricism, see E. P. Thompson, *The Poverty of Theory and Other Essays* (New York and London, 1978).

7. See Alfred Cobban's review of Charles Tilly, *The Vendée* (1964) in *History and Theory* 5 (1966): 201. For a fuller treatment of this problem and the historiography of the French Revolution, see Cobban, *The Social Interpretation of the French Revolution* (Cambridge, 1971), pp. 17–21.

8. Fustel de Coulanges, quoted in Harold T. Parker, "Some Concluding Observations," in Parker and Georg G. Iggers, eds., *International Handbook of Historical Studies: Contemporary Research and Theory* (Westport, Conn., 1979), p. 421.

9. In selecting insightful works from leading historians of the last two centuries for his excellent anthology, *Varieties of History from Voltaire to the Present* (Cleveland, 1956), Fritz Stern discovered that even the great historians have been "reluctant to articulate their views about history" or to identify their presuppositions. Many renowned historians, including Tocqueville and Maitland, had to be omitted from the anthology because at no place in their works had they left explicit statements of the essence of their historical thought. See Stern's introductory essay to the volume, p. 15.

10. For a general overview of these philosophers of history, see Joseph Maier, "Cyclical Theories," in Werner I. Cahnman and Alvin Boskoff, eds., *Sociology and History: Theory and Research* (New York, 1964), pp. 47–57.

11. Elias H. Tuma, *Economic History and the Social Sciences: Problems of Methodology* (Berkeley and Los Angeles, 1971), pp. 174–175.

12. G. R. Elton, *The Practice of History* (New York, 1967), p. 36.

13. We have the immediate pre-Reformation examples of Wyclif, Hus, the Waldensians, and the Albigensians.

14. Gordon Leff, *History and Social Theory* (University, Ala., 1969), pp. 35–37.

15. One important exception is Marc Ferro's *The Great War 1914–1918* (London, 1973), which explains developments in broad sociological terms.

16. In a witty and insightful assessment of his long life as a diplomatic historian, A. J. P. Taylor emphasized the importance of accident (the ultimate contingency) in history as an offset to *"les forces profondes."* A war between Germany and much of the rest of Europe was likely in the early twentieth century, he wrote, but "the actual war that broke out in 1914 would not have occurred as it did if Archduke Franz Ferdinand had not gone to Sarajevo on June 28 or even if his chauffeur had not taken a wrong turning." A. J. P. Taylor, "Accident Prone, or What Happened Next," *Journal of Modern History* 49 (1977): 1–18.

17. A classic example of this is a *Wall Street Journal* article entitled "Why Demographers Are Wrong Almost as Often as Economists," 29 January, 1985, p. 35.

18. Willard V. Quine, "The Scope and Language of Science," *British Journal for the Philosophy of Science* 8 (1957): 17, quoted in Peter D. McClelland, *Causal Explanation and Model Building in History, Economics, and the New Economic History* (Ithaca, 1975), p. 21.

19. The need for historians to cultivate a keener awareness of the theoretical foundations of their work should involve them in closer liaison with social science disciplines that are already steeped in theory. So argues Gareth Stedman Jones. However, he adds, historians should not consider these disciplines academic department stores where pre-tailored concepts can be secured to meet any specific requirement. This will only render them dependent. Much social science theory is inappropriate to history, and the indiscriminate shopper will likely wind up with theoretical merchandise that members of the dispensing discipline no longer prize. The time has come for historians to participate more fully in the formulation of the theoretical precepts that undergird their own studies: "theoretical work . . . is too important to be subcontracted to others." Gareth

Stedman Jones, "From Historical Sociology to Theoretical History," *British Journal of Sociology* 27 (1976): 295. This is an extremely valuable article on the relationship between sociology and history. Also see Raphael Samuel and Gareth Stedman Jones, "Sociology and History," *History Workshop* 1 (1976): 4–8.

2

The Framework of History

Two aspects of theory are particularly important for historians: propulsion and periodization. The first concerns the forces that promote change. The second involves mental architecture: the chronological framework within which we set our history. Since all periodization presumes a theory of change, these are linked theoretical properties.

Despite its importance, periodization may be the least scrutinized theoretical component of history. Scholars assert that history constitutes a seamless garment, but they cannot render the past intelligible until they subdivide it into manageable and coherent units of time. Periodization operates at two levels: individual and institutional. Individually, each writer chooses the chronological parameters for his or her work of history. Whether that work covers ten years or ten centuries, its beginning and ending dates are chosen because they coincide with significant watersheds that set the era of the study apart, provide it a composite character, and enable the writer to focus on particular aspects of the human experience. At the institutional level, historians in the Western world have adopted a tripartite form of periodization that separates the past into three vast compartments—ancient history, medieval history, and modern history—with epochal breaks at roughly A.D. 500 and A.D. 1500. These compartments are further subdivided for convenience and manageability. The Middle Ages are divided three ways—early, central, and later—with breaks around A.D. 1000 and A.D. 1300. The modern epoch is split into early and late modern, with a break falling at the end of the eighteenth century.

This chapter will concentrate on institutional periodization. When, why, how, and by whom was tripartite periodization adopted? What are its implications for historical thinking and writing?

Although periodization is founded on disciplined concepts of continuity and change, change occurs at different rates in different areas of human experience. It occurs quickly in politics, slowly in systems of value.[1] All aspects of human activity are interrelated: technology is affected by what happens in politics; religion is influenced by what happens in science. But the internal rhythms of science and religion, of politics and technology are different. Our judgment on periodization depends, therefore, upon the *priorities* we assign to different areas of human endeavor. For Hegel, history was the dialectical evolution of the *absolute idea*; for Marx, it was the dialectical unfolding of *modes of production*. For both, the structure of the model used to explain the process of change—the dialectic—was similar; but Hegel and Marx emphasized different aspects of human experience, and their periodization reflected those differences.[2]

Periodization is profoundly affected by social orientation. Should we emphasize a top-down or a bottom-up approach to past societies? Until recently, historians have focused on elite groups, and the circa 1500 medieval/modern watershed is partly a result of that. Were we to examine European history in terms of the longevity, labors, physical circumstances, and mentalities of ordinary men and women, we might conclude, as one French historian has done, that the dawn of a new epoch in Europe did not arrive until the eighteenth century.[3]

Any division of time, however meaningful, will cut and separate important on-going historical processes. The treatment accorded the bubonic plague by different groups of historians serves as a case in point. Descending upon Europe in the 1340s, the Black Death recurred continuously in pandemic proportions, remaining Europe's leading killer until the eighteenth century. Human devastation was heaviest in the early period, but the demographic, social, and psychological impact of the plague was profoundly felt for several centuries. Historians of the Middle Ages give it great attention. Scholars of the modern world frequently neglect it. The latters' time clock generally commences around 1500. They break into the epidemiological cycle at midstream, and with some exceptions they are largely oblivious to its monumental societal ramifications.

All periodization is arbitrary. All periodization is flawed. But some forms of periodization are more arbitrary and more flawed than others. More than any other aspect of historical theory, periodization resists change. Once firmly drawn and widely accepted, period frontiers can become intellectual straightjackets that profoundly affect our habits of mind—the way we retain images, make associations, and perceive the beginning, middle, and ending of things. Powerful vested interests inevitably arise to perpetuate accepted practices. Nowhere is the rigidifying power of periodization more evident than in the modern university. We staff departments of history, organize graduate training, and structure undergraduate curricula largely in terms of tripartite periodization. Textbooks reinforce this pattern,[4] and professional journals scrupulously adhere to standard epochal frontiers.[5] Faculty carefully partition the historical terrain to avoid intruding upon places and periods that "belong" to their colleagues. As a result, standard periods have become self-contained entities. Writers and publishers, teachers and students regard them as immutable features of the intellectual landscape, and this influences the way issues are identified and emphases applied.

In the main, two conceptual approaches have been used to justify period frontiers: (1) an *aggregate* approach, and (2) a *leading sector* approach. Aggregate theory identifies converging developments in several areas of human activity. Leading sector arguments focus upon one overwhelming source of change that exercises decisive pulling power on all others. Those advancing an aggregate view might contend that within several decades of 1500 the Ptolemaic perception of the universe was undermined; printing and gunpowder assumed wide importance; Columbus discovered America; the Portuguese opened a sea route to the Indies; the Protestant Reformation erupted; Constantinople fell to the Turks; and the monarchies of France, Spain, and England were consolidated. Together, it is argued, these events wrenched Western man sufficiently from the continuities of an earlier time to merit the establishment of an epochal frontier.

A proponent of the leading sector concept might argue instead that the discovery of America with its alluvial wealth; its effect upon the European power structure; its extraordinary impact on the intercontinental transfer of diseases, plants, and animals; and its influence on Europeans' perception of the physical world, philosophy, and religion catapulted the whole of Western society from one set of norms toward another. Both examples are *episodic* views of periodization wherein a single chance event (e.g., the discovery of America) or the coincidental convergence of many discrete happenings produced exceptional change in human affairs.

An alternative to the episodic approach is one that focuses on *process*. Adam Smith believed that commercial forces were the main engine driving history and that historians should identify major watersheds at climactic points in an evolving international division of labor. Other scholars contend that the rhythmic action of demographic forces has constituted so dynamic an engine of change that epochal divisions can be measured by the ebb and flow of population. Marxists declare that economic affairs dominated and determined all others and that history proceeded from epoch to epoch according to a precise and predictable dialectical process based on modes of production.

If propulsion and periodization are linked theoretical properties, then our periodization should be governed in large measure by our understanding of the forces that drive the historical process. In subsequent chapters, the theories of change currently used by historians will be examined in some detail. Each will be assessed in terms of its compatibility with standard tripartite periodization. In this chapter, however, my objective is to determine how Western tripartite periodization took shape. That, in itself, is an object lesson in the subjective and theoretical character of history.

EARLY CHRISTIAN PERIODIZATION

Medieval chroniclers demonstrated familiarity with several concepts of periodization, all extrapolated from Holy Scripture or other religious writings. The Book of Daniel envisioned a world order of four universal monarchies. The fourth of these, "dreadful and terrible, and strong exceedingly," was expected to give way to a new dominion of glory (a fifth age) in which all people, nations, and languages would be everlastingly united [Daniel (7:14)]. The four universal monarchies were commonly identified with Assyria, Persia, Greece, and Rome.

After the Christianization of the Roman Empire, Rome was viewed increasingly as God's instrument for universal proselytization. Orosius's *Seven Books of Histories against the Pagans* (early fifth century) endorsed the four-monarchy concept, linking Rome with the sacred history of Christianity. Germanic invasions of the Roman Empire were explained as God's means of carrying the Gospel of Christ to all peoples. A century later, Cassiodorus contended that the fourth and final universal monarchy, Rome, was being perpetuated by the Germans. This view persisted through the Middle Ages: the Holy Roman Empire of the German Nation was a continuation of the early Roman Empire and a central force in the sacred history of Christianity. It was destined to survive to the end of the world.[6] That end was near. The decline of Roman political power since the early Caesars and the withering of towns and trade after the fifth century seemed mere confirmation to many Christians that they lived in the final years of a weary and senile world whose end would be accomplished by the second coming of Christ.

Another widely approved periodization was extrapolated from biblical texts during the first centuries of the Christian era. It contemplated six ages of history in geometric symmetry with the six days of creation:

1. From creation to the flood
2. From the flood to Abraham
3. From Abraham to David
4. From David to the Babylonian captivity
5. From captivity to the birth of Christ
6. From the birth of Christ to the second coming.

As a rule, Christian scholars who wrote general surveys of "world history" began with a summary of holy scripture from Genesis through the New Testament, then proceeded to narrate, in greater detail, the events of the sixth age. The exceptional regularity of this scheme gained reinforcement from St. Matthew's gospel, where it is declared that fourteen generations separated Abraham from David, David from the Babylonian captivity, and the captivity from the birth of Christ [Matthew (1:17)]. The seventh glorious age, the gathering of the elect in an eternal sabbath, was expected to commence with the second coming.[7]

INTERVENTION OF THE HUMANISTS

Early Christian concepts of historical periodization encountered no sustained challenge until the fourteenth century, when Italian humanists made the first major revision. Annoyed by German claims to Roman succession and inspired by the growing wealth and power of their own states, Italian humanists launched a relentless attack on the centuries that stretched between the collapse of Rome and their own time. For Italians, Rome was the ancestral civilization. Like no other Europeans, Italian humanists expressed a near-tribal pride in the accomplishments of their

classical forebears. They drew sharp distinctions between the cultural
magnificence of Roman civilization and the "barbarous darkness" that
followed the Empire's demise. Having resisted the overlordship of Germanic Holy Roman emperors since the eleventh century, Italians firmly
rejected the moral foundations upon which that overlordship rested—that
is, the Germans' claim to be legitimate successors to the emperors of
Rome.

Italian humanists did not inaugurate modern tripartite periodization.
That would not happen for several centuries. They did create the forward
epochal frontier of the tripartite scheme, and they laid important conceptual groundwork for the backward parameter. In his *History of the Florentine People,* a work in twelve books that provided a model for other
humanist scholars, Leonardo Bruni (d. 1444) insisted that the Roman
Empire fell under the onslaught of barbarian invaders. It was never
revived, neither in Italy nor Germany. When the long succession of
northern incursions into Italy finally subsided, Italians began a remarkable
recovery, which by the fourteenth century had produced numerous
flourishing and powerful city-states.[8] Flavio Biondo's history of Europe
from the fifth to the fifteenth century (published 1439–1453) emphatically
declared that the Roman Empire fell in A.D. 412. He lamented that fall,
but like Bruni and other Italian humanist historians, he took consolation in
the rise of the new Italy whose great cities, he thought, had restored to the
peninsula its lost dignity.[9]

For Italy's secular historians, the fifth-century fall of the Roman
Empire was *the* watershed event in the history of Western mankind. Bruni
and Biondo assumed the view of Petrarch that from the fifth century to
their own day Europe had been enveloped by darkness. All three were
passionately committed to recovering the lustre of an earlier age, but none
of them developed the concept of a third, modern age.

IMPACT OF THE REFORMATION

The achievements of Italy's humanist historians were blunted in up-
coming centuries by the Protestant Reformation. The greatest of the northern humanists, Erasmus, insisted that purity of religion depended upon
purity of good letters and that purity of letters had subsided in Europe
with the demise of the classical writers and the early Church fathers.[10]
His view furnished intellectual fodder for Lutherans. By the 1520s
Lutheran writers were identifying the fifth-century collapse of both classical literature and evangelical Christianity with the beginning of the

thousand-year reign of the papal antichrist. Rejecting the secular orientation of Italian humanists, Lutherans reaffirmed the union between history and theology. God was directly involved in human affairs, and the chief function of historians was to identify His interventions and to interpret their meaning. At the same time, Lutheran historians agreed with Italian humanists that the millennium from the fifth through the fifteenth century was a period of cultural darkness. For them, however, it was religious corruption, not the Germanic invasions of Italy, that occasioned the darkness. Protestant reform offered the world one last chance at redemption. Time was short. "We clutch at a tiny last corner of the world," wrote the Lutheran Andreas Musculus in 1561; "it is certain that the end of the world is on our doorstep, for Luther has preceded the second coming of Christ as John went before the first."[11]

Lutheran writers generally adhered to the four-monarchy plan.[12] Outside Germany, however, the four-monarchy concept came under attack. Jean Bodin, the French humanist-historian, rejected it on the same grounds as the Italians. The notion that Germans had assumed the mantle of Roman authority and perpetuated the Empire for a thousand years was, for Bodin, a monumental fiction. Growing knowledge about the empires of Asia rendered consideration of a universal Roman Empire (or any other universal empire) futile.[13] Bodin urged historians to abandon religious mythology in order to focus attention on explaining, in a purely secular manner, the ebb and flow of civilizations and the rise and fall of great political states.[14]

As long as religious issues dominated social consciousness, a religious ordering of historical time was likely to prevail. That dominance waned in the seventeenth century. Even the last of the so-called religious wars—the Thirty Years War—was driven less by religious loyalties and more by the political opportunism of secular rulers bent on consolidating territorial states. Those states enjoyed greatly enhanced power in the seventeenth century. Tax revenues increased; trade expanded; mercantile empires were formed; and centralized bureaucracies assumed greater control over a host of social institutions. Historians adjusted their thinking accordingly. Greater attention was given to scientific and technological developments and to the oceanic discoveries of the fifteenth and sixteenth centuries that wrought changes in the conduct of trade, the distribution of power, and the spatial orientation of Europeans toward the world at large. Protestants considered the Reformation a momentous epochal event, and by the end of the Thirty Years War, Catholics conceded that the rupture of Western Christianity, now permanent, represented a major break in historical continuity.[15] New terms had already crept into the common language of

Europeans identifying the millennium following the fall of Rome: *media tempestas* (1469), *media tempore* (1531), *media aetas* (1518), and *medium aevum* (1604).[16] By the late seventeenth century, all of the ingredients for tripartite periodization were at hand.

EIGHTEENTH-CENTURY ADOPTION
OF TRIPARTITE PERIODIZATION

The scholar who first assembled the pieces was a German philologist, Christof Keller, commonly called Cellarius (1638–1707). Author of numerous linguistic and geographical studies, Cellarius composed a brief overview of ancient history in 1675, following it the next year with a work entitled *Nucleus of Middle History between Ancient and Modern*. Thereafter, he published a more extensive treatise on the Middle Ages and another on modern Europe.

Cellarius's chief historical publications passed through at least eight editions, but the tripartite model he adopted gained ground very slowly.[17] Early eighteenth-century scholars generally accepted the fall of Rome as an epochal frontier, but many of them acknowledged no other break. All that preceded the fall of Rome was ancient history; all that followed was modern. This was the understanding that prevailed at Oxford and Cambridge in the 1720s when George I established the Regius Chairs of Modern History.[18]

Enlightenment rationalism intensified the hostility of eighteenth-century intellectuals to the Church, to superstition, to willfull ignorance, and to constraints artificially imposed upon individual human freedom and rationality—all of which were thought to be characteristic features of the millenium following the fall of Rome. Voltaire's well-known prejudice against the so-called Middle Ages was shared by the most noteworthy of British historians, David Hume, William Robertson, and Edward Gibbon.[19] The latter's luxuriant seven-volume *Decline and Fall of the Roman Empire* (1776–1788) combined formidable criticism of medieval Christianity, deep skepticism concerning human nature, and an Enlightenment optimism that man could bring order and coherence to his life through the exercise of reason. For Gibbon, the fall of Rome represented "the triumph of barbarism and religion." That fall, he thought, was "the greatest, perhaps, and the most awful scene in the history of mankind," the baleful consequence of the slow decay of ancient virtues.[20] Gibbon's history comprises two nearly equal parts—the history of Rome to 476, and the ensuing ten centuries to the fall of Constantinople in 1453. It was entirely compatible with tripartite periodization. In fact, all the grand historians of the eighteenth century, including Bolingbroke and Muratori, distinguished between ancient, medieval, and modern times. They were, however, imprecise about dating those epochs.

Precision was a concern of the first distinguished body of academic historians, established at the University of Göttingen in the eighteenth century. History was not a primary branch of learning in European universities, but Göttingen, founded in 1737, became an exception.[21] Johann Christoph Gatterer, who assumed the Chair in history in 1759, had an extraordinary range of historical interests and, for his time, exceptional historical vision.[22] What, he asked, are the determining forces that give unity to the experience of all peoples on this planet? In terms of the entire human experience, how should historical time be marked out?

Gatterer began his periodization with the creation. He identified four great epochs in the history of the world: (1) the age of creation, which included the era of the flood; (2) the age of the founding of nations, including Assyrian, Persian, and Roman nations; (3) the age of the *völkerwanderung,* beginning with the fifth-century movements of Germans and Slavs and continuing thereafter with the conquests of Moslems and Mongols; and (4) the age that commenced with the discovery of America.[23]

If we delete from Gatterer's scheme the one element that reflects literal acceptance of Old Testament scripture—namely, the age of creation—we are left with a tripartite structure not dissimilar from that of Cellarius. Gatterer and his colleagues pursued a universal form of history in which the chief overriding factor since 1500 was the unparalleled dominance of Europe in world affairs. Göttingen historians advocated the primacy of politics, insisting that the central theme of European history in the three centuries after 1492 was the rise of the great powers and the formation of the modern states system. It was this, above all else, that rendered Europe's experience unique and gave Western peoples the vigor, direction, and material prowess to dominate the remaining quarters of the globe.

THE CREATION OF THE RENAISSANCE

Thus far, no mention has been made of the Renaissance. Nor did historians of the eighteenth century have any perception of a distinct segment of time, a general European experience, that might be designated "the Renaissance." As an organizing abstraction, "the Middle Ages" had already taken shape. It was the creation of a second abstraction, "the Renaissance," that put the final seal on Western man's collective conceptualization of the thousand-year period following the fall of Rome.

The modern concept of the Renaissance is largely the gift of Jacob Burckhardt, the eminent Swiss scholar whose *Civilization of the Renaissance in Italy* (1860) constitutes a major historiographical event. Numerous eighteenth-century writers, including Voltaire, had taken humanists at their word and accepted their view that the revival of classical learning represented an intellectual revolution of the first magnitude. But not until Burckhardt did that revolution transcend the realm of artistic and literary achievement.

Burckhardt transformed the Renaissance idea into a comprehensive revolution in the civilization of Italy, a revolution that radiated its light across much of Western Europe and drew the final curtain on the Middle Ages. The revival of classical learning was a necessary but insufficient explanation for the Italian Renaissance, Burckhardt contended. Writers and artists of the ancient world merely provided the guidelines, the models, that this virile society elected to pursue in its effort to shed the "fantastic bonds of the Middle Ages."[24]

Italy's development of a unique civic life uniting noblemen and burghers in societies that rewarded wealth, not birth, encouraged the assertion of human individuality. Dynamic individualism became the touchstone of Italian life. Individualism inspired the discovery of beauty in nature. It stimulated investigation of the wider reaches of the globe, and it rendered Italians increasingly secular. Medieval civilization reached its highest development in France; it never achieved a comfortable fit in Italy. After the fourteenth century, Italians rebelled against it and created a new, modern civilization.[25]

Burckhardt's vision pervaded historical thinking through the late nineteenth century, and it remains today, with numerous corrections and revisions, the basis of our understanding of the Renaissance. Burckhardt's vision of the Renaissance was elitist. His emphasis on Italian individuality resonated with the sense of rugged individualism expressed by Western Europe's expanding bourgeoisie.[26] Although he emphatically distinguished between medieval and modern civilization, Burckhardt did not attempt to create a distinct epoch in human history called "the Renaissance."[27] Rather, he affirmed the Renaissance as a breakwater between medieval and modern times. It was the first flowering of modernity, a bulwark of the tripartite formula.

HISTORY AS AN ACADEMIC DISCIPLINE

Burckhardt's contribution is doubly important because it was during the halcyon years of his interpretive revolution that history came of age in the universities of Britain, France, and the United States. Before 1873, only two persons were formally teaching history at Cambridge University. History was an adjunct of philosophy and politics.[28] A decade later, only twenty people were fully engaged in university-level history teaching in the United States.[29] Thereafter, the discipline expanded rapidly. National associations of historians were formed, and national journals of history quickly made their appearance.[30] A surge in the publication of monographs generated growing demand for collaborative syntheses. The most famous of these—possibly the most influential collaborative work ever to appear in Western historiography—was the twelve-volume *Cambridge Modern History,* which commenced publication in 1902.

Responsibility for orchestrating this massive history fell to Lord Acton, Regius Professor at Cambridge, who declared that Western historical continuity had sustained an abrupt break around 1500:

> The modern age did not proceed from the medieval by normal succession, with outward tokens of legitimate descent. Unheralded, it founded a new order of things, under a law of innovation, sapping the ancient reign of continuity. In those days Columbus subverted the notions of the world, and reversed the conditions of production, wealth, and power; in those days Machiavelli released government from the restraint of law; Erasmus diverted the current of ancient learning from profane into Christian channels; Luther broke the chain of authority and tradition at the strongest link; and Copernicus erected an invincible power that set for ever the mark of progress upon the time that was to come. . . . It was an awakening of new life; the world revolved in a different orbit, determined by influences unknown before. After many ages persuaded of the headlong decline and impending dissolution of society, and governed by usage and the will of masters who were in their graves, the sixteenth century went forth armed for untried experience, and ready to watch with hopefulness a prospect of incalculable change.[31]

In succeeding decades, the *Cambridge Modern History* became a reservoir of information for graduate students, a quarry mined by innumerable college professors for class lectures, and an inspiration for writers of single-volume college textbooks.[32] The periodization established in that history was affirmed in subsequent series of similar magnitude and influence: the *Cambridge Medieval History* (eight volumes, 1911–1936) and the *Cambridge Ancient History* (twelve volumes, 1923–1939). Tripartite periodization has continued to dominate the Western conceptualization of historical time ever since.

Should it?

Historical orientations have changed since Lord Acton initiated the *Cambridge Modern History*. Egalitarianism has triumphed over elitism. Social history has taken prominence over political history. Religious divisions have lost their sting under ecumenical pressures, and great religious movements, like the Reformation, are now thought to have been as much a consequence of economic and social forces as of spiritual or intellectual strivings. Less attention is given to the ideas of great thinkers of the past, more to the mentalities of "the people." New areas of study have arisen— for example, women's history and the history of the family. If we view history from the perspective of women or of common folk, the era around 1500 has little to distinguish it. Not until industrialization, we are told, did patterns of life for common people change significantly in Europe. Between 1500 and 1800 annual per capita income could not have increased by more than 0.2 to 0.3 percent. Yet, in the early nineteenth century, per capita income was growing at a rate of 0.5 to 0.7 percent per annum, and by the mid-nineteenth century, that rate had risen to 1.2 percent.[33]

The few scholars who have written on periodization in recent decades have rejected 1500 as a suitable watershed in European history. In their view, a period break around 1500 severs the vital continuity of European life from the tenth to the eighteenth century.[34] In defense of their position, it can be argued that the Industrial Revolution of the eighteenth century constitutes the great economic and technical divide in Western history. The unprecedented modern surge in population began in the eighteenth century, and the democratic revolutions of the late eighteenth century probably outweigh any comparable experiences of the fifteenth or sixteenth centuries.

Still, the circa 1500 watershed has much to recommend it. It may be the product of episodic thinking, and clearly some of the episodes that gave it significance have faded in historical importance. At the same time, new historical significance has been attached to the most prominent event of this era: the European discovery of America. For Lord Acton, this was a major geographical revelation that eventually altered political balances in Europe and provided a virgin arena for Western economic development. Recent scholarship has emphasized the connection between European exploitation of America, the rise of Western capitalism, and the establishment of a Western world hegemony. Many contemporary scholars consider capitalism the very essence of modernity. Equally important is the work of Alfred Crosby, who has disclosed the startling inter-hemispheric transfers of flora, fauna, and disease that transformed life on this planet in the wake of the Columbian voyages.[35]

Whether circa 1500 can hold up as a pivotal watershed era or whether it should give way to some other divide is an issue that concerns us in this book. If circa 1500 holds up, its success will not hinge upon historical accident, the result of some untoward event or events that befell Western people, broke essential continuities, and altered their orientations. The Europeans' discovery of America may have been accidental to the extent that in 1492 Columbus initiated a wholly different venture—a westward crossing to Asia. Nevertheless, his participation in overseas exploration was part of a long process that involved politics, economics, technology, and a host of other elements in a broad historical context. The same might be said for the eighteenth century. The simultaneous occurrence of the industrial, demographic, and democratic revolutions was not accidental or mere coincidence. These revolutions were integrated aspects of a complex historical process.

For historians, the overriding issue is fathoming the nature of that process: determining how change occurred, what the chief engines of change were, and how various engines of change, primary and secondary, were interwoven to generate significant events. When this is achieved, it will be possible to identify with greater confidence those protracted "moments" in history when old continuities dissolved and new continuities were formed.

NOTES

1. George Duby, "L'Histoire des systèmes de valuers," *History and Theory* 11 (1972): 15–25.

2. The internal structure of Roman history has been periodized in response to political phenomena, but one distinguished ancient historian contends that emphasis upon other aspects of Roman life would have occasioned a different order of periodization. M. I. Finley, "Generalizations in Ancient History," in Louis Gottschalk, ed., *Generalization in the Writing of History* (Chicago and London, 1963), p. 24.

3. Emmanuel Le Roy Ladurie, "Motionless History," *Social Science History* 1 (1977): 131–134.

4. One of the leading texts in modern history, now in its seventh edition, delivers the standard view: "In general, it is agreed that modern times began in Europe about the year 1500. Modern times were preceded by a period of 1000 years called the Middle Ages, which set in about A.D. 500, and which were in turn preceded by another 1000 years of classical Greco-Roman civilization." See R. R. Palmer and Joel Colton, *A History of the Modern World* (New York, 7th ed., 1992), p. 12.

5. For example, *Medieval Studies* or the *Journal of Medieval History* rarely, if ever, step beyond 1500, and the *International Medieval Bibliography* has fixed parameters (500–1500). The same concern for period frontiers applies to the modern history journals. Journals having universal scope (e.g., *American Historical Review*) commonly divide their book review sections into ancient, medieval, modern.

6. Ernst Breisach, *Historiography: Ancient, Medieval, and Modern* (Chicago, 1983), pp. 86, 89, 104, 143–144.

7. This concept was favored by St. Augustine, Venerable Bede, and numerous writers of the medieval chronicles. Denys Hay, *Annalists and Historians: Western Historiography from the VIIIth to the XVIIIth Century* (London, 1977), p. 28.

8. Donald J. Wilcox, *The Development of Florentine Humanist Historiography in the Fifteenth Century* (Cambridge, Mass., 1969), pp. 11–12.

9. For an analysis of Biondo's work, see Denys Hay, "Flavio Biondo and the Middle Ages," *Proceedings of the British Academy* 45 (1959): 97–128.

10. Wallace K. Ferguson, *The Renaissance in Historical Thought* (Boston, 1948), p. 44.

11. Quoted in Gerald Strauss, *Luther's House of Learning: Indoctrination of the Young in the German Reformation* (Baltimore, 1978), p. 82.

12. Johann Philip of Schleiden's universal history, *On the Four World Empires,* passed through sixty-five editions and provided a staple of Lutheran education for several generations. At least three other historians of note in the sixteenth century— Wimpheling, *Epitome of German History*; Nauclerus, *Memorabilia*; and Aventius, *Bavarian Chronicle*—adopted the four-monarchy plan. See Breisach, *Historiography,* p. 163. Luther himself was inconsistent in his use of periodization. See John M. Headley, *Luther's View of Church History* (New Haven, 1963). The four-monarchy plan actually persisted among many German writers until the end of the eighteenth century despite repeated and devastating assaults upon its legitimacy by both German scholars and foreign luminaries, including Voltaire.

13. Bodin's great work, published in 1566, effectively dismantled the theoretical supports of the four-monarchy scheme. Jean Bodin, *Method for the Easy Comprehension of History,* trans. Beatrice Reynolds (New York, 1945), p. 292.

14. Bodin provided a model for several French historians of the sixteenth century, including Louis Le Roy, Nicholas Vignier, and Henri Voison de La Popelinière. George Huppert contends that Vignier was probably the first author of universal history who did not view the coming of Christ as an epochal event. See Huppert, *The Idea of Perfect History: Historical Erudition and Historical Philosophy in Renaissance France* (Urbana, 1970), pp. 88ff.

15. Hubert Jedin et al., *History of the Church*: vol. 5, *Reformation and Counter Reformation* (New York, 1980), p. 644.

16. George L. Burr, "How the Middle Ages Got Their Name," *American Historical Review* 20 (1914–1915): 813–814. Also see Ferguson, *The Renaissance in Historical Thought*, pp. 73–74.

17. Cellarius's role has too often been exaggerated and his merits as a historian unnecessarily demeaned by those who object to the tripartite mode of periodization. In a widely read passage, Geoffrey Barraclough referred contemptuously to Cellarius as "a very indifferent German scholar." He attributed to this "mediocre" scholar the discovery of the idea of the Middle Ages, contending that Cellarius "fitted it, like a straight-jacket over all future historical thought." See Barraclough, *History in a Changing World* (Oxford, 1955), pp. 54–56. In reality, Cellarius neither created the Middle Ages nor coined the term. He was simply the first well-published writer to gather together in a single conceptual package the many threads of a tripartite division that had been accumulating since the fifteenth century.

18. Herbert Butterfield, *Man on His Past: The Study of the History of Historical Scholarship* (Cambridge, 1955), p. 46. Also see G. P. Gooch, "The Cambridge Chair of Modern History," in Gooch, ed., *Studies in Modern History* (Freeport, N.Y., 1968; reprint of 1931 ed.), pp. 289–325.

19. Hume (1711–1776), an economist, philosopher, and essayist, produced an eight-volume *History of England*. His comparison of Anglo-Saxon history with the battles of kites and crows resonates with Voltaire's comment that the early Middle Ages required as little attention as the ramblings of wolves and bears. Hume perceived the millennium before the Renaissance as a profoundly depressing one when humankind wallowed in barbarism and superstition. Robertson (1721–1793), the historian of Scotland, shared this negative view, though he perceived the Middle Ages—at least in their later stages—as preparation for the flowering of civilization in sixteenth-century Europe. For an analysis of the work of both authors, see J. B. Black, *The Art of History: A Study of Four Great Historians of the Eighteenth Century* (New York, 1926). J. H. Brumfitt's *Voltaire, Historian* (London, 1958) remains a valuable and comprehensive analysis of Voltaire's purposes and method.

20. Edward Gibbon, *The Decline and Fall of the Roman Empire*, vol. 7 (London, 1909), p. 308; David P. Jordan, *Gibbon and His Roman Empire* (Urbana, 1971), pp. 70–122, 183–190, 213–230.

21. Charles E. McClelland, *State, Society, and University in Germany 1700–1914* (Cambridge, 1980), pp. 3, 39–42.

22. Peter Hanns Reill, "History and Hermeneutics in the *Aufklärung*: The Thought of Johann Christof Gatterer," *Journal of Modern History* 45 (1973): 27–28.

23. For a detailed exposition of Gatterer's periodization, see Peter Hanns Reill, *The German Enlightenment and the Rise of Historicism* (Berkeley and Los Angeles, 1975), pp. 77–80.

24. Jacob Burckhardt, *The Civilization of the Renaissance in Italy*, trans. S. G. C. Middlemore (London, 1944), p. 107.

25. The Burckhardt thesis had few foreshadowings. Art historians had long used the term "Renaissance" to denote a style of art, but historians of society at large ignored the wider implications of the word. Five years before the appearance of Burckhardt's study, Jules Michelet (1798–1874) completed the seventh volume of his monumental *Histoire de France*, which, with some originality, he chose to title *Renaissance*. But the Renaissance of Michelet was essentially a French phenomenon. He took a very negative view of Italian society in the fourteenth and fifteenth centuries.

26. In the English-speaking world, Burckhardt's vision was effectively confirmed and elaborated by John Addington Symonds, who produced a seven-volume, highly readable masterwork, *Renaissance in Italy* (1875–1886), filling in the roughly sketched terrain of the Burckhardt treatise.

27. Efforts by later scholars to denominate the Renaissance as a separate transitional period between the medieval and modern times have failed to gain acceptance. The most notable attempt was made by Wallace Ferguson, who strongly advocated the concept of the Renaissance as a period of transition. His article, "The Interpretation of the Renaissance: Suggestions for a Synthesis," *Journal of the History of Ideas* 12 (1951): 483–495, preceded a full treatment of this view in Ferguson, *Europe in Transition, 1300–1520* (Boston, 1962).

28. G. Kitson Clark, "A Hundred Years of the Teaching of History at Cambridge, 1873–1973," *Historical Journal* 16 (1973): 541.

29. Arthur S. Link, "The American Historical Association, 1884–1984: Retrospect and Prospect," *American Historical Review* 90 (1985): 2.

30. *Revue Historique* in 1876, *English Historical Review* in 1886, and *American Historical Review* in 1895. Germans were well ahead of the pack. *Historishe Zeitschrift,* the model professional journal, had been established in 1859. For development of the French historical profession, see William R. Keylor, *Academy and Community: The Foundation of the French Historical Profession* (Cambridge, Mass., 1973), pp. 60, 219. Doris Goldstein, "The Organizational Development of the British Historical Profession, 1884–1921," *Bulletin of Historical Research* 55 (1982): 180–193.

31. Lord Acton, *Essays in the Liberal Interpretation of History,* ed. William H. McNeill (Chicago and London, 1967), p. 304. Acton died shortly before the first volume appeared, but he firmly affixed his stamp to the project. Contributors to the *Cambridge Modern History* echoed Acton's aggregate and impressionistic vision. Introducing the series, Mandell Creighton, Anglican bishop, a professor of ecclesiastical history at Cambridge and the first editor of *English Historical Review,* referred to the "extraordinary change of mental attitude" that distinguished the sixteenth from the fifteenth century. For commentary on Creighton and his reliance upon Acton, see Doris Goldstein, "The Origins and Early Years of *The English Historical Review,*" *English Historical Review* 101 (1986): 3–11. Repeatedly, contributors to the first volume of the *Cambridge History* identified the advent of modernity with the growth of nation-states, of individualism, of capitalism, and of secular attitudes.

32. The distinguished historian and historiographer, G. P. Gooch, summed up early twentieth-century opinion of the *Cambridge Modern History*: it was, he wrote, "beyond comparison the best survey of the modern world in any language." Gooch, *History and Historians in the Nineteenth Century* (London, 1913), p. 390.

33. Paul Bairoch, "Europe's Gross National Product: 1800–1975," *Journal of European Economic History* 5 (1976): 276–279.

34. Barraclough, *History in a Changing World,* pp. 54–63; Dietrich Gerhard, "Periodization in European History," *American Historical Review* 61 (1956): 903; Gerhard, *Old Europe: A Study of Continuity, 1000–1800* (New York, 1981), p. 139; William A. Green, "Periodization in European and World History," *Journal of World History* 3 (1992): 13–53.

35. Alfred W. Crosby, Jr., *The Columbian Exchange: Biological and Cultural Consequences of 1492* (Westport, Conn., 1972).

Part II

The Dynamics of Historical Change: Europe

Introduction:
Search for a Governing Dynamic

This section of the book will examine four engines of change employed by historians in our time. In keeping with the priorities of the twentieth century, three of them—the commercial, demographic, and Marxian explanations—are materialist. The fourth, which advocates the religious roots of change, was conceived in response to materialist models, particularly the Marxist one.

The most influential historians and social scientists of this century have identified modernity with the rise of capitalism. Fashioned to create wealth, capitalism transformed the physical structure of Europe, its social psychology, institutional patterns, and outreach to the wider world. All explanatory models in this section of the book concentrate on the advent of capitalism. They are exclusively concerned with Europe and chiefly focused on historical developments during the late Middle Ages and early modern period.

Historians may agree that capitalism is virtually synonymous with modernity, but they do not agree in detail on how capitalism, as a historical abstraction, should be defined. Some are content to define it as the use of mobile property for the purpose of achieving profits. Yet, under so limited a definition, almost all forms of market activity qualify as capitalist. Marxists deny that merchants and markets necessarily indicate the presence of capitalism; for them, capitalism is a mode of production, not a process of exchange. Some insist that capitalism involves high adventure and speculation. Dismissing this, Max Weber contends that reckless speculation is an impediment to capitalism, and that capitalism involves the application of reason, discipline, and sober calculation in business enterprise.

Many scholars hold the opinion that numerous preconditions had to exist before capitalism could be consolidated in European society. First, there had to be an accumulation of capital available for investment by private individuals; second, there had to be a class of propertyless wage workers available for hire. Other preconditions include the need for security in commercial transactions, both physical security for traders and legal security for their property. Some would insist that capitalism could not emerge until business techniques and banking facilities had matured or until there was substantial demand for moveable goods in the marketplace. At some point, it becomes difficult to discern between the preconditions for capitalism and capitalism itself.

How a scholar defines capitalism dictates when he or she thinks it took hold in Europe. Henri Pirenne, a leading figure of the commercial school, identified the presence of capitalism in the merchant community of the twelfth century. Max Weber thought it emerged in the sixteenth century, and the Marxists advocate a seventeenth- and eighteenth-century transition.

Perhaps the term "capitalism," being so diversely employed, has ceased to have value. Fernand Braudel, a leading expert on the rise of capitalism, confronted that possibility, then drew back. If you throw the term out the door, it comes in the window, he argued. It is ambiguous. It is used indiscriminately. It is laden with controversies, past and present. Any use of it for the pre-industrial world may be anachronistic. But we are stuck with it.[1]

Each of the explanations offered in this section is introduced by its theoretical founding father: for the commercial school, Adam Smith; for the demographic school, Thomas Malthus; for the Marxian school, Karl Marx. It can hardly be said that either Sombart or Weber founded schools of history, but their influence was widespread, and they will speak for themselves on the religious origins of capitalism. Smith, Marx, Weber, and Sombart reacted strongly to political and economic stimuli in their own lives. Smith advocated laissez-faire economics in reaction against eighteenth-century mercantilism. In the political struggles of the twentieth century, his approach has been judged highly complimentary to capitalism. Marx reacted against the harsh and exploitative character of mid-nineteenth century capitalism, and of course his work provided the intellectual foundations for modern communism. Responding to the particular needs of Germany at the end of the nineteenth century, Sombart and Weber expressed opposition to laissez-faire capitalism and vehement hostility to the materialist determinism of Karl Marx.

Part II commences with an examination of the commercial dynamic. This mode of explanation is presented as persuasively as possible. Unlike the other chapters, Chapter 3 contains no criticism of the explanatory formula under discussion. The reason is not that I am partial to the commercial explanation. Rather, all other schools of thought— demographic, Marxian, and Weberian—take many of their cues from the commercial dynamic. In developing their own lines of argument, they provide appropriate criticism of it. Apart from affording a clear assessment of the commercial interpretation, Chapter 3 attempts to introduce the salient historical issues that provide the nucleus for debate in succeeding chapters.

Readers will discover that every mode of interpretation identifies particular centuries or parts of centuries as being significant watersheds in the history of Europe. The period around A.D. 1000 is especially significant for both the commercial and demographic schools because it is possible to date aggregate economic growth and secular population growth from that time. The fourteenth century is a critical time for historians of the Marxian and demographic schools. Both argue that Europe confronted a grievous crisis in that century. The sixteenth century is critical for Weber. It is also significant for both the demographic and commercial schools because economic and population growth was renewed after the long hiatus associated with the plague.

The Black Death is an event of major importance in these chapters. Some proponents of the demographic explanation have been tempted to integrate it into the rhythm of their model. Others have considered it an exogenous force. It cannot be ignored, and the reader of these chapters may conclude that none of the explanations offered in Part II accommodate it effectively.

Three modes of explanation identify the specific trajectory of history through time. The commercial mode is linear and progressive. Human affairs evolve continually from the less complex to the more complex. The demographic mode posits a homeostatic equilibrium in which every flow is followed by an ebb, every growth by a subsidence. Marxian analysis is progressive and millennial. Progress is achieved by stages, and the nature of each stage is determined by the inexorable operation of the dialectic.

Some things are noticeably absent in these chapters. No one introduces God as an active force in history. Sombart and Weber argue that religious impulses drive human affairs, but both of them distinguish between God and religious belief. Race and heredity form a part of Sombart's explanation, but his only. Geography as a factor in history is manifestly important only to the commercial school.

I conclude this introduction with a word about language. Among the many abstract terms that suffer from ambiguity of meaning, the word "feudal" is one of the most problematic. For many professional medievalists, the word connotes a relationship between a lord and his vassal by which each party pledges to exercise responsibility to the other in a particular way. Marxist historians use the term to define a mode of production that existed in medieval Europe. In either case, the word is an abstraction intended to facilitate communication between historians concerning a body of similar, though not identical, practices. Marxists take no offense when non-Marxists use the term "feudal" to identify vassalage relationships. Non-Marxists have been very prickly on the matter. Like "capitalism," the word "feudal" has its ambiguities. We shall simply have to live with them.

NOTE

1. Fernand Braudel, *Civilization and Capitalism, 15th–18th Century*: vol. 2, *The Wheels of Commerce* (New York, 1982), p. 231.

3

The Commercial Model

Capital was the solvent of the Middle Ages and the engine of modern progress. So declared the first edition of the *Cambridge Modern History*.[1] This pillar of scholarship embodied the commercial view of historical change in classical form. It determined that early medieval Europe was a "natural economy" comprised of self-sustaining, rural communities that, with few exceptions, produced a narrow range of coarse goods for local consumption. Beginning in the eleventh century, this economy was transformed, expanded, and refined by the unrelenting pressure of commercial forces. Long-distance trade emanating from the Mediterranean altered social habits, cultivated new tastes, and laid the institutional foundations for modern capitalism. From the Dark Ages to the Industrial Revolution, commerce was the primary engine of change in European life.

The commercial explanation for the rise of the modern world is the oldest and most firmly rooted body of concepts employed by scholars. It embodies a linear, progressivist concept of human development and provides economic girding for what Herbert Butterfield called the Whig interpretation of history, the notion that history is the record of man's relentless progress toward liberty.[2] Its main theoretical foundations were elegantly and abundantly set forth in Adam Smith's *Wealth of Nations*, first published in 1776. Professional historians have painstakingly assembled documentary and other evidence to flesh out Smith's theory. In recent years, the theoretical structure has been reworked and revised by the British economist Sir John Hicks.

Writers of the commercial school share several assumptions about human nature and human history. Human beings have always been motivated primarily by self-interest. They are naturally acquisitive. They prefer more goods to fewer, and wherever incentives exist, they will strive to improve their material well-being. Economic forces are the primary, though not the only, factors governing the direction of history. Significant changes in the material circumstances of life trigger changes elsewhere. It is assumed, for example, that human refinement, manners, and good taste are directly linked to the accumulation of property. Abbé Raynal made the point two centuries ago when he argued that "commercial states have civilized all others."[3] Propelled by an innate "propensity to truck, barter, and exchange one thing for another,"[4] men and women have achieved a steadily expanding division of labor. Progressive division of labor both elevates and renders more complex all aspects of human endeavor.

Adam Smith believed that the mode by which people achieve subsistence determines the character of their social order. Humankind, he declared, had passed (or was passing) through a hierarchy of four distinct historical stages differentiated by their relative social complexity. The most primitive, the hunting stage, was characteristic of early man and of some contemporary Indian tribes of North America. The second, a herding stage, was historically evident among Arab tribesmen, Mongols, and the Germans who invaded and undermined the Roman Empire. The third, an agricultural stage, involved the establishment of settled societies like those of Europe in the central Middle Ages. The fourth and highest level was the commercial stage to which Western Europe had ascended in recent centuries.

Germanic invaders of the Roman Empire introduced massive disorder, Smith wrote. Communications broke down; cities shrivelled; buildings, monuments, river ports, and roadways fell into disrepair. Even Rome, its aqueducts cut, saw its population shrink from a half million to 50,000 in the mid-sixth century. By the time St. Benedict withdrew to Monte Casino to establish a rigorous monastic order, circa 529, barbarian darkness had settled across the western continent. All lands were divided among a few great proprietors who, by recourse to laws of primogeniture[5] and entail,[6] deliberately prevented the subdivision of their estates.

> Every great landlord was a sort of petty prince. His tenants were his subjects. He was their judge, and in some respects their legislator in peace, and their leader in war. He made war according to his own discretion, frequently against his neighbours, and sometimes against his sovereign. The security of a landed estate, therefore, the protection which its owner could afford to those who dwelt on it, depended upon its greatness. To divide it was to ruin it, and to expose every part of it to be oppressed and swallowed up by the incursions of its neighbours.[7]

Preoccupied with the defense or extension of their territories, great landlords were not great improvers. Neither were the servile occupiers of the land who lacked both leadership and incentive. In the absence of towns or foreign commerce, whatever surpluses landlords extracted from their tenants had to be consumed "in rustick hospitality at home." If the lord's agricultural surplus enabled him to maintain a thousand men, he had no means of exploiting that surplus other than by maintaining a thousand men, all of whom being supported by his largesse were compelled to obey his commands.

Security was the critical need of all persons in this state of life. The desire for security eventually encouraged lesser landlords to enter feudal contracts with greater lords as, indeed, the greater lords established similar arrangements with the king. Occurring between the ninth and eleventh centuries, these developments provided greater security and tranquility to Western Europe, but lingering violence between lords and the prevailing absence of economic incentives rendered the early medieval economy incapable of growth.

Growth waited upon commercial towns. If economic growth depended upon an expanding division of labor, as writers of the commercial school contend, significant division of labor could not occur in the absence of active and reliable markets. The few concentrations of population that existed in early medieval Europe did not have a commercial character. Lacking merchants and artisans, they were little more than places of residence for bishops, great lords, and their numerous retainers.

The most influential medievalist of the twentieth century, Henri Pirenne, adopted Adam Smith's views on the central importance of towns, trade, and the division of labor. Pirenne's explicit commercial ori-

entation so profoundly shaped the views of two generations of medievalists that most textbooks used in English and American universities from
the 1930s through the 1960s boldly embraced his market-driven division-
of-labor model, even to the point of borrowing his anecdotes.[8] Pirenne
rejected Smith's baleful characterization of the Germanic invasions, but he
adopted Smith's argument on towns. Prior to the appearance of Pirenne's
celebrated *Mahomet et Charlemagne* (1937), only a few scholars had
challenged the conventional cataclysmic explanation for the end of the
ancient world. One of them was Fustel de Coulanges, a nineteenth-
century historian who provided evidence that German invaders had not
undertaken wholesale dismantling of Roman institutions.[9] After World
War I, sensitivity was running high in Germany concerning assertions of
barbarism, both past and present; in 1924 a German scholar, Alfons
Dopsch, produced an influential, though exaggerated, work emphasizing
the continuity between Roman and German Europe.[10] Dopsch argued that
Germans who invaded the Roman Empire were vastly more civilized than
conventional wisdom allowed, that they attempted to preserve, not to destroy, the structure of imperial government and trade, and that significant
institutional continuity was preserved through the early Middle Ages,
providing a basis for cultural and economic revival in the eleventh century.

Pirenne concurred with Dopsch. Germans, he argued, had attempted to
perpetuate Roman civil institutions, trade relations with the East, and
classical culture. Despite disorders associated with the German migra-
tions, the unity of the Mediterranean had been preserved well beyond the
fifth century. It was the Arab expansion of the seventh century, Pirenne
believed, that divided the Mediterranean by planting hostile Moslem forces
in the Levant, across North Africa, in Sicily, and throughout Iberia to the
summits of the Pyrenees. Apart from a thin thread of exchange between a
few Italo-Byzantine towns and the Orthodox East, Christian communication via the inland sea was destroyed. The Western Mediterranean became
a Moslem lake, and Christian settlements along its northern shore were
perpetually harassed and pillaged. Overwhelmed by successive disasters,
West Europeans turned inward, away from the sea, to the cold and
forested North. Trade, towns, and the merchant class disappeared;
seignorialism became entrenched; and cultural refinement all but vanished.
The Middle Ages did not commence with barbarian invasions, Pirenne
concluded. They began with Charlemagne. His coronation in 800 represented a symbolic break with the past. The essential quality of ancient
civilization—its Mediterranean character—had been rejected. All that remained of the Roman Empire was the Byzantine state at Constantinople.

The Carolingian West, isolated and impoverished, had begun its inexorable slide toward Europe's cultural nadir.

For writers of the commercial school, the existence of a primitive "natural economy" in a rich, temperate region of the earth was a negation of man's natural acquisitive instincts. It could be explained only by great social catastrophe like the barbarian invasions, or as Pirenne would have it, by the Moslem conquests. To discover how and why Europe recovered from the Dark Ages, it would be necessary to determine why the barbarian invasions or the Moslem conquests of the seventh century had plunged Western Christendom into such profound economic and cultural stagnation. For Pirenne, the answer was clear. The negation of Mediterranean influences and the collapse of long-distance trade were responsible. Revival could only occur through the renewal of commerce from Mediterranean sources.

This revival was achieved at the expense of powerful vested interests. The Christian Church sanctioned prevailing economic structures. Its vast estates dwarfed those of individual noblemen; its members constituted a tiny literate elite; and its ascetic ideals were precisely suited to an agrarian culture. God, the Church taught, had planted man on earth to work out his salvation. To seek profits or to devote energy to the accumulation of worldly goods was deplored as the sin of avarice. Those who inherited wealth were expected to make generous distributions of their riches, preferably through Christian charity. Usury[11] was forbidden; the concept of a "just price"[12] was supported. European culture had become so intensely anticommercial, Pirenne argued, that it could be jolted from its introverted stupor only by the action of some strong external force. Long-distance trade provided that force.

Proponents of the commercial argument for change have consistently recognized the importance of navigable water. No waters have better served the interest of traders than those of the Mediterranean. Sir John Hicks determined that the best explanation for the divergence between European and Asian history is "the fact that European civilization has passed through a city-state phase." The reason is geographical: "The city-state of Europe is a gift of the Mediterranean." Rich in "crannies, islands, promontories, and valleys . . . which have been readily defensible, the Mediterranean," Hicks declares, "is incomparable."[13]

Hicks sketched out a theoretical model of the city-state. That model is too elaborate to reproduce here, but a few fragments may help clarify some of the theoretical underpinnings of the commercial explanation.

When two communities having different resource endowments produce surpluses of different kinds, mutual advantage is gained by both communities if each of them exchanges its form of surplus for that of the other. At the outset of such exchanges, merchants may enjoy high profits, but as the volume of trade grows, the rate of profit diminishes. The reason is twofold. Merchants have to offer higher prices to stimulate a larger output of surplus from producers. Second, by the natural order of supply and demand, a steady increase in the supply of a commodity tends to depress its market price. Facing diminishing returns, merchants will attempt to expand their range of trade, opening new markets or encouraging the development of new commodities in the older market. They will also attempt to reduce *transaction costs,* the costs of conducting business, so that despite falling margins between buying and selling prices, the profitability of trade will remain the same or nearly the same.

Among other things, reducing transaction costs involves creating legal and quasi-legal institutions to protect the property of traders, to guarantee contracts, to facilitate the settling of disputes, and to provide for special arrangements such as the insuring of trade goods. Legal structures appropriate to an agrarian economy are not suited to a commercial one. The rulers of large regional states comprised of great landed estates are unlikely, at first, to appreciate the needs of merchants or to adopt readily the legal institutions needed to protect trade.

It is here that the city-state structure is superior. The European city-state was by its nature a trading community. Its political leadership was involved in trade, and traders enjoyed social prominence. In contrast to large regional states, independent city-states could shape their legal and institutional structures to provide security for the private property of traders. The legal institutions of different city-states may not have been identical, but they were sufficiently similar that security and commercial facilities were provided to merchants operating between city-states. Hicks concluded that the city-state structure, having the ability to facilitate a diversity of trade and to provide institutional securities to such trade, offered an exceptional means of extending trade into backward regions of the continent.

COMMERCIAL REVOLUTION OF THE TOWNS

Among the Italian city-states, Venice led the way. Situated on sandy islands at the head of the Adriatic, the town was protected by water from mainland powers, far removed from Moslem predators, and politically linked with the Byzantine Empire.[14] At first the community merely exchanged fish and salt for landside agricultural provisions. But townsmen quickly diversified their commodity base and cultivated new markets, extending their mercantile interests up the Po Valley and over the Alps. By the eleventh century, Venice had become the principal maritime supplier of Constantinople. Genoa and Pisa followed its example. Having been periodically sacked by Moslem corsairs, they counter-attacked during the early eleventh century, seized Saracen ports in Sicily and Sardinia, then carried their battle to the coast of North Africa. This Christian resurgence anticipated the Crusades, a movement that would monumentally advance the commercial interests of Italian cities during the next two centuries. Italian merchants conveyed waves of troops as well as pilgrims to the Holy Land, supplied them, and secured weighty economic concessions in the bargain. Eastern trade to Europe flourished, and other Mediterranean communities, like Marseilles and Barcelona, hastened to join it. By the thirteenth century, the inland sea from Gibraltar to the Levant was dominated by Christian fleets.

Both Genoa and Venice established maritime empires in Eastern waters. Colonies were planted in the Black Sea, and Genoese ships sailed on the Caspian. Italian overlords developed large plantations on Crete, Cyprus, and other Eastern islands, producing sugar with slaves imported from the Crimea and Africa.[15] In order to pay for Eastern luxuries, the West developed export industries. The Lombard Plain produced grain and wine for overseas sale, and cities throughout northern Italy initiated the manufacture of linens, woolens, and silks. In time, the commercial vitality of the Mediterranean spread over the alpine passes into Germany and up the Rhone Valley to France.

In transalpine Europe, concentrations of population were gradually transformed into commercial towns by the catalytic action of long-distance traders. So argued Pirenne. Hardy adventurers, bearing a limited assortment of goods, appeared in the environs of castles (bourgs) or other formidable structures located at critical intersections of communication, particularly river crossings. Their activities drew the attention of rural artisans, and in time, growing commercial communities established their own suburbs (faubourgs, or outside bourgs) with the blessing of local lords. As towns grew, walls were extended to secure each additional suburb.

The Flemish lowlands, cut by great rivers and adjacent to the sea, enjoyed an industrial renaissance in the tenth century. An ancient woolens industry predating the Roman conquest existed in the valley of the Scheldt, where lush meadows sustained great numbers of sheep. Although Viking raiders of the ninth century destroyed the few important settlements specializing in the sale of woolens, the Flemish industry swiftly recovered, supplementing its own wool supplies with a superior product imported from England. Originally a rural enterprise, clothmaking was gradually concentrated in a growing number of industrial towns. By the twelfth century, Flemish woolens, distinguished above all others by their soft texture and brilliant colors, were being sold in the Baltic by German traders and throughout the Mediterranean by Italians.[16]

Towns grew in Europe because they conferred some benefit on everyone. Commercial towns expanded the division of labor and revolutionized the operation of agricultural estates. New business techniques evolved in the towns, laying the foundations for modern commercial capitalism. Towns provided a haven for serfs fleeing from rural estates.[17] Some serfs became artisans, more of them proletarians. By the fourteenth century, intense class battles were occurring in major industrial towns between impoverished proletarians and the manufacturing elite. Substantial towns introduced a new and complicating element in the long-standing power struggle between kings and nobles. In the main, kings and urban elites consummated alliances of convenience at the long-term expense of the nobility. Trade promoted the restoration of Roman Law and satisfied the material demands of the great courts for unprecedented indulgence in luxury expenditures.

COMMERCE AND THE DECLINE OF FEUDALISM

The revival of long-distance trade and the introduction of a money economy freed Europe's great landlords from the necessity of expending their agricultural surpluses on retainers. Adam Smith made the point emphatically:

what all the violence of the feudal institutions could never have effected, the silent and insensible operation of foreign commerce and manufactures gradually brought about. These gradually furnished the great proprietors with something for which they could exchange the whole surplus produce of their lands, and which they could consume themselves without sharing it either with tenants or retainers. All for ourselves, and nothing for other people, seems, in every age of the world, to have been the vile maxim of the masters of mankind. As soon, therefore, as they could find a method of consuming the whole value of their rents themselves, they had no disposition to share them with any other persons. For a pair of diamond buckles perhaps, or for something as frivolous and useless, they exchanged the maintenance . . . of a thousand men for a year, and with it the whole weight and authority which it could give them. . . . Thus, for the gratification of the most childish, the meanest and the most sordid of all vanities, they gradually bartered their whole power and authority.[18]

Whether the landlords truly bartered their whole power and authority is an issue to which we will return in subsequent chapters. Suffice it to say, life on the estates changed for tenants as well as lords. Towns created new markets for agricultural products, offering rural serfs the incentive to exchange their meager surpluses for money. By earning money in the marketplace, serfs were able to meet obligations to their lords through money payments rather than payments in kind. In time, many lords commuted the labor services of their serfs in favor of rents. Serfs had long been obliged to perform coerced labor at critical seasons on their lord's demesne.[19] With the rise of towns and a money economy, the lords could release serfs from labor obligations in exchange for money payments, shifting the full burden of marketing manorial surpluses onto the peasants. By the end of the thirteenth century, relatively few large landlords in northwestern Europe were directly engaged in agriculture. Instead, they farmed out their demesnes to third parties or rented demesne lands in small parcels to their own serfs. They had become landowners living on rents. In different ways, the rise of towns, commerce, and a money economy had increased the freedom of both lords and peasants.

THE EVOLUTION OF BUSINESS TECHNIQUES

The growing business acumen of Europeans receives admiring attention from economic historians of the commercial school. Beginning with the tenth century, they argue, the improvement of business methods systematically absorbed Western Europe into the money economy. Innovations in the instruments of credit most dramatically fostered the extension of trade. If capital was to be employed to generate greater wealth, it had to be transferred from those who hoarded it or expended it thriftlessly to those who wished to employ it to make money. In the tenth century, Italians developed *commenda,* a plan whereby a party not directly engaged in trade could advance money to a person conducting trade—generally foreign trade—in return for a portion of the profits of that commerce. An Italian merchant might engage any number of people in contracts of *commenda,* large and small, to expand his cargo and increase his potential for profit. Apart from facilitating trade, *commenda* enabled rich men, craftsmen, even widows with a small savings to invest their money in the activities of traders with a clear expectation of gain.[20]

The most pervasive problem for long-distance merchants was physical insecurity. It was risky to carry large sums of metallic coin. Individual lords, motivated by short-term advantage, often pillaged the property of traders or charged ruinous tolls for rights of passage. Moreover, the perpetual shortage of gold and silver depressed commercial activity. The bill of exchange, developed either at Genoa or Florence, was created to relieve both of these difficulties. One of the most important instruments in business history, the bill of exchange enabled a buyer of goods in one country to pay for his purchases through a promissory note, which the seller could redeem in his own city.[21] Non-negotiable bills of exchange were widely employed by the fourteenth century, and at the end of the Middle Ages they were discounted and circulated as negotiable instruments among parties altogether unassociated with the original transaction. In this sense, they became a substitute for cash, expanding the money supply as well as the volume of trade.

COMMERCE AND THE TRANSFORMATION
OF POLITICAL STRUCTURES

The rise of commercial towns produced major adjustments in the political structure of Europe. It enhanced the power of great princes while reducing the relative strength of the Church and nobility. There was a natural alliance between secular princes and the urban bourgeoisie. The growth of a money economy liberated monarchs from restraints associated with traditional forms of feudal tenure. It accelerated changes in military organization, and it altered relationships between kings and nobles, empowering the former at the expense of the latter. The grant of fiefs in return for service became obsolete by the fourteenth century. Instead, princes granted incomes—money fiefs—to vassals who pledged their homage and performed essential public services. By the fifteenth century, retainers were offering their loyalty to princes under contracts of indenture whereby they served a lord for a specific period in return for an agreed sum. Armies that fought the Hundred Years War were raised in large measure through indenture. As the institutions of chivalry disappeared, the growing cash nexus permitted kings to hire mercenary armies and keep them in the field for longer periods. The pervasive use of metallic money facilitated tax collection; larger, more reliable revenue enabled powerful rulers to exploit fourteenth-century innovations in weaponry, particularly gunpowder and cannons.[22] The medieval warrior had brought his own weapons and armor into battle. By the fifteenth century royal arsenals had begun to appear, and in the sixteenth century the Spanish government began furnishing uniform weapons. The growing size of royal armies and fleets made it increasingly difficult for feudal lords to defy their kings. At the same time, large royal armies increased the problems of supply. Only the great merchants could organize provisioning on a scale required by ambitious monarchs.

The alliance between royalty and the urban bourgeoisie is evident in the revival of Roman Law. Customary law with its insistence on the principles of conditional property had satisfied the needs of a feudal agrarian society. It did not accommodate the political ambitions of kings, nor did it satisfy townsmen and traders who required firm assurances for the rights of private property. Roman civil law admitted the concept of absolute private property. Roman public law justified the absolute authority of the sovereign. The diffusion of Roman civic and public law across Europe in the final centuries of the Middle Ages betokened the converging interests of rising monarchs and the merchant class. The relative position of the nobility declined.[23]

COMMERCE AND CULTURAL SOPHISTICATION

The growth of trade, towns, and urban manufactures went hand in hand with the development of manners and high society. The rich were the best customers of the merchant class; indeed, the consumer demands of the wealthy elite, particularly royalty, substantially enhanced the growth of commerce and the prosperity of traders. Werner Sombart, a renowned German sociologist-historian, argued that the luxury spending of the great courts constituted a fundamental impetus to the growth of modern capitalism. The first extravagant court, he observed, was established under papal rule at Avignon in the fourteenth century. Ecclesiastical princes and noblemen with "no vocation other than that of serving the court's interest" kept the company of clever, witty, and beautiful women who gave court life its distinguishing sensuous and erotic quality.[24] In the age of the Renaissance this papal extravaganza moved to Rome, where the court of Paul II (1464–1471) exceeded all others in magnificence. Secular courts sprang up in Milan, Ferrara, Naples, and elsewhere. Across the Alps, Francis I (1515–1547) inaugurated the first elaborate French court, gathering around him "ladies of noble birth who before then had pined away behind the gray walls of their ancient castles."[25] Other European courts became slavish examples of the French. Castiglione's *Book of the Courtier* instructed contemporaries in the style, etiquette, dress, and other requirements of princely life. This book passed through a hundred editions by 1600. The demand for luxuries was immense, and whole cities rose up in service to princely courts—Naples, Sombart noted, "was never anything but the residence of a prince," and Paris and London owed much of their populations to people engaged directly or indirectly in service to the royal courts.[26] Under Louis XIV, Versailles provided the ultimate example of a social system that exalted monarchy and employed the nobility as expensive ornamentation. Courtly life may have indulged the aristocratic elite, but it transferred wealth to the bourgeoisie, partly in return for the supply of luxuries and partly through the indebtedness that kings and noblemen incurred to merchants in order to pay for their luxuries.

OLD WORLD EXPANSION

Expansion was the watchword of commercial society. In no sphere is the impact of commerce more evident than in the world-wide extension of European power and influence. As commercial firms grew in size they extended their interests into new, more profitable forms of business. Trade and investment required geographical outreach: old territories were exploited more thoroughly; new lands were opened to trade; and the tentacles of European commercial society began to wrap around a shrinking planet. As a matter of course, successful trading houses engaged in banking, securing the deposits of creditors and lending money under concealed interest arrangements. Italian firms dominated medieval banking, dispersing their agents throughout Europe and the Mediterranean. In the fourteenth century, the Peruzzi house of Florence had branches in other Italian cities, Sardinia, Sicily, Cyprus, the Balearics, Tunis, Bruges, Paris, and London.[27] Bankers became tax collectors for the Church as well as for European princes. Successful firms sold maritime insurance and organized manufacture in various industries. When trade floundered in one area, they transferred investments elsewhere. The Genoese lost most of their Eastern colonies to the Turks in the middle years of the fifteenth century, but by that time they had already cultivated new fields for investment in the Western Mediterranean.[28] After 1462 they gained the right to farm the great alum mines discovered at Tolfa, near Rome.[29] Having lost access to the slave trade of the East, they tried to acquire black slaves from North Africa; they sought Malagueta pepper from the west coast of Africa; and they cultivated a silk trade in Grenada before and after its reconquest by Spanish Christians. They financed fruit growing in Andalusia, mercury production in Castile, and iron mining in Biscay. With Genoese financing, the Portuguese colonized Madeira and the Azores, introducing sugar culture from the Mediterranean.[30] This spirit of enterprise, as well as the new focus on Atlantic opportunities, was evident in the young Genoese mariner, Christopher Columbus, who left the Aegean in 1451, ventured to Madeira, then shipped from West Africa to Iceland before launching his great trans-oceanic voyages of discovery.

The energy of Italians in the trans-Mediterranean and north-south trades was matched in the North Sea and Baltic by a remarkable expansion of German commercial power. By the twelfth century, Cologne led a field of developing cities in the Rhine Valley—the main axis of the north-south trade. These Rhenish and Westphalian towns served as nuclei from which German burghers launched an unprecedented eastward urban migration, planting towns beyond the Elbe and along the Baltic coast in lands devoid of urban life. Lubeck, Danzig, Riga, and Reval are only the most noted eastern cities established in the late twelfth or thirteenth centuries by parties of German merchants with the approval of great Slavonic princes.

This eastward migration, coinciding with a similar movement of German agriculturists into the lightly populated East Elbian plain, consolidated German control of the sea approaches to Novgorod, the principal Russian emporium for the fur trade. Unlike West German cities from which they sprang, these eastern towns had no Church heritage. They were, from their founding, organized and dominated by burghers engaged in long-distance trade. A century before the Hanseatic League was formed, the towns that would ultimately constitute it were informally united through interlocking family connections and mutual self-interest.

THE ESTABLISHMENT OF CAPITALISM

Had Western Europe become capitalist? Pirenne, for one, had no doubt of it. Only those completely blinded by preconceived ideas, he thought, could deny the importance and influence of commercial capitalism in Europe by as early as the twelfth century.[31] In the late Middle Ages, Europe was knitted together by a hierarchy of increasingly efficient markets. Village folk sold their small surpluses at local market towns; townsmen traded those goods at regional markets; and large-scale traders accumulated surpluses from regional markets to exchange for scarce or exotic goods at the great fairs. International fairs, originating in the eleventh century, were an enormous asset to long-distance traders. The celebrated Champagne fairs, held four times a year for nearly three centuries, provided a convenient meeting point for the exchange of Mediterranean and Flemish goods. The great fairs became financial markets. Debts incurred in trades not related to the exchange of goods at a particular fair could, nevertheless, be settled there. All obstacles to trade were met and surmounted. By the thirteenth century, Italian business practices were more sophisticated than those of Byzantium, and moral anxiety over such concerns as avarice and usury was fading fast. In the sixteenth century, traders in the Eastern Mediterranean generally accepted the superiority of Italian mechanics, metallurgy, and weaponry.[32] Lynn White, a historian of technology, declares that by 1500 Europe's industrial skill as well as its industrial capacity exceeded that of any world culture.[33] In the language of the *Cambridge Modern History,* capitalism "swept away local exclusiveness." It broke down ancient restrictions, overtook industry, and gave powerful impetus to the formation of national monarchies.[34]

Even the most ardent advocate of the commercial model acknowledges that the expansion of trade and the progressive evolution of inter-regional division of labor did not continue unabated throughout European history. In the fourteenth century, economic growth subsided. The Flemish cloth industry, ravaged by labor strife, suffered decline, and an alarming number of Italian banking firms collapsed. German traders, concerned by general trends, established the Hanseatic League to defend and consolidate their interests. Famine descended between 1315 and 1317, and in 1346–1347 the Black Death began its inexorable migration from the Middle East. During the next five years plague devoured up to a third of the European population. Plague was complicated by strife. In 1337, the English and French began their Hundred Years War, laying waste a large part of France. Political anarchy reigned over much of Germany. Although the Italian states retained some of their vigor, the fourteenth century was for most of Europe a time of despair, anguish, and economic stagnation.

Despite these setbacks the essential ingredients of a dynamic new economy were in place in Europe. The Italians had taught others efficient methods of conducting business. The Flemish, having pioneered in the cloth industry, had passed their methods to the English, who at long last were utilizing their immense herds as the basis for a highly successful export industry in finished woolens. When the ravages of plague and war subsided, Europeans possessed the material and commercial instruments required for rapid economic recovery. The opening of mines in Germany, Bohemia, and Hungary after 1450, made possible by improved pumping, extracting, and smelting techniques, rapidly expanded the trade in minerals. Silver production in Europe increased fivefold between 1450 and 1530.[35] French wine, salt, fruits, and linen; Scandinavian timber, iron, and forest products; Russian fur; Spanish wool; Roman alum; German minerals; Dutch herrings—these and innumerable other products were traded in growing volume across Europe. The flow of Baltic grain to the West, though not terribly large, permitted the transfer of manpower from farm to workshop in critical industrial areas, particularly the Lowlands. Most important, the opening of a direct sea route to India and the discovery of the Western hemisphere suddenly expanded the international division of labor and offered unprecedented opportunities for profit.

NEW WORLD EXPANSION

European exploitation of America provides emphatic evidence of the power of commerce and the deepening alliance between monarchs and merchants. From the start, Europe's monarchs asserted administrative authority over the process of overseas expansion. Prince Henry the Navigator pursued his explorations of West Africa and initiated colonization of the Atlantic islands under dispensation from the Portuguese Crown.[36] Shortly after the discovery of America, Spanish monarchs asserted supreme authority over the process of colonization, centralizing all American trade at Seville. The fact that events in America outran the superintending power of Madrid or that regulations issued in Spain were neglected in the Indies was more a function of distance and time than of disregard for the monarchy. The Crown was universally perceived as the fount of privilege, the ultimate authority that any aspirant to high position must conciliate. When the French and English launched exploring or colonizing probes during the sixteenth century, they too acted under patent or charter from the Crown.

How were these overseas probes to be financed? Being aware that American bullion strikes enriched the Spanish Crown, English and French monarchs were prepared to support endeavors to find alluvial wealth or to discover a northwest passage to India. But their resources fell short of costs. Money had to be raised from merchants or courtiers or syndicates of the two. London became the propaganda center for every variety of English "venture." Its merchants were clearly the principal underwriters of overseas endeavors,[37] and in France, overseas adventures, slave trading, and colonization were almost exclusively the province of merchants residing in the coastal cities.[38]

Colonization required prodigious capital resources, and trans-Atlantic investment accelerated the evolution of capitalist institutions. The planting of colonies was always speculative: not only was it big business, but it was a form of big business that required a generous investment of capital as well as considerable lead time before investments could bear fruit. In contrast to routine European trading, the establishment of colonial positions involved the construction of port facilities, forts, villages, and all the physical paraphernalia of permanent habitation. Both the costs and the risks of such ventures were high, and investors required commercial institutions that would attract abundant capital while permitting an equitable sharing of the greater risks of long-distance operations.

Existing business structures did not fulfill all these requirements. In northwestern Europe, the concept of incorporation had not advanced beyond the regulated company, a form of merchant guild by which an association of merchants was granted a royal charter giving it monopoly trading rights in a particular area. The regulated company was akin to a privileged chamber of commerce representing multiple forms of business ownership. It was not a unified company with a single mode of ownership. To meet the exceptional requirements of overseas expansion, Europeans developed the joint stock company, an institution that accepted capital investments from a large number of shareholders in order to minimize risks and conduct business under a single unified directorship.[39] Although early English joint stock companies—the Muscovy Company, the Virginia Company, the Hudson's Bay Company, and the East India Company—possessed vestigial remains of earlier forms of business operations, they were formative structures that laid the groundwork for subsequent monuments of Western capitalism such as the Bank of England.[40]

CONCLUSION

Commerce had drawn Europe from the dismal quiet of the Dark Ages to the conquest of world markets. Europe's experience was unique. Only once in world history has such a natural evolutionary transformation from agrarian backwardness to dynamic urban capitalism occurred. All subsequent breakthroughs to modern capitalism have been, in one degree or another, force-fed by the pressure and example of Europeans. In Europe, man's natural acquisitiveness was aided by a temperate climate, rich soils, and natural highways of communication. Rent by numerous navigable rivers and surrounded by seas, the continent afforded relatively easy movement of men and trade goods, even in times of primitive technology.

It was, however, the Mediterranean that provided the economic well-spring for Western Europe, first in Roman times and later in the tenth and eleventh centuries when Italian city-states began their illustrious career as purveyors of products and culture to backward fellow Christians across the Alps. What transformed Venice from a shabby community of fishermen to the great port of Christian Europe was trade. Venice's example ignited similar strivings elsewhere in Italy. In trans-Alpine Europe, a keen acquisitive outlook was belatedly and slowly aroused by merchants who tramped from region to region, huddling in the shadow of great stone fortresses. Gradually, trade increased the use of money; the money economy gave life to towns; and towns became catalysts of change across the countryside. By 1600, the center of economic power and cultural influence had passed from Italy to northwestern Europe. Spain may have been the great political power of the period, but the Low Countries were the nucleus of an expanding commercial world. Antwerp, the great emporium of the sixteenth century, gave place after 1585 to Amsterdam. Both stood at the maritime crossroads of Europe, opposite Great Britain, halfway between the Baltic ports and Iberia, at the terminus of rivers that drained Eastern France and Germany. The explosion of wealth was evident in European ports; in the vast growth of shipping; in the size and character of armies, navies, and bureaucracies; and in conspicuous expenditure on country houses and royal palaces.

Commerce was the engine that drove every momentous change in European life. It facilitated the rise of monarchical power while it eroded the power of the Church and the ascetic principles upon which the Church relied. Every obstacle to the expansion of trade was met and overcome by new devices, new technology, or new modes of business organization. By the sixteenth century, desire for profit had occasioned the great maritime discoveries, the establishment of trans-oceanic colonies, and the extension of European commercial activity to the far reaches of the world. European culture had become distinguished above all other world cultures by its superior arms and marine technology, by its commitment to the development and use of machinery, by its sophisticated business methods, and by its self-confident bravado. The instruments as well as the mentalities of modern capitalism had triumphed, and European society, the master of an advancing world-wide division of labor, was marching inexorably toward its eighteenth-century Industrial Revolution. For all its diversity, the culture of Europe was fundamentally the product of commerce.

NOTES

1. William Cunningham, "Economic Change," in *The Cambridge Modern History:* vol. 1, *The Renaissance* (Cambridge, 1902), pp. 494, 497, 500.

2. Herbert Butterfield, *The Whig Interpretation of History* (London, 1931). This was the viewpoint of countless series histories and university textbooks during the first six decades of the century. Textbooks like Carl Stephenson's widely read *Medieval History* (New York, 1935) and Sidney Painter's *History of the Middle Ages* (New York, 1952) pursued that approach, and volumes of the influential *Rise of Modern Europe* series, edited by William Langer, were unabashedly market oriented. See, for example, Edward P. Cheyney, *The Dawn of a New Era 1250–1453* (New York, 1936).

3. Abbé Guillaume-Thomas Raynal, *Histoire philosophique et politique des établissemens et du commerce des Européens dans les deux Indes,* vol. 1 (Geneva, 1782), p. 4. The French wording is as follows: "*les peuples qui ont poli tous les autres, ont été commercans.*"

4. Adam Smith, *An Inquiry into the Nature and Causes of the Wealth of Nations,* vol. 1 (1776; Oxford, 1976), p. 25.

5. A law of inheritance by which the entire real estate of a deceased person passes to the eldest son.

6. A legal settlement by which the inheritance of a landed estate is limited to an unalterable succession of heirs. Entail prevents the person currently enjoying landlord rights from bequeathing the property at his or her pleasure.

7. Smith, *Wealth of Nations,* vol. 1, p. 383.

8. Pirenne's commercial orientation is delineated in *Medieval Cities: Their Origins and the Revival of Trade* (Princeton, 1925) and *Economic and Social History of Medieval Europe* (London, 1937).

9. Fustel de Coulanges, *Histoire des institutions politiques de l'ancienne France* (Paris, 1975). This work is discussed in Bryce Lyon, *Henri Pirenne: A Biographical and Intellectual Study* (Gent, 1974), p. 443.

10. Alfons Dopsch, *Wirschaftliche und Soziale Grundlagen der Europäischen Kulturentwicklung* (Vienna, 1923–1924), 2 vols. The work has been condensed in English translation, *The Economic and Social Foundations of European Civilizations* (London, 1937).

11. In modern times, usury involves the taking of exorbitant interest on a loan. In the Middle Ages, any interest taken on a loan was considered usury.

12. In theory, the "just price" of a product should be equal to the cost of the materials and labor required in its making; in practice, it was perceived as fair market price.

13. Hicks observed that the inland Sea of Japan was relatively small and that the lands around it did not generate the variety of natural resources of the Mediterranean. The coastline of India, largely unbroken, provided less attractive opportunities for trade. Only the South China Sea linking Indo-China, Indonesia, and the Philippines offered conditions approaching those of the Mediterranean. Hicks did not speculate on why this area had been less productive of active commercial city-states than the Mediterranean. Sir John Hicks, *A Theory of Economic History* (Oxford, 1969), pp. 138–139.

14. Before the eleventh century, a number of south Italian towns (Naples, Gaeta, Amalfi, Solerno, and Bari) as well as Venice recognized the emperor at Constantinople.

15. Fernand Braudel, *The Mediterranean and the Mediterranean World in the Age of Philip II,* vol. 1, trans. Sian Reynolds (New York, 1972), p. 115.

16. Braudel contends that the urban population of Flanders and Brabant was about 50 percent by 1400. The proportion of townspeople for Western and Central Europe by the end of the eighteenth century was only 20–25 percent. Fernand Braudel, *Capitalism and Material Life 1400–1800* (New York, 1975), p. 376.

17. It was a common medieval expression that the air of the city made one free. If a runaway serf was able to escape capture for one year and a day, he or she was granted freedom.

18. Smith, *Wealth of Nations,* vol. 1, pp. 418–419.

19. Demesne was the land of a manor held by and worked in behalf of the lord. Non-demesne lands were distributed to serfs who worked those lands for their own maintenance.

20. Pirenne, *Economic and Social History,* p. 18.

21. Herbert Heaton offered an example of a bill of exchange: "I, A.B. (Genoese importer), have accepted from you, C.D. (Alexandrian exporter), goods to the value of xyz pounds of Genoese money, and I promise to pay to you in Alexandria, in bezants of Alexandria, pq bezants to the pound, before (a certain date)." Heaton continued: "This bill was sent to C.D. He sold it for bezants to some Alexandrian importer (E.F.) who owed pounds to G.H., an exporter in Genoa. E.F. sent the bill to G.H., who presented it to A.B. and collected pounds. Thus two debts between two remote towns were settled with one document and two local transfers of money." Herbert Heaton, *Economic History of Europe* (New York, 1948), pp. 177–178.

22. Carlo M. Cipolla, *Guns, Sails and Empires: Technological Innovation and the Early Phases of European Expansion, 1400–1700* (New York, 1965), pp. 24–26.

23. It might be argued that nobles were compensated for their diminished influence by the establishment of private property rights over lands distributed to their antecedents under the usufruct conditions of fiefdom.

24. Werner Sombart, *Luxury and Capitalism* (Ann Arbor, 1967), p. 52. This work was first published in German in 1913.

25. Ibid., p. 3.

26. Ibid., pp. 22–28.

27. Gerald A. J. Hodgett, *A Social and Economic History of Medieval Europe* (London, 1972), pp. 67–68.

28. Ruth Pike, *Enterprise and Adventure: The Genoese in Seville and the Opening of the New World* (Ithaca, 1966), pp. 6–9, 17–19, 145–147.

29. Alum was a vital chemical used in the woolen industry. Western supplies had come from Phocaea near Smyrna, but the Turks gained control of the eastern mines in 1455 and imposed weighty taxes on the product. The Tolfa concession was, therefore, a valuable asset to the Genoese.

30. Robert Lopez, "Market Expansion: The Case of Genoa," *Journal of Economic History* 24 (1964): 456–462.

31. Pirenne, *Economic and Social History,* pp. 160–168.

32. Braudel, *The Mediterranean,* vol. 2, pp. 799–800; Carlo Cipolla, *Before the Industrial Revolution: European Society and Economy, 1000–1700* (New York, 1976), p. 207.

33. Lynn White, Jr., *Medieval Technology and Social Change* (Oxford and New York, 1962), pp. 128–129.

34. Cunningham, "Economic Change," pp. 494–500.

35. Heaton, *Economic History*, p. 232.

36. Charles Verlinden, *The Beginnings of Modern Colonization* (Ithaca, 1970), pp. 204–209.

37. Theodore K. Rabb, "Investment in English Overseas Enterprise, 1575–1630," *Economic History Review*, 2d ser., 19 (1966): 70–81.

38. Gabriel Debien, *Les Engagés pour les Antilles (1634–1715)* (Paris, 1952), pp. 38–39. Attempts by the French Crown to encourage the participation of nobles were rejected on grounds that commerce was a socially degrading activity. See Guy Richard, *Noblesse d' affaires au XVIIIe siècle* (Paris, 1974).

39. Italians had developed prototypes of the joint stock company to administer imperial holdings in the Eastern Mediterranean in the fourteenth century. E. L. J. Coornaert, "European Economic Institutions and the New World: The Chartered Companies," in E. E. Rich and C. H. Wilson, eds., *The Cambridge Economic History of Europe*, vol. 4 (Cambridge, 1967), p. 221.

40. K. G. Davies, *The Royal African Company* (London, 1957), pp. 24–33.

4

The Demographic Model

Although the commercial explanation enjoyed absolute dominance among Western historians during the first half of this century, that dominance was challenged in the decades after World War II. Medievalists led the charge. For all its appeal, the linear and progressive commercial model failed to explain the unevenness of medieval economic life. Despite expanding markets and increasing division of labor, things did not "grow bigger and better from generation to generation": indeed, wrote M. M. Postan, there was "no continuous ascent from barbaric primitivity . . . to the glorious efflorescence of the renaissance." As we have seen, the fourteenth and fifteenth centuries were a time of commercial failure, bankruptcy, and retrenchment. Markets shrivelled, and the international division of labor was thrust into reverse. If market activity and the money economy were unable to counter Europe's fourteenth-century tailspin, then perhaps commercial forces had not been primarily responsible for the growth that occurred earlier.[1]

Historians have lavished attention on markets and money, but most of the medieval economy was not involved in long-distance trade. Inter-regional commerce does not account for some of the most significant changes in a fundamentally agricultural society: the rise of new villages; the increase in crops, animals, and men in agriculture during the thirteenth century; or the disappearance of villages and the decline of agricultural production in the fourteenth and fifteenth centuries. Nor can expanding trade or the "rise of the money economy" account adequately for the commutation of the serfs' labor services or for the elimination of serfdom itself. Postan demonstrated that commutation was not a continuous and progressive process. The typical chronology of lord-serf relations in England was a change from labor services to money rents in the twelfth century, a return to labor services in the thirteenth century, and a wave of commutations in the fourteenth and fifteenth centuries. Serfdom had ended in Western Europe by the sixteenth century. Labor services were commuted first in those regions of England that were least commercial, not in trading districts adjacent to London.[2]

In the early modern period as well, Europe's vital signs were irregular. The sixteenth century was a time of commercial and demographic expansion, the seventeenth one of stagnation. In Eastern Europe, the growth of long-distance trade and the expansion of the international division of labor neither increased human freedom, stimulated urban life, nor enhanced the general well-being. Instead, the rise of international commerce proved socially regressive. From the Baltic to the Black Sea, peasants who for centuries had enjoyed relative freedom were systematically reduced to serfdom upon the advent of large-scale inter-regional trade in the fifteenth and sixteenth centuries. In Poland, agricultural ownership became concentrated in the hands of great lords; peasants were confined to survival-sized plots; artisanal groups withered; interior towns declined; and the few large manufactories that arose employed serf labor.[3]

Because the linear commercial model seemed ill-equipped to accommodate these realities, scholars have sought alternative theories of change more sensitive to the unevenness of material life in Europe. For some, the celebrated essays on population of the English parson, Thomas Robert Malthus (1766–1834), provided inspiration. Malthus challenged Adam Smith's trade-based division-of-labor model, arguing that material progress was possible only within the narrowest limits. Likewise, he rejected the optimistic speculations of French revolutionaries and Enlightenment philosophers concerning the perfectibility of man and of society. History was not a linear account of human progress. The material existence of humankind had ebbed and flowed like ocean tides. Every surge to the fore was followed by a retreat, albeit this ceaseless oscillation occurred around a slowly rising trend of material wealth. The key to understanding the historical process was not commerce. It was population pressure.

Malthus determined that stable agrarian societies having fixed land resources and limited technological skill confronted upper limits, or ceilings, to population size. These ceilings were determined by the maximum amount of food that could be drawn from the land at a particular time. Malthus offered two fundamental postulates: first, that food is necessary for human survival; second, that passion between the sexes is both necessary and enduring. He observed, however, that the procreative power occasioned by human passion is vastly greater than the power of the land to supply subsistence. When unchecked, population naturally increases geometrically (1–2–4–8–16–32), while subsistence increases only arithmetically (1–2–3–4–5–6). Using these ratios and assuming that humans could double the bounty of their lands every twenty-five years, Malthus determined that without checks the natural growth of population would be 315 times greater than the growth of the food supply over a period of three centuries.[4]

Such imbalance is inconceivable. In reality, observed Malthus, population is kept in homeostatic balance with food supply by the operation of preventive and positive checks. Preventive checks were voluntary actions taken to control fertility. They included contraception, celibacy, late age of marriage for women (a practice peculiar to European society), the delay of property transfers between generations, and out-migration. Preventive checks alone had never preserved a stable equilibrium between population and subsistence, Malthus believed. Given natural passion between the sexes, population rose whenever subsistence was ample, and rising population ultimately placed excessive pressure on food resources, ensnaring the masses of humankind in subsistence crises. Such crises triggered positive checks (famine, epidemic disease, and war over scarce resources), sharply increasing mortality. When the painful operation of these checks finally restored equilibrium between population and food supplies, a new cycle of growth and subsidence would commence. With each succeeding cycle, population ceilings drifted upward. This drift was made possible by agricultural and technological innovations introduced under the pressure of successive crises.

The Malthusian model was highly pessimistic. For all historical time, the lives of common people had oscillated between mere sufficiency and extreme misery. Humankind was capable of moderating the severity of overpopulation by exercising "moral restraint," but the inexorable logic of the Malthusian principle insured that the upward drift of material progress would be painfully slow and erratic.

Although numerous refinements and adjustments have been made to Malthus's theory, his principle of population continues to provide an intellectual cornerstone for modern historical demography. Malthus worked under enormous handicap. He had no reliable population statistics. Nineteenth-century Britain became the world's leader in recording demographic information, but the country's first national census was not taken until several years after Malthus's essay appeared. Not until 1838 did the law require public registration of births, deaths, and the causes of all deaths. In the absence of such records it is extremely difficult, if not impossible, for historical demographers to determine with certainty the relative importance of fertility and mortality in producing demographic change. Thomas McKeown, a renowned demographer, doubts that we will ever have an acceptable interpretation for the modern rise of population.[5] Yet McKeown's work concentrates on the last three centuries, a period for which vital statistics are relatively abundant! What about the twelfth or fourteenth or sixteenth centuries? For them, wrote Michael Flinn, we must resort to "hypothesizing on an heroic scale."[6]

THE POPULATION HISTORY OF EUROPE

It is ironic that the demographic explanation for historical change has been most persuasively advocated by scholars focusing on the Middle Ages and the early modern era. We will never know the actual population figures for Europe (or for even the smallest regions of Europe) in the Middle Ages, but the relative simplicity of medieval life enables us to draw some conclusions about the ebb and flow of population and material life. J. C. Russell estimated the population of western and central Europe to have been 9 million in A.D. 500. At that date, the whole Mediterranean basin from Iberia and Morocco eastward to Syria may have supported 35 million people.[7] In A.D. 541, bubonic plague entered the inland sea from East Africa, killing up to a third of the Mediterranean population. The weakened Byzantine government was unable to achieve Justinian's goal of restoring the Roman Empire, and the decimation of stable populations in North Africa enhanced the seventh-century conquest of Arabs, whose nomadic habits rendered them less vulnerable to plague. Northern Europe was largely spared the effects of the ancient plague. By A.D. 1000, the gradual recovery of Mediterranean populations and the slow demographic advance of transalpine peoples provided all Europe a total population estimated in the range of 36 to 38.5 million.[8]

After A.D. 1000, Europe's population expanded. On a graph, this upward movement would show a saw-tooth configuration, indicating sharp short-term fluctuations, yet the overall direction of demographic change was unmistakably upward. During three centuries, total population may have doubled, reaching as much as 74–78 million by 1300. Some historians think this growth slowed in the thirteenth century and stopped around 1270; others believe that growth continued at reduced rate until the 1340s. In the late 1340s bubonic plague swept over Europe, producing catastrophic loss of life. Initial mortality may have been a third of the population, but successive recurrences of plague increased losses.[9] By 1410, England may have lost half of its pre-plague population, and similar losses occurred elsewhere in Europe. At some point in the later fifteenth century, population growth resumed. Precisely when this recovery began and how it was staggered across Europe is disputed, but once under way, the recovery continued vigorously through the sixteenth century.

In the seventeenth century population retreated once again, but in the absence of universal catastrophe on the scale of plague, the retreat was uneven and comparatively modest. The Iberian countries suffered significant decreases in the seventeenth century; population declined in Italy in the first half of the century; it stagnated in France. In German-speaking Europe where the Thirty Years War occasioned widespread devastation, population fell as much as 40 percent. Growth continued in England and the Netherlands during the first half of the seventeenth century, then stabilized for another hundred years.

By 1750, population growth had, once again, resumed almost everywhere in Europe. Growth has continued to the present day (see Figure 4.1). Europe's population was about 140 million in 1750. It rose to around 180 million in 1800, to 390 million by 1900, and it is expected to reach 700 million by 2000.[10]

Figure 4.1
European Population Growth, A.D. 100–2000 (Estimated)

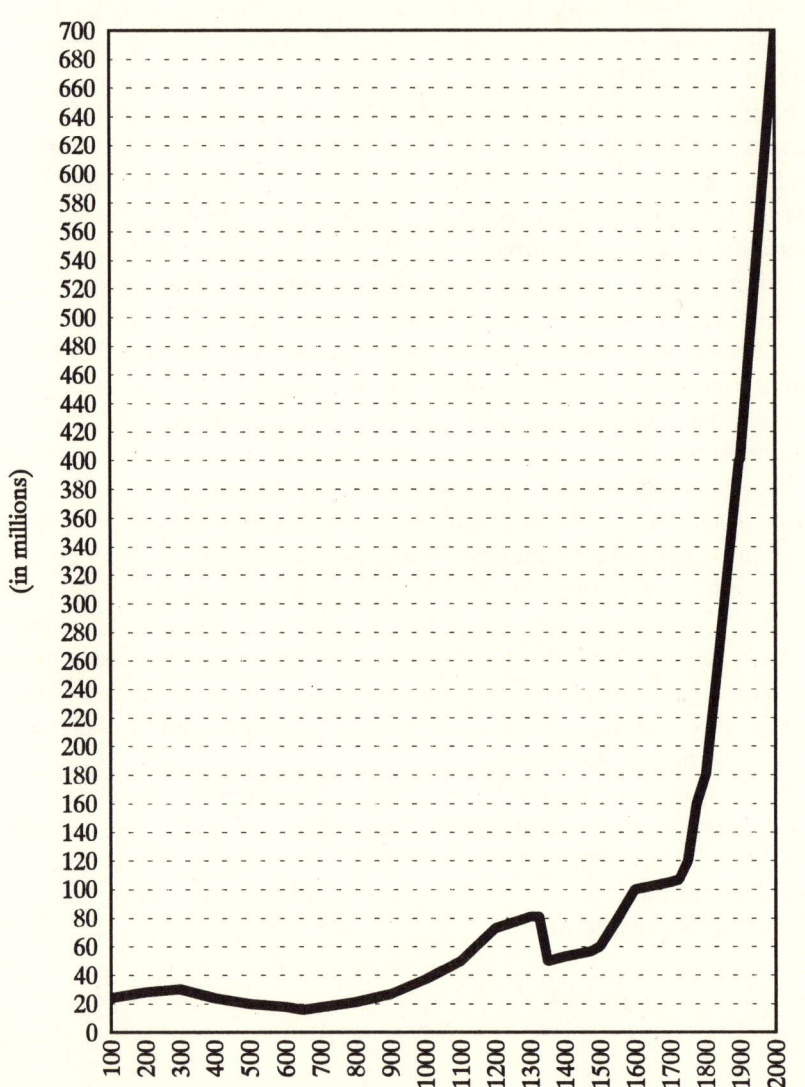

Sources: Colin McEvedy and Richard Jones, *Atlas of World Population History* (Harmondsworth, 1978), p. 19; Roger Mols, S. J., "Population in Europe 1500–1700," in Carlo M. Cipolla, ed., *The Fontana Economic History of Europe:* vol. 2, *The Sixteenth and Seventeenth Centuries* (Glasgow, 1974); J. C. Russell, "Population in Europe 500–1500," in Carlo M. Cipolla, ed., *The Fontana Economic History of Europe:* vol. 1, *The Middle Ages* (London, 1972).

Can a pattern be discerned in these figures? Arguing in the affirmative, D. B. Grigg has identified the following population trends since A.D. 1000.[11]

Years	Trend
1000–1100	Increase
1100–1200	High Growth
1200–1300	Growth Rate Cooling
1300–1347	Stagnation
1347–1450	Decline
1450–1600	Growth
1600–1740	Stagnation in Northern Europe
	Decline in Southern Europe
1740–	Growth

For neo-Malthusian historians, the two cycles of growth and subsidence—1000–1450; 1450–1740—represent Malthusian rhythm writ large. In agricultural societies, rising population imposes pressure on land resources, requiring the progressive fragmentation of arable land into smaller and smaller parcels. By the simple action of supply and demand, landlords are able to extract higher rents from their tenants. The number of landless people grows, and those having no land or too little land must obtain their livelihood (or part of it) through wage labor. When the number of wage workers competing for employment grows, wage levels fall. Food costs rise both as a reflection of increasing land values and as a response to intensified demand by an expanding population. Because people are compelled to spend a larger share of their wealth on daily sustenance, they have fewer resources to expend on manufactures. Therefore, in periods of growing population pressure, the terms of trade run against industry and in favor of landlords.

When a population ceiling is reached and the land is unable to sustain the demands placed upon it, a self-correcting mechanism is triggered, and all the trends are reversed. Land empties out. Marginal lands occupied under a regime of high pressure are abandoned; land values fall; rents fall; and the terms of trade begin to favor industry. Wages rise, and bargaining power passes from the landlord to the tenant and from the employer to the wage earner. To the extent that political power is based upon economic power, the power of landlords is increased in times of high population pressure and compromised in times of population decline.

THE DEMOGRAPHIC MODEL AND THE MIDDLE AGES

Neo-Malthusians contend that European history after A.D. 1000 offers a vindication of Malthus. The upward trajectory of population after the year 1000 was possible because Europe's abundant virgin land permitted the establishment of new villages and new settlements. Population grew, but yields from the land did not increase significantly.[12] Medieval farmers were not profit maximizers, and it stands to reason that the ready availability of land during the eleventh and twelfth centuries discouraged technological innovation. As the land gradually filled with people and population pressure mounted, pasture was converted into arable, reducing the numbers of grazing animals and limiting the availability of manure. Increasingly, marginal agricultural lands were brought under the plow, but such lands were particularly subject to the law of diminishing returns. In brief time, poorer lands punished the men who worked them with failing crops and cattle disease.

Symptoms of overpopulation were abundantly evident by the fourteenth century. Land was being subdivided through inheritance and fragmented through exchange into smaller and smaller holdings. Despite intense cultivation, the land could not produce enough food to supply an expanding population. As demand for land increased, so did its price. Rents rose; wages fell. Landlessness increased, and with it, banditry, vagrancy, and pauperism. Food prices soared, trapping people in a wage-price scissors and leaving them vulnerable to any type of natural disaster. All that was needed was some combination of adverse circumstances—a few years of drought or crop disease—to set off a crisis. Occasional bad harvests in the late thirteenth century sent preliminary shock waves across the continent. These were mere portents of the disaster that befell England in 1317–1319 or southern France in 1335–1347 when failing crops produced severe famine. With the arrival of bubonic plague in the 1340s, a society already experiencing a Malthusian check suffered demographic catastrophe.

Plague relieved pressure on the land, and the whole bundle of social and economic trends surged into reverse. Food prices fell; wages rose. Great landlords, who in the thirteenth century had benefitted from high rents and low wages, found themselves hard-pressed to obtain suitable tenants to occupy their properties. Exploiting their advantage, tenants demanded and received lower rents and long-term leases. At the abbey of

Saint-Germain-des-Prés, rents averaged 84 deniers per arpent from 1360 to 1400, 56 deniers from 1422 to 1461, and 31 deniers from 1461 to 1483.[13] Leases of twenty and forty years' duration became common, and a few estates, like Chertsy Abbey in England, granted leases for 200 and 300 years![14] The most enterprising peasants seized the opportunity to purchase customary or freehold property as well as to lease demesne land. During preceding centuries, a growing disparity had emerged in the size of holdings occupied by peasants. The dislocations of plague enabled prosperous and vigorous peasants who preserved their health to accumulate extensive land holdings. By the sixteenth century, many of these rich peasants—so-called kulaks—had become country gentlemen.

Changing demographic conditions in the late fourteenth and fifteenth centuries also served the poorer peasants by reversing bargaining power between employers and workers. Food had become cheap; labor dear. When the lords enacted laws to keep peasants bound to the land and their wages low, peasants rebelled. The most dramatic example of this is the celebrated Peasant's Revolt in England in 1381. In the chaotic period following the fall of Rome, peasants had sacrificed their personal freedom in exchange for the protection of feudal lords. This situation no longer applied, and lords who insisted upon extracting onerous obligations were viewed as mere exploiters. Peasants were highly mobile. Since their possessions were few, they were able to assemble their modest belongings and be on the high road in a matter of minutes. Landlords who resisted the reasonable demands of peasants risked losing their services altogether, and by the fifteenth century, there was no shortage of competing landlords willing to hire them. In these conditions, the constraints of serfdom, which for centuries had bound individuals to the soil, were peeled away across Western Europe.

These developments prompted a sea-change in political power relationships. The end of serfdom and the assertion of greater independence by leading elements of the peasantry weakened the relative power of the landed nobility. A diminished nobility was less capable of resisting the attempts of Europe's monarchs to consolidate their power through the extension of royal taxation and the expansion of royal bureaucracies, royal armies, and royal courts. It is no accident that the monarchs of England, France, and Spain consolidated their power at the end of the first great Malthusian cycle.

In formulating the demographic model, neo-Malthusian historians have not ignored the growth of markets, towns, and manufactures; nor are they insensitive to the importance of division of labor. Being pre-modern historians for the most part, they view the subject of economic growth differently from their modernist colleagues. Modern economists and economic historians have distinguished two categories of wealth—per capita (individual) and aggregate (collective)—observing that increases in the production of aggregate wealth need not generate an increase in per capita wealth if the number of individuals who must share the aggregate product grows at a rate faster than aggregate production itself. For this reason, economists determine that *real* economic growth occurs only when a society experiences sustained increases in *both aggregate and per capita wealth*.

This definition has little relevance for European society during most of the pre-industrial age. Because medieval people had no inclination to maximize profits and because they experienced no technological or structural changes far-reaching enough to revolutionize production, economic output in medieval society depended overwhelmingly on the number of labor inputs—that is, on the number of people working. Rising population meant rising aggregate output. Yet, as Malthus observed, rising population also meant reduced average income per capita. In spite of this, argue neo-Malthusian historians, long-term demographically driven oscillations did not occur around a fixed axis. In other words, when a population reversal occurred, it did not return the European economy to the place it had been prior to the last long-term surge of population growth. Long periods of rising population—which is to say, long periods of aggregate economic growth—generated important structural changes in society, even though such changes occurred at an almost glacial rate. The rise of markets offers a case in point.

In England, rural markets were established in profusion during the thirteenth century. These markets, held at specific locations once a week, did not initiate exchange among villagers. Village trade had always existed. Formal markets, established by local lords, merely regularized and regulated rural trade when it become apparent that such trade was large enough to benefit from formalization. Often, rural markets served as collection centers from which raw materials were funneled into market towns and thence to the long-distance trade. For this reason, advocates of the commercial model have long contended that it was the rise of long-distance trade that stimulated the establishment and growth of rural markets. Not so, writes R. H. Britnell: it was population growth that prompted the founding of rural markets by promoting division of labor and stimulating local demand for manufactures, services, and foodstuffs. Economic specialization requires a significant density of population. As population pressure mounted and increasing numbers of people suffered from landlessness or from insufficiency of land for family maintenance, their sustenance had to be achieved through specialized wage work: for example, threshing, thatching, ditching, carting, or employment in trades. Moreover, population growth naturally increased the absolute number of craftsmen who served the community—the smiths, millers, tailors, carpenters, potters, tanners, clothworkers—and, of course, these people depended upon the sale of their goods or services to buy food and raw materials.[15] Rural markets provided the necessary vehicle for exchange. Like towns, however, markets were sensitive to population trends, and population decline in the fourteenth and fifteenth centuries caused the contraction of market activity, a falling-off of long-distance trade, and the shrinkage of towns.

THE DEMOGRAPHIC MODEL
AND EARLY MODERN EUROPE

The decades around 1500 witnessed a quickening of activity. Among other things, there was new buoyancy in long-distance trades. The great discoveries permitted direct trade to the Orient as well as the founding of colonies in the New World. Neo-Malthusians consider this renewed vigor highly predictable. Population growth had resumed in the late fifteenth century, initiating this vitality. The transportation and business infrastructure so carefully delineated by scholars of the commercial school was already in place by the late fifteenth century. Moreover, legal recognition of individual property rights by many European governments enabled enterprising persons to pursue economic gain with greater security. These developments permitted a swifter acceleration of aggregate economic growth when the growth of population resumed.

Of course, Europe was riding to a fall. Aggregate growth in the sixteenth century occasioned a revival of towns and trade, but this was offset by higher rents, higher food costs, and lower wages—in effect, by declining per capita wealth. Europe was being drawn toward another Malthusian trap, and by the century's end, Spain, Europe's greatest political power, was enduring repeated famines. In fact, much of Mediterranean Europe was confronting a grain crisis by 1600.[16] Only England and the northern Netherlands escaped a Malthusian check in the seventeenth century. There, population growth continued through the first half of the century and remained stable during the second half. The ramifications of these developments for international politics were profound. Spain began its long and tortured decline as a great power; Italy's economic and strategic importance withered; and the center of European political and economic power passed from the Mediterranean to northwest Europe.

Exponents of the demographic model, Douglas North and Robert Paul Thomas, explain why England and the Netherlands escaped the seventeenth-century Malthusian trap and emerged as Europe's economic nucleus. During the growth surge of the sixteenth century, rising aggregate demand for goods and services reduced the transaction costs borne by Europe's leading merchants. As noted in the previous chapter, transaction costs are the expenses incurred in acquiring information about markets, in negotiating commercial exchanges, and in enforcing compliance with business contracts. Although per capita incomes fell in agriculture, incomes rose in the trading sector as a result of declining transaction costs. Only those countries that earned a substantial part of their income through trade could increase population levels and concurrently enjoy both aggregate and per capita economic growth.[17]

Britain and the Netherlands were Europe's leading commercial countries. By the seventeenth century, England possessed a large uninterrupted national market; its urban growth was second only to that of the Netherlands; and institutional factors favored the expansion of commerce. The Netherlands already possessed a capital market and a long history of trading activity. The material interests of Dutch society were manifestly connected to international trade, and laws governing property rights reflected that fact. New business procedures had reduced transaction costs, and innovations in agriculture had integrated the countryside in a mutually beneficial relationship with the cities.

It was different in Europe's agrarian regions. In his study of Languedoc, the rural province stretching across Mediterranean France from the Rhone to the Pyrenees, Emmanuel Le Roy Ladurie bore witness to successive demographic cycles, what he called the "immense respiration of a social structure." At the end of the medieval cycle of expansion and contraction, Languedoc experienced vigorous population growth. With some irregularity, population climbed steeply until about 1570, then leveled off. Production levels were low and production per capita grew slowly. As farm land was subdivided, people struggled more and more to make ends meet. By 1680, there was no slack left in the system. Demographic growth ceased, and for the first time in two centuries, Languedoc sustained long-term decline. It was a decline, writes Le Roy Ladurie,

> provoked not so much by the repeated famines—which were perhaps less serious than in the center and in the north of France—as by joblessness and poverty; by chronic undernourishment; by the

low standard of living which favored the spread of epidemics; by the primitive sanitary conditions of the poor; and—very accessorily—by emigration, late marriages, and even a little birth control.[18]

Le Roy Ladurie does not contend that population pressure was the sole engine driving provincial affairs or that the timing of great demographic cycles was consistent across Europe. Political dictates from Paris, tax laws, religious disputes, warfare, changing trends in regional and international trade: these and other forces affected the lives and the livelihoods of Languedoc's peasants. Each of these forces had some bearing on provincial fertility rates. As for timing, vigorous population growth began later in Languedoc than elsewhere during the second great Malthusian "respiration," and the Malthusian check arrived later. Population sometimes stabilized at a low level even though the prospects for growth were abundant. This was true of Languedoc in the final decades of the first great cycle, 1470–1500. All that was needed was a catalyst—a series of good harvests—to trigger the mechanism. Once the mechanism was operative, however, the cycle moved inexorably along its course despite the action of secondary forces—that is, tax laws or political conflicts—that might delay or accelerate the process. In Languedoc, as in other agrarian regions, the ultimate constraints upon human affairs, the parameters that determined what was possible and what was not, were demographic.

Ironically, the demographic rhythm identified by Malthus lost its predictive value during his own lifetime. "Malthus was a clear-headed theoretician of traditional societies," wrote Le Roy Ladurie, "but he was a prophet of the past."[19] From one cycle to another, the cumulative upward drift of technical knowledge, physical and social infrastructure, financial institutions, and business acumen finally equipped Europeans—particularly northwest Europeans—with the ability to increase per capita production dramatically. Beginning in the eighteenth century, the productive, social, and institutional changes that we identify as the Industrial Revolution gave rise to an unprecedented and sustained increase in the rate of economic growth, both aggregate and per capita. A few statistics graphically demonstrate the degree to which rising per capita production outdistanced the growth of population, even at a time when population was growing at an unprecedented rate. During the three centuries from 1500 to 1800, the average annual increase of gross national product (GNP) per capita could not have exceeded 0.2–0.3 percent. In the early nineteenth century—the beginning phase of the Industrial Revolution—annual per capita income for all of Europe was growing at a rate of 0.5–0.7 percent. Between 1830 and 1910, the annual rate of growth of GNP per capita was 1.98 percent in the industrialized European countries. Over the same period, population grew at an annual rate of 0.82 percent per year.[20]

By the nineteenth century, Europe had surmounted the Malthusian trap: aggregate growth no longer dictated per capita impoverishment. Enjoying backward vision, it is much easier for us to identify this breakthrough than it was for contemporaries. Neither Adam Smith nor Malthus, two acute observers of the contemporary scene, were aware that they were living through the early stages of the Industrial Revolution, perhaps the greatest watershed since the Agricultural Revolution, B.C. 8000–3500!

Demographic forces are a factor in the interpretation of late modern history. However, the model conceived by Malthus and refined by neo-Malthusians has little utility for the history of Western society since the Industrial Revolution. Whether it is still suitable for the study of pre-industrial societies of the Third World where rising population, overstrained resources, and shrinking productivity impede development is a matter for debate.[21]

CHALLENGING THE DEMOGRAPHIC MODEL: THE ROLE OF PLAGUE

The integrity of the demographic model as a macrohistorical mode of explanation depends upon the ability of its practitioners to demonstrate that the two great Malthusian checks of the fourteenth and seventeenth centuries were predictable crises in a recurring pattern of growth and subsidence. The two crises were dissimilar in important respects. The fourteenth-century crisis was a universal catastrophe of the first magnitude, and its effects lingered in Europe for at least a century and a quarter. The seventeenth-century crisis was briefer; it was less severe, and it did not have a uniform result.[22] For this reason, many historians deny that the so-called crisis of the seventeenth century was prompted by demographic pressures. Some argue, for example, that Spain's decline in the seventeenth century was a result of injudiciously assumed political commitments that overextended the national economy. Others contend that the collapse of population in seventeenth-century Germany was a consequence of the last great religious war and that religious warfare in Europe was not prompted primarily by population pressure.

Most historians concede that Europe confronted population pressure in the fourteenth century. Advocates of the demographic model generally agree that famines in the early fourteenth century constitute evidence that a positive check was under way. There is disagreement on the role of the Black Death. Postan separated the fourteenth-century famines from the Black Death, deliberately minimizing the importance of plague in the operation of the late-medieval Malthusian check.

> The Black Death could perhaps be regarded as a biological catastrophe; yet it is doubtful whether the Black Death, even if taken in conjunction with other great epidemics of the fourteenth century, could by itself account for the population trend of the later Middle Ages. . . . [S]igns of falling trends appear before the Black Death and do not disappear after the direct effects of the great pestilences should no longer have been felt.[23]

Other historians link famine with plague, sometimes explicitly, sometimes vaguely. Famine, argue North and Thomas, "set the stage for disease" and often accompanied it. Echoing such sentiments, Le Roy Ladurie referred to the Black Death as a "holocaust of the undernourished."[24]

Because plague coincided in time with what neo-Malthusians perceive as a positive check and because it occasioned enormous loss of life over an extended period, the relationship between the check and the plague must be clarified. Malthus argued that a positive check could take the form of famine, epidemic disease, war over scarce resources, or some combination of the three. If excessive demographic pressure begot famine in the fourteenth century, did famine, in turn, beget plague?

Plague entered Europe from the Black Sea port of Caffa where a Mongol army, laying siege to the city, had been overcome by the disease in 1346. Striking swiftly at Constantinople, plague progressively extended its deadly presence around the continent, reaching England in 1348 and the Baltic by 1350. Devastation was not confined to Europe. From the 1320s, plague had worked its way along the trade routes of Central Asia. China was hard hit. One authority contends that the population of China may have declined from around 125 million to 90 million by the 1390s.[25] The leading scholar of plague in the Middle East believes that by the early fifteenth century that region may have lost more than a third of its population.[26] North Africa and much of Eurasia experienced plague in the fourteenth century. Yet only a few of the victimized areas had suffered famine in the period preceding the pandemic.

In the mid-1960s, Jean Meuvret contended that there was no simple or necessary cause-effect relationship between famine and epidemic disease.[27] His position was affirmed by Jean-Noel Biraben in a monumental study of the plague. Biraben showed that although bubonic plague often followed famine, there were numerous cases in which famine followed plague and others in which plague was altogether unaccompanied by famine or famine by plague. He concluded that in the case of the Black Death there was no cause other than the disease itself that could have brought about plague.[28] There may have been a relationship between famine and plague, he writes, but it was not because famine aggravated the virulence of plague; rather, it was because plague, after striking, induced famine as a result of the violent interruption of agriculture and the disorganization of the economy. In all the abundant recent literature on plague, there is no direct linkage established between malnutrition and plague.[29]

If Biraben's views are correct, the unparalleled demographic blowout of the fourteenth and fifteenth centuries was not related to famine or to population pressure. Rather, demographic collapse was occasioned by an extraordinary and unpredictable epidemic that would have befallen Europe whether population was at, above, or below its presumed ceiling.

Minimizing the role of plague and maximizing the effects of demographic rhythm, Postan argued that Europe was already experiencing a Malthusian check before the onset of plague and that plague does not explain protracted demographic stagnation at the end of the Middle Ages. Others would disagree. One historian of plague considers the fourteenth-century pandemic "the worst disaster that has ever befallen mankind."[30] For the modern United States to sustain a demographic tragedy of similar proportions, 75 million people would have to die of disease in a few years' time. That is more than 200 times the number of U.S. troops killed in World War II. Yet, despite the incomprehensible scale of such a disaster, scholars believe that the recurrent nature of plague, not the initial die-off, was its most devastating feature. Writing about the early modern era, a time when the worst ravages of plague had eased, Michael Flinn asserted the following:

> The key to population growth or decline in early modern Europe lay, beyond doubt, both in the ebb and flow of epidemic tides of particularly infectious diseases and in the secular shifts of endemic levels of diseases. Of all the infectious diseases taking part in these processes bubonic plague was the preeminent arbiter of population growth rates. Until the middle of the seventeenth century this terrifying disease was seldom absent on an epidemic scale from any part of Europe for much more than a decade and was mostly present permanently at a low endemic level, at least in the great cities. More than any other single factor, the comings and goings of bubonic

plague determined whether and where population would grow, stagnate, or decline.[31]

In fairness to neo-Malthusian historians, fourteenth-century Europe may have undergone a population reversal had plague never occurred. It is hardly possible, however, that a fourteenth-century crisis uncomplicated by plague would have been as grave as the disaster that actually befell the continent. It stands to reason that without so devastating and recurring a force as plague, less arable land would have been abandoned. Rents would have held up better, and wages would have risen less. The nobility would have remained stronger, the kings weaker, and the ability of the peasants to throw off serfdom and acquire property rights would certainly have been jeopardized. Presumably, these altered social and economic relationships would have occasioned different responses to the stimulus of population growth whenever growth resumed. If, as Biraben contends, the plague pandemic was a chance epidemiological episode, only partially if at all related to the state of subsistence in Europe, then plague profoundly exaggerated any medieval Malthusian check.

This conclusion raises doubt about the general utility of the demographic model. Historians of Europe have identified only two macro-historical cycles. The apparent symmetry and universality of the medieval cycle may only be a reflection of distortions occasioned by plague. As for the second cycle, 1470/1500–1750, it lacks both symmetry and universality, and many historians remain dubious about the demographic roots of the so-called crisis of the seventeenth century.

CHALLENGING THE DEMOGRAPHIC MODEL: POPULATION AND INNOVATION

One of the sternest critics of the neo-Malthusian argument, Ester Boserup, acknowledges that population pressure has been vitally important to human development, but she rejects the neo-Malthusian concept of predictable, recurring cycles of growth and subsidence.[32] Rather, argues Boserup, a gradually rising population has been the normal condition for humankind throughout history. Historians of the pre-industrial West should not view rising population as a harbinger of famine and privation. Rising population has been the chief engine of technological innovation; in turn, technological innovation has consistently raised population ceilings and permitted a consistent upward trend in population figures. If Europe suffered dramatic demographic reversals over the last two thousand years, the explanation must be sought in unpredictable incursions of disease, not in Malthusian checks.

For a thousand years, writes Boserup, Europe lagged behind China in technology. Why? Because China had sufficient population to sustain a relatively high level of technology. Europe did not. When the population of a society is small, it is difficult to effect economies of scale. Specialization (division of labor) is rendered problematical, and the creation and maintenance of collective capital assets (bridges, walls, dikes) is harder to achieve and more costly for each of the people being served. Higher levels of technology, like degrees of specialization, require high densities of population.

At no time was pre-industrial Europe overpopulated. If anything, it was underpopulated, writes Boserup. As population density increased, declining supplies of land and other resources stimulated people to discover more efficient means of utilizing existing resources. Either by invention or by the borrowing of new technologies, Europeans found ways to enhance productivity. In Roman times, much of Western and Central Europe was cultivated by means of long fallow. Long fallow involved burning off a bit of bush or forest, planting and replanting the land as long as it remained fertile, then moving on to do the same in another place. Suited only to a thin population, this system allowed lands to lie fallow for five or more years. By the eighth century, a two-field short fallow was being used across Western Europe; subsequently, in densely populated areas, the more sophisticated three-field system replaced it. By the nineteenth century, fallow had been abandoned altogether.[33] Each adjustment involved the adoption of innovations and new technology to accommodate the needs of a larger population. Whereas the only tool needed for long fallow was the hoe, short fallow required the plough. Long fallow permitted tribal tenure systems; short fallow necessitated systems of secure tenure in which permanent investments in land and water supply could be guaranteed. It was in Tuscany and the Low Countries, both densely populated districts, that Europeans first developed intensive systems of agriculture.[34] Likewise, in Tuscany and the Low Countries sophisticated systems of trade and industry first developed.

Boserup's thesis on the relationship between population size and technology raises many questions. Why, for example, did population pressure in Europe produce innovation and advancing technology when rising population did not evoke equivalent innovations elsewhere in the world? At the same time, Boserup's analysis directs us back to a debate among historical demographers. If, as Malthus argued, passion between the sexes naturally produced overpopulation, what was the principal mechanism of population control? Was it the positive check generating high mortality, or the preventive check achieving fertility control?[35] Neo-Malthusian historians place their chief emphasis on positive checks. Yet we know that West Europeans adopted social patterns to control fertility. Most West European families were nuclear. Marriage usually involved the creation of a new household, and marriage could not occur until the economic base for a new household existed. By the seventeenth century, the average age of first marriage for women was 26 years, and between two-fifths and three-fifths of women of childbearing age (ages 15–44) were unmarried.[36] Not surprisingly, Boserup would observe, this unique marriage pattern was present in densely inhabited Tuscany as early as the fourteenth century. Scholars like Boserup are prone to emphasize fertility control. Fertility-lowering adjustments in family structure and marriage customs, like adjustments in fallow, are perceived as innovative responses to population pressure that precluded the necessity for positive checks.

CONCLUSION

Both Boserup and the neo-Malthusians consider population pressure the chief propellant of historical change in pre-industrial Europe, but they draw opposite conclusions concerning the nature of the changes wrought. The neo-Malthusians consider high pressure a portent of subsistence crises, demographic decline, and aggregate economic stagnation. Boserup deems high population pressure a vital goad to technological innovation and, as a consequence, to further population growth. Both views are deterministic: a particular condition, it is inferred, produces a particular result. In Boserup's case, it is not clear that Europeans consistently responded to high population density with new technologies. In fact, many of the most revolutionary technological innovations in European history occurred during periods of low population pressure. Notable examples are the fifteenth-century introductions of printing, gunpowder, and navigational instruments as well as the development of the superior sailing ships that enabled Europeans to establish maritime hegemony throughout the world. Even when new technologies emerged in Europe, their diffusion tended to be painfully slow before the nineteenth century. Likewise, changes in cultural values and social customs that were capable of relieving population pressure were adopted slowly. Among all areas of human experience, the slowest to change is our system of values.[37]

As for neo-Malthusian theory, it is clear that there are close historical correlations between the movement of population, prices, wages, and rents, and it is reasonable to deduce that in pre-industrial times an equilibrating mechanism like that discerned by Malthus generally kept population in line with subsistence. At best, however, such a mechanism would have worked asymmetrically. Fertility, mortality, and the material and social conditions of daily life were organically interconnected. If fertility and mortality shaped the circumstances of community life, they were also influenced by them. In such an interactive relationship, it is difficult to discern where the driving force resided, if indeed it resided in the same place throughout historical time. Different communities behaved differently. Some communities lived perpetually on the edge of Malthusian crises: marriage was early, living standards low, and there was little land per head. Elsewhere, communities maintained marriage and inheritance patterns that preserved a wide margin over subsistence.[38] For some, the prevailing vital force was mortality; for others, fertility.

An equilibrating model like that conceived by Malthus provides important explanatory power, especially for early agrarian societies. Does it offer predictive power? The expansion-contraction mechanism was always vulnerable to distortion from random exogenous forces such as epidemics or geographical discoveries that might accelerate or reverse prevailing trends. This may have been the case during the fourteenth and fifteenth centuries when plague intensified what neo-Malthusians have considered a predictable subsistence crisis. Similarly, the unforeseen introduction of New World food crops to Europe (potatoes, maize, and tomatoes, to mention a few) might have moderated the so-called crisis of the seventeenth century by increasing yields on European farms. By elevating the Malthusian model to a macrohistorical level, have neo-Malthusians stretched the predictive power of the principle of population beyond the limit of its utility?

NOTES

1. M. M. Postan, *Essays in Medieval Agriculture and the General Problems of the Medieval Economy* (Cambridge, 1973), pp. 41, 196.

2. M. M. Postan, "The Chronology of Labour Services," first published in 1937, reprinted in *Essays in Medieval Agriculture*, p. 90.

3. These developments occurred after Poland had become heavily involved with the West in the exchange of grain for finished products. Marian Malowist, "Poland, Russia and Western Trade in the Fifteenth and Sixteenth Centuries," *Past and Present* 13 (1958): 26–39; "The Economic and Social Development of the Baltic Countries from the Fifteenth to the Sixteenth Centuries," *Economic History Review*, 2d ser., 12 (1959): 117–189.

4. Thomas Robert Malthus, *An Essay on the Principle of Population,* ed. Philip Appleman (1798; New York, 1976), p. 23.

5. Thomas McKeown, *The Modern Rise of Population* (New York, 1976), p. 17.

6. Michael Flinn, *The European Demographic System, 1500–1820* (Baltimore, 1981), p. 1.

7. J. C. Russell, "Population in Europe 500–1500," in Carlo M. Cipolla, ed., *The Fontana Economic History of Europe,* vol. 1 (London, 1972), p. 39.

8. The 36 million figure appears in Colin McEvedy and Richard Jones, *Atlas of World Population History* (Harmondsworth, 1978). J. C. Russell, "Population in Europe 500–1500," offers 38.5.

9. Spain, for example, suffered sixteen recurrences of plague between 1362 and 1497. Rural England fared somewhat better, but London had twenty recurrences during the fifteenth century.

10. This modern surge of population in Europe has been mirrored elsewhere in the world. In 1750 world population may have been 750 million. Humankind reached one billion around 1830, two billion in the 1930s, three billion by 1960, four billion in 1975. Currently, world population is around five billion, and it is expected to reach 6.2 billion by the year 2000. McKeown, *Modern Rise of Population,* p. 1; Richard Gardner, "Bush, the U.N., and Too Many People," *New York Times,* 22 September 1989.

11. D. B. Grigg, *Population Growth and Agrarian Change: An Historical Perspective* (Cambridge, 1980), pp. 7, 64, 65, 281.

12. In England, the average gross yield of food grains per grain of seed sown was about 3.7 in the early thirteenth century, perhaps 4.7 in the fifteenth century. Yields only doubled in midland and southern England between 1200 and 1820. Carlo Cipolla, *Before the Industrial Revolution: European Society and Economy, 1000–1700* (New York, 1976), pp. 119–120; Grigg, *Population Growth and Agrarian Change,* p. 36. The best record of yields in medieval Europe is analyzed in J. Z. Titow, *Winchester Yields: A Study in Medieval Agricultural Productivity* (Cambridge, 1972).

13. Karl F. Helleiner, "The Population of Europe from the Black Death to the Eve of the Vital Revolution," in E. E. Rich and C. H. Wilson, eds., *The Cambridge Economic History of Europe,* vol. 4 (Cambridge, 1967), p. 14.

14. Gerald A. J. Hodgett, *A Social and Economic History of Medieval Europe* (London, 1972), p. 206.

15. For a stimulating discussion of early rural markets, see R. H. Britnell, "The Proliferation of Markets in England, 1200–1349," *Economic History Review* 34 (1981): 209–221.

16. Fernand Braudel, *The Mediterranean and the Mediterranean World in the Age of Philip II,* vol. 1, trans. Sian Reynolds (New York, 1972), pp. 588–606.

17. Douglas C. North and Robert Paul Thomas, *The Rise of the Western World: A New Economic History* (Cambridge, 1973), pp. 93–113.

18. Emmanuel Le Roy Ladurie, *The Peasants of Languedoc* (Urbana, 1974), p. 295.

19. Ibid., p. 311.

20. Paul Bairoch, "Europe's Gross National Product: 1800–1975," *Journal of European Economic History* 5 (1976): 275–282.

21. In the 1970s, world population was rising at a rate of 2.05 percent a year, and few countries in the underdeveloped world had a rate below 2 percent. The significance of this becomes apparent when we acknowledge that in the century between 1750 and 1850 the population of England and Wales nearly tripled, albeit the average increase per

year was only about 1 percent. A 3 percent rate of growth will produce a thousandfold increase in population in two centuries.

22. Most scholarly literature on the "crisis of the seventeenth century" subordinates demographic factors among a host of other causes of crisis. See articles by E. J. Hobsbawm and H. R. Trevor-Roper in Trevor Aston, ed., *Crisis in Europe, 1560–1660* (New York, 1967). Theodore K. Rabb's analytical treatise on the crisis of the seventeenth century devotes little attention to demographic forces: *The Struggle for Stability in Early Modern Europe* (New York, 1975).

23. Postan, *Essays in Medieval Agriculture*, p. 12.

24. North and Thomas, *Rise of the Western World*, p. 72; Le Roy Ladurie, *Peasants of Languedoc*, p. 13. Charles Frederic Mullett offers a similar view. Having observed that Europeans had undergone a number of famine years, he argued: "The Black Death thus attacked a population wholly susceptible to the bubonic plague." *The Bubonic Plague in England: An Essay in the History of Preventive Medicine* (Lexington, 1956), p. 13.

25. Robert S. Gottfried, *The Black Death: Natural and Human Disaster in Modern Europe* (New York, 1983), pp. 34–36.

26. Michael W. Dols, *The Black Death in the Middle East* (Princeton, 1977), p. 223.

27. Jean Meuvret, "Demographic Crises in France from the Sixteenth to the Eighteenth Century," in D. V. Glass and D. E. C. Eversley, eds., *Population in History* (Chicago, 1965), pp. 510–513.

28. Jean-Noel Biraben, *Les hommes et la peste en France et dans les pays européens et méditerranéens,* vol. 1 (Paris, 1975), pp. 148–154. Plague is primarily a disease of rodents, not humans. The bacillus, *Pasteurella pestis,* lives in the bloodstream of warm-blooded animals, particularly rodents, more than 200 species of which are susceptible to the disease. The disease organism is transmitted from rodent to rodent by the flea, especially the flea *Xenopsylla cheopis.* When fleas draw blood from a host infected by the disease organism, the bacilli multiply in the gullet of the flea, sometimes blocking the digestive tract. Such "blocked" fleas become ravenously hungry. In their desperate attempt to feed, they regurgitate bacteria into the bloodstream of their host. When a diseased rat dies, his fleas migrate to other rats, progressively devastating the rat community. When, through such decimation, insufficient rodent hosts are available, the fleas migrate to other warm-blooded creatures, including man, thereby transmitting plague to the human population. Because fleas stray little distance from their hosts and because rat populations travel very slowly, plague epidemics will, as a rule, spread only if infected rats and fleas are transported from region to region. Grain is a favorite food of the black rat, and the *Xenopsylla cheopis* breeds best in the debris of cereal grains; consequently, grain transports were a major means of spreading contagion. At the same time, infection could be dispersed by the transfer of flea-infected cotton, wool, hides, or furs. For clear and brief descriptions of the etiology of plague, see Robert S. Gottfried, *Epidemic Disease in Fifteenth Century England* (New Brunswick, 1978), pp. 58–63; John T. Alexander, *Bubonic Plague in Early Modern Russia: Public Health and Urban Disaster* (Baltimore, 1980), pp. 2–12; L. Fabian Hirst, *The Conquest of Plague: A Study of the Evolution of Epidemiology* (Oxford, 1953), pp. 28–31, 266–271.

29. John D. Post makes the point firmly: "The clinical evidence . . . indicates no biological interaction between plague bacillus and nutritional levels." "Famine, Mortality, and Epidemic Disease in the Process of Modernization," *Economic History*

Review, 2d ser., 29 (1976): 37. D. B. Grigg confirms the point, observing that medical science currently demonstrates that it is difficult to trace any causal link between disease and hunger. *Population Growth and Agrarian Change: An Historical Perspective* (Cambridge, 1980), p. 13.

30. Dols, *Black Death in the Middle East*, vii.

31. Flinn, *The European Demographic System*, p. 55.

32. Ester Boserup, *The Conditions of Agricultural Growth* (London, 1965); *Population and Technological Change: A Study of Long-Term Trends* (Chicago, 1981).

33. Soil-enriching fodder crops were being sown on lands that in former times would have been left fallow.

34. According to Ester Boserup,

In the eleventh century, draining, irrigation, and other investments needed for intense agriculture were undertaken in northern Italy, and dikes and polders were built in the Netherlands as early as the tenth century. In the fourteenth and fifteenth centuries, fallow in these densely populated areas was replaced by fodder crops for domestic animals and by industrial crops. In most other parts of Western and Central Europe, similar changes had to await the wave of population increase in the eighteenth and nineteenth centuries.

Ester Boserup, *Population and Technological Change: A Study of Long-Term Trends* (Chicago, 1981), p. 103.

35. For most of modern history, scholars have held that population regulation was primarily a function of high mortality. See, for example, Carlo Cipolla, *Economic History of World Population* (Baltimore, 1962), pp. 76–77. An emphatic defense of the role of fertility control is made in Roger S. Schofield, "Through a Glass Darkly: *The Population History of England* as an Experiment in History," in Robert I. Rotberg and Theodore K. Rabb, eds., *Population and Economy: Population and History from the Traditional to the Modern World* (Cambridge, 1986).

36. Flinn, *European Demographic System*, p. 27; E. A. Wrigley, *Population and History*, (New York, 1969), p. 90.

37. Georges Duby, "L'Histoire des systèmes de valuers," *History and Theory* 11 (1972): 15–25.

38. H. J. Habbakuk, *Population Growth and Economic Development since 1750* (Leicester, 1972), pp. 17–20; Michael Anderson, "Historical Demography after *The Population History of England*," in Rotberg and Rabb, eds., *Population and Economy*, pp. 41–44.

5

The Marxian Dynamic

Marxist historians dismiss the neo-Malthusian model. Subsistence crises were not occasioned by inexorable Malthusian forces. They were not even necessary. The crisis of the fourteenth century was brought about by *an exploitative system of feudal class relations* that permitted lords to consume conspicuously and to fight interminably while it precluded technological and organizational changes in agriculture that would have generated ample food for an expanding population. The neo-Malthusian model may account for alternating booms and slumps in aggregate economic activity, but it offers little or no illumination about how a new social order, like capitalism, takes its rise within an old social structure.

Marxists consider the commercial model to be no better. In its tendency to conceive history as no more than the progressive evolution of efficient markets, the commercial model muffles the heartbeat of the historical process. Adam Smith and Henri Pirenne saw merchants, markets, and commercial towns as external agents that persistently and systematically pulled a primitive economy toward ever-expanding levels of technological and institutional complexity. Their approach was compellingly simple, but it leads to the anachronistic imposition of modern bourgeois mentalities upon medieval peoples—and, argue the Marxists, it fails to discern that traders and townsmen, far from being external agents of change, were conservators of an abiding social structure.

More than any other thinker, Karl Marx has fashioned the intellectual landscape of modern historical scholarship. Marxists and non-Marxists alike have adopted his historical vocabulary, his categories of analysis, and his emphasis upon social and economic forces. To the extent that historians identify the modern age with capitalism, they reflect the Marxian view that capitalism constitutes a distinct social structure whose existence, from its advent to its demise, represents a major historical epoch. One of the most influential thinkers of our time, Michel Foucault, describes the impact of Marx:

> It is impossible at the present time to write history without using a whole range of concepts directly or indirectly linked to Marx's thought and situating one's self within a horizon of thought which has been defined and described by Marx. One might even wonder what difference there could ultimately be between being a historian and being a Marxist.[1]

Marxism is more than a theory of history. It is a revolutionary ideology—a purposeful, progressivist, even millenarian political philosophy. While interpreting history, Marxists have sought to change the world. Their politics have been informed by their theory of history, and their theory has always been sensitive to the changing demands of contemporary politics. Particular Marxist orientations became official doctrine in the Soviet Union after 1917, and during much of the Cold War, the Soviet position provided a common ideological denominator for communist activists throughout the world. For better or for worse, Marxist intellectuals were drawn into alliance with Moscow. They were dedicated to the destruction of capitalism; they had high hopes for the Soviet experiment; and all too often they served as apologists for its shortcomings. In the West, Marxist scholars were always subject to the criticism that their identity with Moscow or their affiliation with local communist parties compromised their intellectual integrity. None of Britain's distinguished Marxist historians—and there have been many— chose to focus his or her studies on the twentieth century, where a scholar's intellectual integrity and ideological loyalties might be brought into conflict with his or her political attachment to the Soviet Union or to the Party.[2]

If the Cold War imposed constraints upon Marxist theoreticians, it also generated critical scrutiny of Marxist theory by non-Marxist journalists and scholars. Each element of the Marxist canon was tested empirically. As errors or inconsistencies were exposed, Marxist historians adjusted their models and redirected their emphases. The revisions undertaken by innumerable Marxist scholars have been anything but uniform; consequently, the intellectual landscape of modern historical Marxism has become bewilderingly diverse. Marxist theory continues to divide Marxist historians from non-Marxists, and the nuances of theory separate one brand of Marxist from another.

All Marxism derives from a common source: the corpus of Karl Marx's written work. It is important, therefore, that we examine Marx briefly in the hope of understanding something of his objectives, his achievements, his shortcomings, and his relationship with Friedrich Engels, his co-author, intellectual companion, and survivor. Marx's attention swung alternately between philosophy and activism. Professor Robert Daniels discerned five distinct periods in his forty-year working life.[3] From 1841 to 1847, Marx made a philosophical migration from idealistic Hegelianism to materialism, focusing on economic conditions, class struggle, the role of the proletariat, and the concept of an ideal communist society. The years 1847–1852 were years of activism: participation in the revolutionary events of 1848, and co-authorship with Engels of *The Communist Manifesto*. With revolutionary movements in retreat across Europe after 1852, Marx repaired to the British Museum, where he undertook his greatest work, *Capital,* a three-volume exegesis upon the structure of capitalism, in particular British capitalism. From the mid-1860s to 1872, Marx devoted increasing energy to political activism, to the International Workingmen's Association, and during 1870, to the revolution in France. After 1872 his creative energies declined. He died in 1883.

Marx studied mature capitalism. His occasional forays into earlier historical periods were undertaken primarily to shed light on the origins and development of capitalism. Our knowledge of his historical periodization and our understanding of his concept of historical dynamics in the precapitalist era derive from limited, often sketchy, writings or by way of analogy from his detailed analysis of capitalism. At the root of Marx's theory are several cardinal principles. Most important, he was a doctrinaire materialist. People must eat and be sheltered before they can contemplate God, he argued: life is not determined by consciousness; consciousness is determined by the rigors of life. Two key concepts derive from his materialism: mode of production and class struggle. Unlike historians of the commercial school who focus on the distribution of scarce resources, Marx concentrated on production. That which distinguished one form of society from another was the mode by which wealth was produced. For Marx, history constituted the progressive journey of humankind through successive modes of production. The motor of change within each mode of production was class struggle, and the process by which change occurred was dialectic.

In his most compact and most oft-quoted theoretical statement on the dynamics of historical change,[4] Marx declared that mode of production, the system of work and of social relations by which material wealth is generated, "determines the general character of the social, political and spiritual processes of life." In other words, legal and political institutions as well as religious, family, and educational practices represent a social superstructure that is erected upon and derived from the economic base of society. This *base-superstructure* model constitutes an extreme example of economic determinism, or economism. Although it was modified by Marx in other writings, twentieth-century Marxists continue to debate the primacy, or at least the degree of primacy, of the economic base.

Each social structure, argued Marx, harbors internal contradictions that manifest themselves in *class relations*. The relationship that different groups of people experience to the process of production and the degree to which they possess productive forms of property determines, in the main, their class identity. In every society some people exercise control over the productive process, extracting ample surpluses for their pleasure. Others acquire relatively little surplus. They are repressed, restrained, or victimized by the productive process, and at some point they unite in opposition to it. The struggle of antagonistic classes over the appropriation of surplus provides the driving force of history.

Class struggle is played out through the predictable operation of "scientific dialectics." Each social structure generates within itself the seeds of its own destruction. In Marxian terms, the dominant class within a mode of production provokes opposition from less advantaged classes. The struggle between opposing classes ultimately leads to revolution and to the displacement of the old dominant class by a successor. That displacement does not occur, however, until the productive forces of the old order have become mature or until the material base for a new dominant order has developed "in the womb of the old society." When a new dominant class takes hold, it gives rise to the opposition of hostile classes. Struggle ensues, and in time that dominant class is replaced by yet another successor. By this means, history, propelled by class struggle, advances through successive modes of production.

In his Preface to *A Contribution to the Critique of Political Economy* (1859), Marx explained the transition from one mode of production to another in economistic terms. Incremental changes in productive technology or changes in the resources used in the productive process gradually undermine the close correspondence between the dominant class and the productive process, thereby rendering the dominant class vulnerable to revolution. In recent centuries, for example, there has been gradual change from the use of hand tools to machines as well as a change from organic sources of energy (e.g., timber) to inorganic sources (e.g., coal, petroleum). The increasing use of machines and inorganic sources of energy powerfully enhanced the prospects of the bourgeoisie in the productive process.

This enhancement occurred at the expense of an older dominant class, the nobility, whose economic roots were embedded in a fading productive order based upon hand tools and organic sources of energy. Because outmoded property relations and outmoded political power relations inhibited the full realization of the new productive order, the class representatives of that incipient order, the bourgeoisie, rose up, seized political power, and consolidated their command over the economy. In this way, one social structure, feudalism, was displaced by another, capitalism. For Marx, the French Revolution of 1789 was a classic transitional episode in which the bourgeoisie forcibly asserted its class control over the new productive system that had developed "in the womb" of the old.

"In broad outlines, " Marx declared, "we can designate the Asiatic, the ancient, the feudal, and the modern bourgeois [capitalist] methods of production as so many epochs." In other words, history was divisible into four stages, each distinguished by its mode of production. Under capitalism, Marx wrote, society was becoming divided into two great hostile classes: the bourgeoisie and the proletariat. When, in accordance with the dialectic, the inevitable proletarian revolution arrived, capitalism would give way to communism, a social structure in which private property was forbidden and wealth was equally divided. Under communism, social classes would cease to exist because class divisions, based on property, could not arise when private property had been abolished and material resources had been equally distributed. Without classes, there could be no class struggle. The new dominant order, communism, would not generate internal contradictions. The dialectical process of historical change would end. The millennium would have arrived.

This is a highly simplified and conservative synopsis of Marx's theory of history. In fact, it is somewhat presumptuous, if not flatly incorrect, to assert that Marx had a single theory of history. His published works, written over forty years, are replete with contradictions, ambiguities of language, and downright obfuscation. Some of the contradictions can be explained by Marx's changing orientations over time; some of them result from the publication of notes that Marx used in his own intellectual development—what he called "clarifying my own ideas."[5] Contradictions in Marx's philosophy are all the more difficult to reconcile because he was given to the use of strident and dogmatic language. In his Preface to the first German edition of *Capital*, for example, Marx claimed to have discovered "the natural laws of capitalist production . . . working with iron necessity towards inevitable results."

The kind of scientism suggested by this passage was even more characteristic of Engels than of Marx. A constant intellectual companion, Engels enjoyed his most productive years after 1872 when Marx's creative energies flagged. It was he, not Marx, who provided a systematic elaboration of dialectical philosophy. Engels rendered the dialectic process highly mechanistic and extended it beyond the realm of human history to encompass the natural world and the process of evolution. Engels's mechanistic emphasis was widely adopted by European Marxists after the Russian Revolution.[6]

In our time, a small academic industry has arisen, probing the depths of Marx's own scholarship, attempting to fathom his "real" intentions, trying to reconcile inconsistencies and to provide meaningful definitions for critical terms. No scholar has difficulty finding quotations from Marx to legitimate his or her particular analysis. On critical interpretive matters, however, the scholars remain in disarray. Clearly, the gospel according to Karl Marx will continue to be interpreted as variously as those of Matthew, Mark, Luke, and John.

ECONOMIC DETERMINISM

At the root of the interpretive muddle is determinism. In Marx's base-superstructure model, do the technical and material foundations of production dictate and determine all else in the social structure? Or do elements of the superstructure—religious tenets, legal traditions, social and political practices—influence, moderate, or even direct aspects of the economic base? If an organic two-way relationship does persist between base and superstructure, what are the dynamics of that relationship? Are they the same in all societies? Or does each historical situation dictate a different dynamic? If it does, can Marxist theory be predictive? If Marxism is not predictive, what do we make of Engels's scientism or Marx's claim to have discovered a natural law that works "with iron necessity towards inevitable results?"

Marx himself did more to confuse than to clarify the issue. Take, for example, a single passage in his 1859 Preface:

> At a certain stage of their development, the material *forces of production* in society come in conflict with the existing *relations of production*, or—what is but a legal expression of the same thing— with the property relations within which they had been at work before. From forms of development of the forces of production these relations turn into their fetters. Then comes the period of social revolution. With the change of the economic foundation the entire immense superstructure is more or less rapidly transformed. [emphasis added]

Apart from the sheer difficulty of this language, Marx never explicitly defined what he meant by "forces of production" or "relations of production." The passage appears to contend that changes wrought in the material circumstances of production (forces of production) evoke and intensify contradictions in the social order (relations of production), ultimately giving rise to social revolution. This interpretation has encouraged many scholars to emphasize economic determinism and the absolute primacy of the economic base.[7]

Theoretically, Marx probably preferred this approach. It accorded with his concept of the future transition from capitalism to communism. Yet he was not able to reconcile his economistic model with past events, most notably the transition from feudalism to capitalism. The historical chapters of *Capital* I and III invert the base-superstructure model, contending that the development of capitalist forces of production (the economic base) was a by-product of the prior establishment of capitalist relations of production—that is, business institutions, authority structures, market facilities, and property relations—which had demonstrated their ability to generate larger material surpluses.[8]

The issue of determinism spills over into every aspect of Marxian historiography. Obvious questions arise concerning Marx's periodization and his theory of progressive historical stages. Must all countries pass through the same, or similar, stages of historical development? Does the movement of peoples through history always involve a unilinear progression from a slave mode of production to a feudal mode of production to a capitalist mode to communism? In his Preface to the first edition of *Capital* I, Marx observed that "the country that is more developed industrially only shows, to the less developed, the image of its own future," a statement that has consistently been used to afirm a unilinear progressivist view of history. Yet, just as stridently, Marx denied having authored a "historiophilosophical theory of the general path every people is fated to tread."[9]

What about human agency in history? Since Marxism is both a revolutionary creed and a theory of history, Marxists have attempted to reconcile economic determinism with voluntarism. What historical role do revolutionary activists play? If the course of history is predetermined, can political activism be of any utility? Marx was more, rather than less, inclined to affirm the value of human agency in determining the course of history. His followers, beginning with Engels, generally encouraged activism as a means of hastening the course of events, albeit with an important qualifier. Political activism, it was stressed, can only be meaningful when it functions in accordance with the natural laws of history. It cannot alter the general direction of history.

CLASS STRUGGLE ANALYSIS

Modern Marxist historians who resist or reject the rigorous economism of the base-superstructure model have generally adopted class struggle as the thematic centerpiece of their work. But class struggle analysis presents its own problems, some practical, some philosophical. Neither Marx nor Engels ever provided a systematic exposition of the concept of class even though Marx's discovery of the "proletariat" prompted his studies of capitalism and inspired his claim that the "history of all hitherto existing society is the history of class struggles."[10] Is class rooted in economic structure, as the base-superstructure model assumes? Conventional economistic Marxists affirm the model: social consciousness derives from social being, and social being is framed by the material circumstances of the mode of production. This seemingly straightforward proposition can be a problem for the historian. How does a historian, working with evidence that is several centuries old, distinguish one class from another? Is occupation a sufficient criterion of class?

This question was addressed in the first systematic investigation of the American class structure undertaken from an explicitly Marxian perspective.[11] Erik Olin Wright and a team of researchers discovered that occupational status was *not* a sufficient criterion of class. In contemporary society at least, occupation would be a highly misleading determinant of class. The research team, working with live subjects, found it necessary to conduct a survey of those subjects in order to validate their class position. If the team had been forced to define the subjects' class by occupational category, it would have misclassified up to 45 percent of the people in the survey![12] Considering the difficulties in discerning class distinctions encountered by contemporary researchers, how can historians hope to achieve a finely tuned understanding of bygone class structures? Because historians rarely have the opportunity to survey living subjects, they are compelled to rely upon the type of empirical data—census records, tax lists, occupational status—that Wright et al. found highly misleading.[13]

Among the philosophical issues raised by class struggle analysis is the problem of anachronism. In recent years, historians have come to realize that the Marxian concept of class, particularly as it relates to class consciousness and class identity, is historically specific *only* to an urban, industrial society. Urban proletarians may have developed an acute sense of class. But peasants living in agrarian societies never possessed strong class identity.[14] Is it possible for people to act together in specifically class ways if they are not conscious of their class identity? Is class struggle a meaningful engine of historical change in epochs that predate the evolution of modern class consciousness?

All of these questions have been examined by E. P. Thompson, a free-spirited English Marxist historian. His masterwork, *The Making of the English Working Class* (1963), demonstrated that genuine class identity only emerged among British workers during the decades between 1780 and 1832. Thompson rejected economic determinism in the formation of class, and he lamented that Marx, Engels, and most Marxists since them had unduly saddled themselves with static models and misguided assertions about iron "laws" of history. Class is not a thing. It is not the automatic by-product of mode of production. It is not a mathematically defined body of people standing in a particular relation to the means of production. Nor can it be defined or discerned by theoretical formulas. Production relations (including occupational status) provide coloration and tonality to the class experience, but class is, above all, a fluid, constantly changing "*historical* phenomenon" experienced by men and women who share the pleasures and the penalties of a common cultural context:

> If we stop history at a given point, then there are no classes but simply a multitude of individuals with a multitude of experiences. But if we watch these men over an adequate period of social change,

we observe patterns in their relationships, their ideas, and their institutions. Class is defined by men as they live their own history, and, in the end, this is its only definition.[15]

As for the problem of anachronism, Thompson offers the following:

To put it bluntly: classes do not exist as separate entities, look around, find an enemy class, and then start to struggle. On the contrary, people find themselves in a society structured in determined ways (crucially, but not exclusively, in productive relations), they experience exploitation (or the need to maintain power over those whom they exploit), they identify points of antagonistic interest, they commence to struggle around these issues and in the process of struggling they discover themselves as classes, they come to know this discovery as class-consciousness. Class and class-consciousness are always the last, not the first stage in the historical process.[16]

In effect, class struggle *can* antedate class consciousness in the sense that exploitative human relationships occasion antagonism between social groups, producing conflicts that are structured in class ways even before self-conscious class formations have arisen.

Thompson has thrown down the gauntlet to Marxist historians and to non-Marxist historians alike. In order to fathom class in a bygone society, the historian must achieve profound intimacy with a bewildering array of people, of groups, of attitudes and beliefs; the historian must mediate between the vocal and the silent, between the advocates of causes and the faceless multitudes whose collective inner will can be discerned only by their actions. Combining empirical research with patience, perception, and "historical logic," he or she must attempt to comprehend how culture has comingled with the material circumstances of life to produce class, and how class (consciously or unconsciously) has served to resist or to promote change.

Thompson's work reset the battleground upon which Marxists contest points of theory and methodology. Economic determinists, even those of moderate disposition, reacted strongly to Thompson's "culturalism," insisting that he gave insufficient attention to the deep structural phenomena that have shaped human attitudes and behavior. Would the English working class have evolved as it did had there been no Industrial Revolution?

At another level, structuralists, following the lead of the French Marxist, Louis Althusser, reject all historical empiricism, especially that of

Thompson, insisting that real history is unknowable and that attempts to fathom the inner consciousness of earlier peoples can only lead to false consciousness and misunderstanding. Since the past is inaccessible, argue the structuralists, theoretical knowledge is the only true knowledge. For Marxism in particular, true theory is discernable only through a critical reading of Marx that discards teleological argumentation and logical inconsistencies. In sum, theory is not an aid to historical understanding. Theory is history.

WHAT IS A MARXIST HISTORIAN?

Considering these sharply divergent viewpoints, how does one define "the Marxist historian"? Some Marxist historians continue to pursue orthodox historical materialism, utilizing an economically determined base-superstructure model while periodizing history in accordance with changing modes of production. Others (like Thompson) deny the paramount directing influence of economic forces and give equal or near-equal weight to superstructural elements in determining the character of social formations. Some self-proclaimed Marxist historians avoid direct encounter with the base-superstructure model although they acknowledge the primacy of material forces. Some pay little heed either to mode of production or to class struggle while, at the same time, they emphasize exploitative social relationships. Some reject empiricism in any form, deriving an understanding of the past through the systematic elaboration of theory. These latter, the structuralists, offer little of value to historians save a sobering reminder of the dangers and limitations of their discipline. Marxists of every stamp share a vocabulary bequeathed them by Marx, but they define common terms differently, causing confusion in their own ranks and bewilderment outside them. Marxists do employ common designations for historical periods, though many would deny Marx's theory of progressive stages, and they do focus scholarly attention upon two epochs—the feudal and capitalist periods. But disagreement abounds concerning when and why the epochal transition from feudalism to capitalism occurred. In its manifold diversity, historical Marxism constitutes a contemporary school of thought only to the extent that its practitioners share some ideological orientations to the past. What is a Marxist historian? It is someone who, in professing to be a Marxist historian, can justify his or her claim by adherence, however small, to some aspect of Marx's historical theory.[17]

THE TRANSITION FROM FEUDALISM TO CAPITALISM

Despite the ahistorical negativism of the structuralists, Marxist historians have been compelled to reconcile their theories of history with the actual record of history. Otherwise, they could never hope to earn the respect of non-Marxist historians or achieve the conversion of others to their points of view. The central problematic for Marxist historians has always been the rise of capitalism. In keeping with Marx's theory of historical stages, how, when, where, and by what agency did the transition from a feudal mode of production to the capitalist mode of production occur? Marx did not undertake a systematic analysis of the internal dynamics of the feudal mode of production; in fact, not until the appearance of Maurice Dobb's *Studies in the Development of Capitalism* (1946) did a Marxist scholar attempt to explain, in comprehensive detail, the process of transition from feudalism to capitalism.[18] Dobb's work evoked an electrifying debate, attracting contributions from leading Marxist luminaries around the world. While agreement on many aspects of theory and interpretation emerged, the debate exposed vital areas of disagreement that continue to divide Marxist writers. What follows in this chapter is an attempt to identify the critical issues raised in that controversy, the main points of consensus, and the chief areas of dispute.

Dobb adopted the logic of the 1859 Preface: Marx's emphasis on the primacy of economic forces, on the dialectical process, on the concept that change occurs through class conflict, on the view that class conflict derives from contradictions within the dominant mode of production, and on Marx's assertion that the transition from one epoch to another must ultimately be consummated by the revolutionary action of a new dominant class. Having subscribed to the proposition that the feudal mode of production must give way to capitalism, Dobb and his allies developed precise definitions for both feudalism and capitalism. Feudalism, Dobb declared, was virtually identical to serfdom. In the feudal mode of production, unfree producers remained attached to the land but in possession of their own primitive tools. They were compelled, independently of their own volition, to render payments to their overlords in the form of labor, dues, money, or goods in kind. The precise nature of the payment was not critical. That payments involved the forced extraction of surplus above that required to sustain the lives of unfree producers was critical. Extractions were made possible by the military, juridical, and political power exercised by the feudal elite.

In the capitalist mode of production, it is argued, ownership of the means of production (e.g., tools, factories, raw materials, sources of energy) is concentrated in the hands of a relatively small class, the bourgeoisie. The rest of society, lacking ownership of the means of production, is obliged to sell its labor as a commodity in order to earn a livelihood. The bourgeoisie acquires the productive labor of the proletariat through freely undertaken wage contracts, not by compulsion, legal or otherwise. The surplus generated by the productive system, above that required to sustain the mere existence of the proletariat, accrues to the bourgeoisie.

Marxists readily appreciate that history does not offer a succession of "pure" modes of production. Nevertheless, each prevailing mode has its own "law of motion." In the feudal mode, the prime mover was the ceaseless struggle between lords and peasants over feudal rent. As the nobles' revenue requirements increased, they extracted ever-expanding levels of surplus from their peasants. Concurrently, the peasants strove to increase the amount of surplus retained by them. Feudal lords did not behave like modern commercial agribusinessmen, minimizing costs and maximizing efficiency. Little or no thought was given to estate management. Feudal properties were the source of social prestige and political and military power. A lord enhanced his prestige and power by expanding his holdings and enlarging the number of his dependents. The former was chiefly accomplished by warfare, the latter by subinfeudation, a process by which the number of vassals owing fealty to a lord was increased. Combined with the natural enlargement of noble families, subinfeudation increased the parasitic class that had to be sustained from the surplus product of serf labor. The Crusades added additional burdens upon the servile class, and the growth of markets multiplied the lords' opportunity for conspicuous consumption. To satisfy their numerous indulgences, the nobles consistently intensified their squeeze on the serfs.

The agrarian economy upon which this burden fell was primitive. Innovations in the productive process were relatively few, and the geographical dispersion of innovation was slow. After three centuries of population growth, land for new settlements was exhausted in Western Europe, and many villages barely survived on inferior soils. At the same time, market activity created greater social stratification among servile producers. The better-off peasants sold more of their surplus at market, acquired more estate land for their own use, and hired the wage labor of poorer peasants. As the lords' demand for revenue increased, the richer peasants objected vehemently to increased demands on their small surpluses. Their antagonism was powerfully reinforced by despairing poor peasants who were driven to (or beyond) the margin of subsistence by the lords' increasing demands for rent. By the fourteenth century, the lords could not extract more and the serfs could not provide more. The feudal mode was in crisis.

Beleaguered peasants fled the manors in increasing numbers. With the onset of the Black Death, labor shortages multiplied. The lords, in their so-called feudal reaction, tried to restore discipline through draconian legislation. Peasant revolts—the Jacquerie in France, peasant rebellion in England in 1381, and risings in Germany, Spain and the Low Countries—were decided in favor of the lords, but demographic realities, the empowered bargaining position of the peasants, and the need of lords to make concessions to retain ample estate labor conspired, over time, to free the peasants from bondage.

Before the end of the fifteenth century, peasants were no longer attached to the soil. Many were still obligated to grind their grain at the lord's mill, to pay entry fines, and to remain subject to the jurisdiction of manorial courts, but the disciplinary prerogatives of the lords had eroded. The feudal order, wrote Dobb, had disintegrated in many ways:

> The ranks of the old nobility were thinned and divided; and the smaller estates, lacking sufficient labour-services, had taken to leasing or to wage-labour as soon as the increase of population and in particular of the ranks of the poorer peasantry had made labour cheap again. Merchants were buying land; estates were being mortgaged; and a *kulak* class of improving peasant farmers were becoming serious competitors in local markets and as rural employers of labour.[19]

THE AWKWARD CENTURIES: 1500–1700

If we accept Dobb's contention that the feudal mode of production was roughly identical to serfdom, then the feudal mode of production was moribund by the fifteenth century. The capitalist mode of production, as defined by Dobb, did not take hold in Europe until the seventeenth century at the earliest, and then only in England. How do Marxist historians categorize the awkward period between 1500 and 1700? Paul Sweezy, an American Marxist, suggested that the period be redefined as a time of "pre-capitalist commodity production," a distinct but lesser stage of historical development lodged between the greater epochs of feudalism and capitalism.[20] Dobb rejected any modification of Marx's stages theory, arguing that Europe was feudal until, by the revolutionary action of the bourgeoisie, it became capitalist. In response to Sweezy, Dobb posed a critical question: what was the ruling class of the awkward centuries, 1500–1700?[21] He answered the question. The ruling class in the sixteenth and seventeenth centuries was the traditional feudal nobility, and the monarchical state in Europe continued to serve as the political instrument of feudal rule.

In *Studies in the Development of Capitalism*, Dobb had tried, within reason, to keep faith with the base-superstructure model. Sweezy's challenge exposed the model's fragility. How long can a superstructure, shorn of its economic base, sustain its independent existence before the logic of the base-superstructure model is undermined? A century? Two centuries? Sensing his weakness, Dobb redirected the focus of attention from judicious economism and mode of production to class. Feudalism persisted from the fifteenth through the seventeenth century *because Europe continued to be ruled by the feudal class.*

Class struggle analysis has increasingly dominated historical explanation among Marxists. Louis Althusser, the structuralist theoretician, observed that the "political regime of the absolute monarchy [was] only the new political form needed for the maintenance of feudal domination and exploitation in the period of development of a commodity economy."[22] Pursuing this idea, Perry Anderson published *Lineages of the Absolutist State* (1974), contending that absolutism, the leading political medium of the early modern period, was essentially the "redeployed and recharged apparatus of feudal domination." It was designed to keep the peasant masses back in their traditional social position despite any gains they had made through their release from serfdom.[23] When the class power of the feudal lords was threatened by the dissolution of serfdom, the nobility deliberately reposed their power with a centralized, militarized monarchy whose "permanent political function was the repression of the peasant and plebeian masses at the foot of the social hierarchy."[24]

The absolutist state was feudalism writ large, argues Anderson. It was a machine built for war. The rationale for feudal warfare was the maximization of power, prestige, and wealth. Land was the chief object of conflict, and the ceaseless squeeze on peasant resources provided nobles the material means to fight. In the absolutist state, these conditions persisted. War was perpetual. Land was the chief object of struggle; tax systems were created to support armies; and the peasants were squeezed to provide the means to fight. Other attributes of the absolutist system further advanced the interests of the nobility. Royal bureaucracies provided public offices to members of the nobility. Such offices were used to stabilize or recoup fortunes, "a kind of monetarized caricature of investiture in a fief."[25] Tax systems were a form of centralized feudal rent. The lords were exempt from many taxes, while tax burdens weighed heavily on commoners. Even the weakening of vassalage relations worked to the lords' advantage. Under the original fief system, land holding by leading members of the nobility and their vassals had been conditional upon service. With the growth of Roman Law and its concept of absolute private property—a condition that conferred primary benefit upon the bourgeoisie—the lords were able to assume unqualified property rights in their estates.

From the beginning of historical Marxism, the length of time between the decline of feudalism and rise of capitalism has been an awkward historical problem. Engels addressed the question. Like Anderson, he attributed the length of the transition to the rise of absolutism, but his conclusions were sharply different from those of Anderson. The class representatives of feudalism and capitalism (the nobility and the bourgeoisie) were stalemated for two centuries, wrote Engels: they were balanced and offset by absolutist monarchs who exercised independence from both classes and mediated between them.[26] Using the same triad, Robert Brenner, a Marxist economic historian, considers absolutist kings the competitors of the nobility, not their protectors and not the mediators between them and the bourgeoisie.[27] Brenner's position bears resemblance to that of the commercial school, whose authors have considered the alliance between kings and the bourgeoisie to have been a means of advancing capitalism and undermining the nobility.

There is something to say for and against each of these arguments. Anderson's position seems least tenable. He declared it his intention to integrate history with theory, but his historical chapters are replete with evidence that could be used to support an opposite conclusion. Did the nobles of Europe consider the absolutist kings their protectors or the usurpers of their traditional powers? There were numerous armed struggles between the nobles and kings, the Fronde being only the most famous, and noble-dominated regional estates across Europe bitterly resisted the grant of taxes to monarchs. In seventeenth-century France, the monarchy responded to this resistance by drawing up to 38 percent of its income from the sale of offices. To whom were the bulk of these offices sold? To wealthy members of the bourgeoisie. There was a massive absorption of the bourgeoisie into the fabric of the absolutist state by the system of purchase. Anderson himself declares that the purchase of offices was so profitable an investment of capital for members of the bourgeoisie that money was diverted from manufacturing and mercantile ventures into collusion with absolutism. For whom, then, was absolutism a shield? The bourgeoisie or the nobility? And what portion of the nobility—those people owning estates and assuming the appearance of a feudal class—were actually of bourgeois origin?

This confusion of classes and class-consciousness constitutes a serious problem for Marxist historians. It would seem that real actors on the world's historical stage frequently failed to recognize what latter-day historians would perceive as their class interest. Nor did they consistently act in conformity with it. Edward Thompson alluded to this in *The Making of the English Working Class,* cautioning that whenever class is presumed to be a fixed condition in which people stand in some relation to the means of production, writers are all too disposed to describe class-consciousness "not as it is, but as it ought to be."[28]

THE ADVENT OF CAPITALISM

It is one thing to argue, as Dobb and Anderson have, that in spite of the erosion of feudal economic structures, feudal class power was preserved in England through the seventeenth century and in France and other continental states through the eighteenth century. It is another thing to identify clearly the economic processes by which a capitalist mode of production came into being. Before capitalism could take hold, three conditions had to be met, argue the Marxists. First, laborers had to be separated from the means of production so that labor itself could become a commodity for sale in the market. Second, capital—real money power—had to accumulate in unprecedented volume, and these accumulated resources had to be invested in revised methods of production. Third, when new productive relations had matured in the "womb" of the old system, the representatives of the new order had to rise up in revolutionary action to assert their class control over political, social, and economic institutions. Since the transition to capitalism occurred first in England, most historical attention has been directed to the English experience.

In order to create a free market in industrial labor, working people had to be displaced from the land. Also, agricultural productivity had to rise in order that displaced workers could be fed. In England, this was achieved in two ways. There was an unparalleled growth in the number of aggrandizing peasant farmers, the so-called kulaks, who amassed power and property at the expense of less successful peasants and who were, in a great many cases, assimilated into the gentry. Kulaks consolidated village lands. Their successes were recorded at the expense of poor peasants who lost land and became propertyless, or near propertyless, agricultural wage workers—a rural proletariat. At the same time, class struggle was under way between the traditional manor lords and their peasants, the former using whatever weapons they still possessed, including entry fines, to pry peasants off their customary plots in the open fields so that those lands could be reorganized and consolidated for more efficient and profitable production. Although major agrarian risings erupted over these matters during the sixteenth century—the northern revolt of the 1530s and Ket's Rebellion of 1549—the power of the landlords prevailed. Much of England's pasture land was consolidated, and arable farming assumed a pattern whereby great landowners subdivided their acreage into large tenant farms, which were leased on long-term contracts to "capitalist" farmers. In turn, the tenant farmers hired agricultural proletarians as wage laborers. By 1700, Robert Brenner observes, 70 to 75 percent of the cultivable land of England was controlled by large landowners. Capitalist relations were evolving on the land; excess proletarians were being displaced to the towns; and the productivity of English agriculture, having become more adaptable to technological innovation and capital inputs, was rising.[29]

The accumulation of capital is the second prerequisite for the transition to capitalism. There is no doubt that money capital had been accumulating for centuries. The histories of Venice, Genoa, Bruges, Antwerp, and a host of other cities bear ample evidence to this. Marx himself declared that European plundering of the New World and the East Indies was the "chief momenta of primitive accumulation." The problem for Marxists is not whether capital was accumulating, but how to define the class role played by the merchants who fostered this accumulation. Marx himself insisted that the replacement of one mode of production by another does not depend on commerce. It depends on the nature of the old mode of production. Each mode of production generates within itself the contradictions that give rise to antagonistic class struggles. In the feudal mode of production, the struggle over rent created a dialectical confrontation between landlords and peasants.

In this confrontation, where did the ever-rising bourgeoisie stand? What role is to be given to the long-distance merchants heralded by Pirenne and the commercial school as an external element that broke into the natural agrarian economy of the Middle Ages and precipitated its destruction? Marxist writers reject Pirenne. Long-distance merchants were not external to the feudal economy, they argue. Far from precipitating the destruction of the system, great merchants sought to preserve it.

The Marxists' argument derives from their emphasis on production. Merchants were engaged in distribution, in conveying articles for sale from one place to another. They did not change the structure of production. They did not alter the character of the articles sold. They earned profits through arbitrage, taking advantage of price differentials prevailing between markets that were distant from one another. The great long-distance merchants formed merchant guilds in medieval towns, and their merchant guilds generally dominated the various craft guilds. In time, leading merchants assumed control over the organization of production. They acquired contracts from distant buyers to deliver specific goods that were fabricated in their towns; they set the craft guildsmen, their fellow-townsmen, to work producing those goods; and ultimately they became de facto employers of the craft guildsmen because they controlled the access to raw materials and the markets for finished goods. The effect of this process was to proletarianize craft guildsmen.

The merchants' activities went further still. They initiated the practice of putting-out; that is, they distributed some forms of industrial work, like wool spinning, to rural people who performed labor in their cottages with raw materials supplied them by the merchants. Putting-out permitted merchants to enlarge the scope of their operations, to evade guild restrictions in the towns, and to obtain labor at a price below that paid to town workers. All the same, neither putting-out nor the merchants' exercise of hegemony over craft guildsmen altered the prevailing mode of production. The prevailing system of petty commodity production remained intact. Only the administration of it was altered. It terms of production, the merchants were not a revolutionary class.

Nor were they revolutionary in social and political terms. From the earliest days, merchants were parasites of the landlord class. They supplied the nobility with consumables and credits, and they lived off the lords' largesse. At no time did they attack the feudal structure. Often, they demonstrated solidarity with the lords in their struggles against the peasants. The goal of long-distance merchants was not to endanger the system but to "muscle in" on the privileged position of the lordly class. Indeed, wrote Dobb, the merchant bourgeoisie, far from being a progressive force for change in history, retarded the development of capitalism as a mode of production.[30]

That retardation was occasioned by commercial monopolies. In the sixteenth and seventeenth centuries, the time when absolutist aspirations excited monarchies across Western Europe, merchants and kings achieved a symbiotic relationship. Great merchants made loans to royalty and engaged in contracts to equip their armies and supply their courts. In exchange, they received monopoly rights over every manner of trade. In England, there was the fifteenth-century Company of Merchant Adventurers, a group of merchants having the exclusive privilege of trading cloth to the Low Countries. A parade of chartered monopolies followed: in 1553, the Russia Company; in 1555, the Africa Company; in 1577, the Spanish Company; in 1600, the East India Company. These are but a few. Monopoly restricted major trading opportunities to a privileged few, and it stifled developmental changes in the structure of production.

Since Marxist historians characterize privileged merchants as parasites and allies of the feudal elite, they must, to fulfill the logic of the dialectic, specify some other bourgeois element to serve as class antagonist to the feudal establishment. In accord with Marxist theory, that class antagonist would, at a decisive moment, rise up, seize power, and set in place the social and political apparatus of a capitalist mode of production. The chief candidate for this role was the enterprising artisan. Marx thought the new mode of production would take hold when commerce was subordinated to production. That would happen when artisans stopped producing merely for local consumption and began, as employers of wage labor, to produce for a larger national or international market. The basis of their earning power would not depend upon monopoly privileges in the distribution of goods but in greater efficiency and higher levels of productivity in the production of goods. This, Marx considered, was the "really revolutionary way," a way that subordinated commerce to production. In practice, however, Marxist scholars have had difficulty demonstrating that the capitalist mode of production emerged via the artisans in this "really revolutionary way." On the other hand, there is ample evidence that the great merchants, despite their monopolies, accelerated progress toward what Marxists define as the capitalist mode of production.

The great discoveries and the opening of direct trade with the East evoked enormous demands for capital investment, for shipping, and for the supply of vital commodities in intercontinental trade. The exploding size of royal armies required the services of large-scale suppliers of weapons. Mines were being driven much deeper, at far greater cost. In England, the first paper mills, cannon factories, and sugar refineries were established in the sixteenth century, each of them requiring relatively high capital investment. There is little likelihood that these industries could have evolved so successfully had the state not provided them with secure contracts and protection from foreign competition. Artisans—even extraordinary artisans—could not expand their operations quickly enough to accommodate the rising scale of demand or to meet the need for regularity and uniformity in the output of armaments. For commerce to become subordinate to production in the "really revolutionary way," production had to become more profitable. Increased profitability could only be achieved through industrial innovation, but even by the early eighteenth century Europe's industrial technology was essentially what it had been in the fifteenth century. In the early eighteenth century, the normal pattern of manufacturing involved a host of tiny shops operated by individual artisans. If the great merchants did not revolutionize production, they did at least coordinate and direct the production of these artisans. The effect of this was to increase output, heighten demand, and encourage a level of consumerism that set the stage for technical innovation at the end of the eighteenth century. Even when Europe entered the Industrial Revolution, utilizing what Marxists would agree was a capitalist mode of production, the industrial innovators were no more likely to emerge from the artisan class than from merchant communities.[31]

THE REVOLUTIONARY SEIZURE OF POWER

The Marxian thesis that representatives of a new mode of production would finalize the process of transition by taking revolutionary action against defenders of the old economic structure has generated intense debate in recent decades. Encouraged by the work of Georges Lefebvre in France[32] and Christopher Hill in England,[33] Marxists ardently adopted the English Civil War, 1642–1649, and the French Revolution, 1789, as critical watersheds when the bourgeoisie forcibly asserted its primacy in society. In his original thesis, Hill conceived the English Civil War as a confrontation between two well-defined and self-conscious class entities, the bourgeoisie and the aristocracy, the former representing trading and industrial interests in the towns as well as yeomen and lesser gentry (kulaks) who were determined to wrest power from the feudal elite and advance the interests of capitalism. The monarchy, allied with the feudal elite, enjoyed the support of the great monopolistic merchants. Marxist historians considered Hill's work the opening gambit in a constructive debate on mode of production in the seventeenth century and on the class configuration of English society. Non-Marxists considered it a call to arms, and in the years that followed they dismantled it piece by piece.[34] We cannot probe these debates here. Suffice it to say, Hill was obliged to modify his position, ultimately affirming only that the Civil War established conditions that were more favorable to capitalism than those that persisted in England before 1642. The debate on the French Revolution has been at least as intense and, on balance, somewhat less baleful to the Marxian position, although in the French case as well the more strident early assertions of Marxist writers have been systematically discredited.[35]

CONCLUSION

The contribution of Marxists to modern historical scholarship can hardly be exaggerated. Marx's identification of modernity with capitalism has taken root across the spectrum of historical opinion, and the specific categories of analysis employed by Marxist scholars, especially the concepts of class and class struggle, have been widely adopted in the profession. No mode of interpretation has been more provocative of debate, either within or without the ranks of the converted. No form of theory has taken so many tangents or offered such kaleidoscopic variation. That Marxism has been a seedbed for both sympathetic and antithetic modes of historical interpretation is a testament to the compelling force of many of its most fundamental propositions.

NOTES

1. Quoted in Jeffrey Weeks, "Foucault for Historians," *History Workshop Journal* 14 (1982): 108.

2. This does not mean that some scholars did not defy the Party. When the British Communist Party refused to condemn the Soviet invasion of Hungary in 1956, three of the leading socialist historians in Britain—Rodney Hilton, Christopher Hill, and E. P. Thompson—resigned from the Party. Two other renowned historians stayed in: Maurice Dobb and Eric Hobsbawm. Harvey J. Kaye, *The British Marxist Historians* (New York, 1984), p. 17.

3. Robert V. Daniels, "Marxian Theories of Historical Dynamics," in Werner J. Cahnman and Alvin Boskoff, eds., *Sociology and History: Theory and Research* (New York, 1964), p. 63.

4. Marx's "Preface" to his *Contribution to the Critique of Political Economy* (New York, 1904; first published, 1859).

5. David McLellan, *Karl Marx: His Life and Thought* (New York, 1973), p. 305.

6. Daniels, "Marxian Theories," p. 72.

7. G. A. Cohen, *Karl Marx's Theory of History: A Defense* (Princeton, 1978), p. 165.

8. Jon Elster, *Making Sense of Marx* (Cambridge, 1985), p. 285.

9. These points are succinctly argued in Tom Bottomore, ed., *A Dictionary of Marxist Thought* (Cambridge, Mass., 1983), pp. 117–119.

10. This statement appeared in the early portion of Marx and Engels's *Manifesto of the Communist Party,* which was published in February 1848. For the original text of the *Manifesto* and a comprehensive introduction to it, see Howard J. Laski, *Howard J. Laski on the Communist Manifesto* (New York, 1967).

11. Erik Olin Wright, Cynthia Costello, David Hachen, and Joey Sprague, "The American Class Structure," *American Sociological Review* 47 (1982): 709.

12. Ibid., p. 719.

13. Numerous scholars have attacked the conventional Marxist position that the French Revolution was a "bourgeois" revolution by demonstrating that the French bourgeoisie was a congeries of highly diverse groups whose attitudes toward the revolution were widely varied. See, for example, Alfred Cobban, *The Social Interpretation of the French Revolution* (Cambridge, 1964), and George V. Taylor, "Non-Capitalist Wealth and the French Revolution," *American Historical Review* 72 (1967): 486–496.

14. A distinguished French sociologist-historian, Roland Mousnier, initiated a major debate in the early 1970s by declaring that the concept of class was inappropriate to pre-industrial Europe. Rather, he argued, Europeans were stratified by a hierarchy of "orders" based upon the dignity that society attached to particular social functions. For his argument on Europe as a "society of orders," see Roland Mousnier, *Social Hierarchies, 1450 to the Present*, trans. Peter Evans (New York, 1973).

15. E. P. Thompson, *The Making of the English Working Class* (New York, 1966), p. 11.

16. Quoted in Kaye, *British Marxist Historians*, p. 201.

17. Paul Hirst, a structuralist, makes the point well: "There is no such thing as 'orthodox Marxism.' All 'orthodoxies'—Kautsky's, Lukacs', Stalin's—are particular theoretical constructions culled out of the possibilities within the complex whole of Marx and Engel's discourse." He says much the same thing about structuralism. See Paul Hirst, "The Necessity of Theory," *Economy and Society* 8 (1979): 420, 443.

18. Maurice Dobb was a leading Marxist theoretician in England. Between 1924 and 1967, he was lecturer, then reader in economics at Cambridge University, where he provided guidance to several generations of young communists and communist sympathizers.

19. Maurice Dobb, *Studies in the Development of Capitalism* (New York, 1984), p. 65.

20. Paul Sweezy, "A Critique," in Rodney Hilton et al., *The Transition from Feudalism to Capitalism* (London, 1978), p. 51.

21. Maurice Dobb, "A Reply," in Hilton et al., *The Transition from Feudalism to Capitalism*, p. 62.

22. Quoted in Perry Anderson, *Lineages of the Absolutist State* (London, 1974), pp. 18–19.

23. Ibid., p. 18.

24. Ibid., p. 19.

25. Ibid., p. 33.

26. Friedrich Engels, *Origin of the Family*, Kerr edition (Chicago, 1902), p. 209.

27. Robert Brenner, "Agrarian Class Structure and Economic Development in Pre-Industrial Europe," *Past and Present* 70 (1976): 63-73.

28. Thompson, *The Making*, p. 10.

29. Brenner, "Agrarian Class Structure," pp. 61–62.

30. Dobb, *Studies*, p. 122.

31. J-F. Bergier, "The Industrial Bourgeoisie and the Rise of the Working Class 1700–1914," in Carlo Cipolla, ed., *The Fontana Economic History of Europe*, vol. 3 (Glasgow, 1973), pp. 408–412.

32. Georges Lefebvre, *The Coming of the French Revolution, 1789*, trans. R. R. Palmer (Princeton, 1947).

33. Christopher Hill, *The English Revolution, 1640* (London, 1955). This essay was first published in 1940 in a three-essay collection.

34. The protracted debate involving Christopher Hill, R. H. Tawney, H. R. Trevor-Roper, Lawrence Stone, and others occupied two decades. J. H. Hexter's "Storm over the Gentry," *Encounter* (May 1958), reproduced in his *Reappraisals in History* (Evanston, 1962) and Perez Zagorin's "The Social Interpretation of the English Revolution," *Journal of Economic History* 19 (1959): 376–401, capped the controversy in a fashion inimical to the interpretive interests of Marxists. For an overview of historiography on the issue, see R. C. Richardson, *The Debate on the English Revolution* (New York, 1977).

35. Many of the most important scholarly contributions to the debate have been collected in a book designed for students. See Ralph W. Greenlaw, ed., *The Social Origins of the French Revolution: The Debate on the Role of the Middle Classes* (Lexington, 1975). William Doyle, *Origins of the French Revolution* (New York, 1980), provides an excellent summary of the state of the question. For an evaluation of Marxist writings on the 1789 experience, see G. Ellis, "The 'Marxist Interpretation' of the French Revolution," *English Historical Review* 93 (1978): 353–376.

6

Weber, Sombart, and the Spirit of Capitalism

Two world-renowned German sociologists, Max Weber (1864–1920) and Werner Sombart (1863–1941), vehemently affirmed Marx's belief that capitalism constituted a distinct social formation in Western history. For them, the advent of capitalism marked the beginning of modern history. All of their historical work was devoted to understanding capitalist culture, its spiritual essence and the particular qualities of Western culture that promoted and sustained its existence. Like Marx, Sombart and Weber grew progressively estranged from the capitalist system, although the level of their estrangement never approached that of Marx. Both deplored the alienation that working people suffered under mature capitalist production, and both lamented the erosion of individual heroism and creativity within bureaucratic capitalist states. Unlike Marx, however, they rejected economic determinism and monocausality. While they admitted that the relative importance of economic factors had increased in modern times, they insisted that history was not the product of impersonal material forces. It was driven by the interaction of numerous forces, some economic, some not. But all such forces were set in motion by ideas—in particular, religious ideas.

In the medieval seedbed where capitalism took root, economic stimuli were powerfully influenced by religion. Weber and Sombart studied the world of religious ideas, contending that spiritual forces were crucial to creating the cultural climate that promoted capitalism. Weber was better disciplined and more profound than Sombart. But it was Sombart who first probed the inner logic of capitalism, arguing that the "spirit" of capitalism called the substance of capitalism into being. Sombart remained a competitor, interlocutor, and foil for his more famous colleague, and together they challenged the theoretical postulates of Adam Smith, Karl Marx, and their respective academic partisans.

Weber, in particular, contended that neither Marx, Smith, nor the schools of historical explanation they fostered fully appreciated the distinctive character of Western capitalism. Yes, capitalism involved private appropriation of the means of production; yes, it involved a money economy and a search for profit through market exchanges; yes, it comprehended the use of free wage labor drawn from a propertyless population that had only its labor to sell; and, of course, it was driven by individual economic self-interest. But capitalism, as a social structure, a culture, a comprehensive code of conduct, is more than these, Weber insisted. Capitalism transcends the free exercise of acquisitive instincts under market conditions. Ardent acquisitiveness has been evident in most social systems since the beginning of recorded time. There is no shortage of examples, East and West, of avaricial entrepreneurs exploiting private property to achieve high profits. Yet only in Europe and only in the sixteenth century was there a breakthrough to capitalism as a distinctive civilization, as a way of life.

Although Weber and Sombart advocated different reasons for the emergence of capitalism, their intense focus on the question was inspired by heated academic debates in imperial Germany. The Germans had experienced industrial capitalism differently from other West Europeans. In England, the Industrial Revolution unfolded gradually but steadily over the eighteenth and nineteenth centuries. In Germany, industrialization descended abruptly in the second half of the nineteenth century. Germany did not undergo a successful bourgeois revolution; consequently, the German middle class exercised substantially less political and cultural influence than its counterpart in France, Belgium, or Britain. Because British industrial capitalism emerged slowly as a natural evolutionary growth, most Britons took it for granted: in fact, the scholarly community in England devoted little attention to capitalism as a distinct social system.

In Germany, on the other hand, rapid and belated industrialization commanded the attention of the nation's social thinkers. Germany's new industrial order was founded at precisely the time that a German nation was being unified under Prussian leadership. New circumstances demanded new policies. In order to cope with the multiple dimensions of the new national order, it was deemed important that scholars fathom the character of capitalism, probe its origins, and identify the principles that sustained it.

Having assumed this charge, German academics became divided on a host of theoretical issues.[1] Among them was the question whether all human beings, in their economic pursuits, exhibited the same motives and behavior. Beginning with Adam Smith, Britain's classical economists had advanced this position, arguing that "economic man" was universally propelled by individual self-interest and the desire to maximize his or her material advantage. The best societal means of achieving maximum economic efficiency was to permit the greatest measure of individual economic freedom. This orientation was well suited to Great Britain, a self-conscious and centuries-old national state whose modern industrial growth had occurred over many generations.

It was not suited to Germany. There, social scientists constituting the German Historical School condemned the classical tradition as unduly abstract, unverified by inductive historical research, and thereby both ahistorical and falsely universal. They found it ethically and pragmatically repellant. It was, many Germans argued, an utterly materialist orientation, indifferent to the special requirements of particular cultures. It failed to acknowledge that in some times and some places individual economic behavior could be significantly constrained by ethical or other non-economic imperatives. More pragmatically, argued the Germans, the laissez-faire component of the classical tradition did not meet the special needs of a newly unified national state in which infant industries required protection and the swift progress of industrialization evoked calls for government interference to protect workers and unravel the worst problems created by rapid economic expansion.

SOMBART: THE SPIRIT OF CAPITALISM

In 1902 Sombart published his two-volume *Modern Capitalism* purporting to show how capitalism had emerged in Europe.[2] He divided European economic development into chronological stages, beginning with "traditional societies" in which people were the sum of all things.

They accepted what was handed down to them; their economic activity was calculated to satisfy natural wants and to achieve self-sufficiency. Leisure was prized over accumulation. By the sixteenth century, traditional economies were giving way to early capitalism (merchant capitalism), and in the nineteenth century early capitalism was supplanted by "high" capitalism (industrial and financial capitalism). Throughout the centuries, human values determined what was acceptable economic conduct, and those values were shaped by an on-going dialectical struggle between opposing principles: a traditional principle and an acquisitive principle. The traditional principle held that people should engage in economic activity only to satisfy fixed needs. The acquisitive principle urged that people pursue unlimited acquisition. Over the last six centuries, the acquisitive principle, embodying the "spirit of capitalism," steadily gained ascendancy over the traditional principle.

The rise of the capitalist spirit was a necessary, though not sufficient, condition for the triumph of capitalism, Sombart thought. He identified a host of political and material forces that promoted changes in production and exchange. The growth of the modern state with its demand for military hardware, troops, and luxury goods stimulated organizational changes in the economy. The introduction of precious metals from America after 1492 increased the money supply and heightened the rate of circulation. There were numerous technological inventions as well as innovations in commercial institutions and business techniques that accelerated economic change. But all material adjustments were preceded by and integrated through an evolving capitalist spirit.

What was this capitalist spirit? It had two dimensions, Sombart thought: on one side, it was dynamic, adventuresome, enterprising, and driven by a ruthless greed for riches; on the other, it was calculating and rational. Neither dimension alone could produce the capitalist spirit or initiate a capitalist order. The capitalist spirit could only be produced when its two components were united. Where did this union first arise? With the Jews, declared Sombart.

SOMBART: ETHNICITY AND CAPITALISM

Sombart's identification of the Jews with early capitalism first appeared in his book *The German Economy in the Nineteenth Century,* which was published the year after *Modern Capitalism.* Together, these works achieve important unity. *The German Economy* amplifies hints in the earlier work that Sombart was becoming hostile to the capitalist system, and the book embodies Sombart's first resort to hereditary and racial explanations for historical developments. Jews had a special propensity for capitalism, he argued. Jewish character demonstrated selfishness and powerful will. Jews were sober. Their family structure was tight, and this permitted the ready transfer of property from one generation to another. Jews had an exceptional capacity for abstract thought, a facility that enhanced their appreciation of the abstraction, money. By the dictates of heredity, they were the ultimate traders. Their religion was highly rational and legalistic. Because the Old Testament did not discourage the accumulation of riches, Jews never formulated an ideal of poverty. Christians did. The New Testament was replete with ominous warnings against laying up earthly treasure and serving two masters: alas, "it is easier for a camel to pass through a needle's eye than for a rich man to enter the kingdom of God."[3] The Book of Deuteronomy enjoined Jews to observe one code of commercial conduct in dealing with one another, and another code, less scrupulous, in treating with Gentiles. This applied to the practice of usury. Christians were formally and universally forbidden to engage in usury; Jews were forbidden usurious undertakings with other Jews. But Jews were free to practice usury in contracts with Christians. Because Jews living in Christian Europe were excluded from traditional modes of advancement, from high state office, or from the dignities of the Church, the only avenue of advancement open to them was the accumulation of wealth. Christian kings and merchants consistently repaired to them for loans of money—at interest, of course. In Venice, Holland, Frankfurt, and many other places where Jews arrived in large numbers, business activity burgeoned. By religion, by temperament, and by circumstance, Jews were particularly fitted to be early agents of the capitalist spirit and educators to those who would follow their example.

In books written before World War I—*The Jews and Modern Capitalism* (1911) and *The Quintessence of Capitalism* (1913)—Sombart emphasized the importance of race and heredity in influencing the course of history. All Europeans had the qualities necessary for capitalism, he contended, but those qualities flourished in different peoples in different ways and to different degrees. Among Europe's ancient tribes, some, like the Celts and Goths, were "under-inclined" by their heredity toward capitalism. Others were "over-inclined." Sombart divided the latter into two categories consistent with the two components of the capitalist spirit. There were the adventurous, enterprising "Heroic peoples" who demonstrated their ruthless acquisitiveness through a special talent for "forcible, all-conquering undertakings on a large scale." These included the Romans and several Germanic peoples: Normans, Lombards, Saxons, and

Franks. The second group, the "Trading peoples," exhibited special gifts of rationality. They exercised this quality in conducting "successful business by peaceful contract-making, by diplomacy and by clever calculation." Among the "Trading peoples" were Scots (descended from Frisians), Florentines (descended from Etruscans and Greeks), and Jews. The latter were, from the first, he wrote, "a pure trading people."[4]

Sombart lamented the ascendancy of trade over heroism in modern capitalism. Man was no longer the measure of all things. Dynamism, enterprise, and adventure had fallen prey to the barren power of rationality. Economic activity was governed by cold reason. Profit had become the only objective. Wealth was not being generated to serve human interests. Everything was sacrificed to the "Moloch" of work. Human beings had become degraded faceless cogs in a productive machine committed to accumulation—accumulation for the sake of accumulation: "all the higher instincts of heart and mind [were] crushed out by devotion to business."[5] In the evolving mentality of Werner Sombart, all the ingredients for what would later become a Nazi worldview were in place before World War I: a sentimental tribalism, a contempt for high capitalism, an emphasis on heredity and race, and an inclination to blame Jews for perceived misdirections in German society.[6]

Sombart has been described as a "weathercock for the creative winds of his age."[7] During his long and colorful career, he passed through at least three distinct phases—from sentimental conservatism, to social democracy, to the advocacy of racialism. Sombart served as a stimulus, sometimes an outrageous stimulus, to the steadier, more systematic Max Weber. For twenty years, he and Weber exchanged ideas as well as critical volleys. Although their books on the rise of modern capitalism located the origins of the capitalist spirit in religious communities, they differed fundamentally on which religious communities embodied it. Scholars often contend that Weber's historical sociology was a direct response to the extreme economism of Marx. In some ways, it was. More emphatically, however, Weber responded to the work of Sombart, a professional colleague with whom he shared similar intellectual roots and orientations but highly dissimilar fruits.

WEBER: THE SPIRIT OF CAPITALISM

Max Weber published his famous work, *The Protestant Ethic and the Spirit of Capitalism*, in 1904–1905 as a two-part article in the *Archiv für Sozialwissenschaft und Sozialpolitik,* a journal for which he served as an editor. The work gave ample evidence of Sombart's influence. Both men considered modern capitalism an epoch-forming and unique historical phenomenon. For both, the spirit of capitalism was paramount in generating the institutional structures of capitalism. That spirit was rooted in religious ideas, and it had a rational dimension. Both considered the capitalist spirit a necessary, but not sufficient, condition for the rise of capitalism. At the same time, Weber rejected Sombart's main conclusions. He denied his argument on the Jews,[8] and he set aside the immediate value of using heredity as a causal explanation in history. Weber did not disavow a hereditary explanation. On the contrary, he admitted that he too was "inclined to think the importance of biological heredity very great," but there was, at his time of writing, no way of knowing either how or to what extent heredity produced different behavior in different races or national groups.[9]

Weber addressed his main criticism to Sombart's two-dimensional concept of the capitalist spirit. According to Weber, Sombart mistook the origins of capitalism because he misrepresented the capitalist mentality. The modern spirit of capitalism has a single dimension. It is exclusively rational, not, as Sombart argued, rational in part. Weber agreed with Sombart that capitalism displaced traditionalism, a condition in which workers, even to some extent businessmen, preferred shorter working hours and more leisure, seeking only to earn enough money to preserve the mode of living to which they had grown accustomed. In traditional society, it served no purpose for an employer to double his worker's pay in hope of stimulating an increased yield. The hired man would work only half as long, earn the same pay, and thereby obtain more leisure. What Weber sought to explain was how this traditional ethos was displaced by a calculating and rational orientation to work, one in which profits were maximized, risks were minimized, idle leisure was despised, and the accumulation of personal wealth was perceived as a duty.

Sombart's dualistic notion of the spirit of capitalism did not help. Enterprise, bold adventure, and the ruthless search for riches—the heroic side of the Sombartian concept—are not especially modern, and they have nothing to do with the transition from traditionalism to capitalism, Weber argued. As the embodiment of rationality in economic activity, capitalism relies on systematic business enterprise that yields consistent profit through careful planning, honest exchange, and repeatable performance. Capitalism is not well served by high adventurism, spoilation, or rapine— the type of avaricial self-interest that propelled Cortez and Pizzaro.[10] High-stakes speculation may, on occasion, exhibit capitalistic qualities, but speculative economic behavior does not produce a culture of capitalism. The two dimensions of Sombart's capitalist spirit were contradictory. The bold adventurer and the calculating profit-maximizer were utterly dissimilar types. To envision their union as achieving the consummation of the capitalist spirit was, to Weber, empirically untenable. Only half of Sombart's analysis was correct, his recognition that capitalism involves the application of rational calculation to economic activity.

Like Sombart, Weber asserted that an array of preconditions was necessary before the capitalist spirit could breathe life into a capitalist economy. These included an entrepreneurial organization of capital whereby business and family accounts would be kept separate; a free labor market; a system of calculable law that offered protection to private property; unrestricted (or minimally restricted) markets in goods and services; and rational technology. A vital facilitating medium through which these and other preconditions evolved was the bureaucratic state. Served by professional administrators and professional jurists, it supplanted the highly personal feudal or patrimonial state. The bureaucratic state pacified large areas, eliminated barriers to trade, standardized currencies, provided the means for reliable banking institutions and dependable courts of law, and increased the demand for goods and services by raising armies and expending large sums on luxuries. However, material development and bureaucratic government, by themselves, did not produce capitalism. In China, elaborate Confucian bureaucratic regimes had functioned for centuries, maintaining armies, enjoying relatively high technology, and exercising strong demand in the marketplace without achieving the transition to capitalism. Something more was needed: namely, a capitalist spirit, an ethos, that could integrate and consolidate the preconditions for capitalism into the reality of modern rational capitalism. For both Weber and Sombart, that spirit was a precondition *for* as well as an abiding condition *of* modern capitalism.

The capitalist spirit was superbly and succinctly expressed in the writings of Benjamin Franklin, Weber contended. Weber quoted Franklin at length:

> Remember, that *time* is money. He that can earn ten shillings a day by his labour, and goes abroad, or sits idle, one half of that day, though he spends but sixpence during his diversion or idleness, ought not to reckon *that* the only expense; he has really spent, or rather thrown away, five shillings besides.
>
> Remember, that *credit* is money.

Remember, that money is of the prolific, generating nature. Money can beget money, and its offspring can beget more, and so on.

The most trifling actions that affect a man's credit are to be regarded. The sound of your hammer at five in the morning, or eight at night, heard by a creditor, makes him easy six months longer.[11]

Franklin enjoined his readers to be attentive to opportunity costs; to keep exact accounts; to maximize profits; to resist all temptation to squander time or capital; to exhibit honesty, punctuality, and commercial dependability; and to be ever vigilant in enlarging capital. Acquisition was the "ultimate purpose" of life. Making money was not merely a virtue; it was a duty. Franklin's advice was more than plain talk to aspiring tradesmen, Weber argued. He was expressing an "ethos," a comprehensive orientation to living, and any infraction of his tenets constituted "forgetfulness of duty."

Franklin's values were different from those of entrepreneurs in China, Babylon, or ancient and medieval Europe. The latter may have exhibited commercial daring; some, especially medieval Christians, would have accumulated their riches at the peril of their souls. But Ben Franklin had no fear for his soul. On the contrary, utilitarian honesty, punctuality, frugality, and industry were doubly enriching because they pleased God while they assured other mortals of one's credit and credibility. Weber not only denied Sombart's assumption that daring speculation and ruthless acquisition constituted a critical component of modern capitalism, but he also contended that any exercise of irrationality or unscrupulousness in the conduct of business was anathema to its spirit. Dishonesty (or even the appearance of dishonesty) in commercial dealings as well as the exercise of dual standards of commercial behavior (a characteristic that Sombart attributed to Jews) were impediments to regular, reliable, and repeatable trade. The ethos of modern capitalism is not to be found in the unrestrained pursuit of gain; it is found in the rational tempering of such impulses in order that renewable, continuous, secure business profit can be assured.

Where did Franklin, in particular, and the modern world, in general, acquire this ethos? Was it, as Marx would have argued, a part of the ideal superstructure that merely reflected conditions prevailing in the economic base of society? Hardly, wrote Weber. Ben Franklin lived in colonial Pennsylvania where money was scarce and barter was common, where there were no large enterprises, and where banking was rudimentary. For Franklin, *ideas* offered guidance for economic practice, not the reverse.

Was the ethos expressed by Franklin simply a product of Occidental rationality? Yes and no, thought Weber. Rationalism comprehends a world of different things, and Occidental rationality has evolved under differing timetables in different places.[12] The task before Weber was to locate the particular source of rationalism expressed in the worldview of Benjamin Franklin.

WEBER: CALVINISM AND CAPITALISM

Weber found the rationalism he sought in the Protestant Reformation. Virtually all Protestants adopted the concept of *the Calling,* a belief that individuals could glorify God by conducting their lives admirably and meeting their obligations fully in this world.[13] It was Calvinism, however, that was chiefly instrumental in forming the capitalist spirit. John Calvin (1509–1564), lawyer, theologian, and father of Puritanism, acknowledged that God was both omnipotent and omniscient. Therefore, he reasoned, not only has God the power to offer salvation, but He knows who will be saved and who will be damned before they are born. To assert that an individual, once born, can alter his or her fate is to assume that the dictates of God can be modified by mere mortals. The individual cannot help himself. The intercession of priests, the sacraments, stained glass, religious statuary—all the sensuous accents of the Catholic Church—offer nothing but sentimental illusion.

In practice, Calvin's doctrine of predestination was all but impossible for his followers to sustain. Because people became obsessed with the question of whether or not they were among the elect, the principle of predestination had to be moderated in pastoral practice. Calvinist pastors enjoined their flocks to glorify God, to consider themselves among the elect, and to fight all doubts about their salvation as if such doubts were temptations of the devil. They embraced worldly activity, demonstrating to themselves and to one another their worthiness. According to Calvin, punctilious conduct may not have had any effect upon an individual's ultimate fate, but it did, in daily practice, provide personal reassurance. It was, as Weber argues, an indispensable "sign" of election—"the technical means, not of purchasing salvation, but of getting rid of the fear of damnation."[14]

Highly ascetic, Calvinists renounced popular amusements on the Sabbath or frivolities like dancing or card playing or theatre. Vanity and ostentation, whether in clothing or decoration, were repudiated as idolatry of the flesh. The accumulation of wealth was considered objectionable only if it tempted the flesh to excess or bred idleness, but if wealth was acquired in the performance of duty, if its accumulation could be seen as a means of glorifying God (as in the parable of the talents),[15] it was both permissible and encouraged.

Wealth is seductive, Weber observed. Medieval monasteries that began with the best ascetic intentions often succumbed to worldly temptations once they had accumulated wealth. This would happen to Calvinists as well, but not before the asceticism that regulated economic behavior in the full flush of Calvinist religiosity was transformed into a sober economic virtue. Calvinists transformed what earlier generations had considered vices into Christian virtues. They renounced idleness; rendered labor a spiritual enterprise; encouraged thrift, diligence, and sobriety in daily life; and identified honest profit-taking as a duty to God. Economic accumulation was encouraged within the bounds of correct moral conduct. While this was most evident in the bourgeois businessman, it manifested itself as well in "sober, conscientious, and unusually industrious workmen, who clung to their work as to a life purpose willed by God."[16] When, after time, the religious veneer was peeled away, what remained of worldly asceticism was rational economic conduct founded on the concept of a Calling. This was the wellspring of Ben Franklin's worldview. It was the key ingredient in the rise of modern European capitalism.

Weber recognized that capitalism may have arisen at another time without the inspiration of aescetic Protestantism. It would never have arisen unless economic, demographic, technological, and monetary preconditions were in place. But, he concluded, in the particular experience of sixteenth-century Europe, Calvinism provided the spiritual spark that ignited material tinder that had been accumulating there throughout the late Middle Ages.

THE WEBER THESIS REFUTED

From the moment of its publication, Weber's essay aroused intense debate. The Marxists, Pirenne, Sombart, and a host of other luminaries rejected his thesis. It would be fruitless to identify more than a few participants in the controversy. Debate has persisted at differing levels of intensity for nearly a century. Almost every historian concerned with early modern Europe has taken some position on Weber's work. Many, perhaps most, have oversimplified his thesis, assuming that Weber believed that ascetic Protestantism was the prime cause of capitalism and that the presence of the former necessarily produced the latter. As we have seen,

Weber's argument was more subtle and more moderate than that. It was no surprise to him that the advent of Calvinism in places like Hungary and Scotland did not inspire the rise of capitalism. Yet many of his critics used the example of places like Hungary or Scotland to discredit his thesis. Historians working on the Netherlands, Rhineland Germany, and Switzerland found no apparent connection between Calvinist religious practice and capitalism. Others demonstrated that Calvinists were as idle as Catholics, that they were as opposed to usury as Catholics and just as hostile to an economic ethos baldly committed to material accumulation.[17]

Weber's critics have challenged him at many levels. Some have derided his advocacy of Calvinism. Others have dismissed his emphasis on the role of ideas, insisting that ideas are derivative of material conditions. Still others have challenged his use of statistics and the factual data employed to support his thesis.[18] Some challenges to Weber arise obliquely, not directly. This is the case with Theodore Rabb, a student of the English merchant class in the sixteenth and seventeenth centuries. Rabb discovered that during the early years of English expansion, whether in exploration, the founding of colonies, slave trading, or piracy, investors—many of them Calvinists—exhibited precious little of the sober rationality identified by Weber as being genuinely capitalist. A lottery mentality prevailed in England, and investors referred to their overseas enterprises, quite appropriately, as "ventures" or "adventures." Men dreamed of great windfalls, eldorados, and they recklessly poured capital into scores of ill-conceived and ill-fated projects. Rabb describes the mood of those years as "irrational and emotional," moved by international competition, national animosities, and zenophobia—an approach quite at odds with the cautious capitalism of the nineteenth and twentieth centuries or the sober, systematic capitalism described by Weber.[19]

Sombart considered Calvinists the least likely religious community to evoke a capitalist spirit. Calvinists were "inimical to acquisitiveness." They were hostile to grandeur in art, decoration, and clothing, and their behavior had the effect of repressing demand in the marketplace. Even Catholics were more likely candidates to raise the capitalist spirit. Early Church fathers may have advocated poverty, Sombart continued, but Thomas Aquinas, uniting Pauline and Augustinian doctrines of love and legalism, established an ethical system based on the rationalization of life. Reason should regulate the world and control the passions, Thomas thought. He deplored idleness. He taught industry, frugality, and honesty: indeed, commercial honesty in Europe owed much to Church teaching.[20] As for Ben Franklin, he was antedated by a host of writers who advocated virtually identical doctrines. Sombart quoted at length from a fifteenth-century Florentine, Leon Battista Alberti, whose book *I Libri della Famiglia* offered homilies advocating thrift, industry, and frugality very similar to those of Franklin. Such doctrines appeared in numerous works throughout the centuries, among them Daniel Defoe's *The Complete English Tradesman* (1727). Defoe, Sombart observed, was among Franklin's favorite authors.[21]

R. H. Tawney, the renowned English economic historian, was sympathetic to some aspects of Weber's work and critical of others.[22] Tawney agreed that the sixteenth century was a watershed in Western history and that the Reformation was a vital factor in Europe's transition to capitalism. But, with Sombart, Tawney believed that Weber overstated the uniqueness as well as the importance of the Protestant concept of the Calling. He undervalued the extent to which the rationalizing impulse of the Calvinists was foreshadowed by Roman Catholic schoolmen, and he failed to appreciate the degree to which changing social and economic needs gave rise to the Reformation and its abiding religious mentalities. Tawney acknowledged the existence of a rationalizing, ascetic Protestant ethic, and he agreed that Calvin provided the first systematic body of religious teaching to recognize and applaud economic virtues. But neither the Protestant ethic nor Calvin's teachings manifested themselves until economic and political change had created a congenial environment for them. Calvinism did not trigger the rise of capitalism. Rather, the existing apparatus of capitalism adopted Calvinism as religious reinforcement. For Tawney, the Protestant ethic was an intellectual capstone, a moral justification for cultural adjustments that were rooted in and advanced by material forces. In this sense, it was more an effect than a cause of historical change.

Marxists have been sterner critics than Tawney, yet their orientation differs in degree, not in kind. Religion is an element of the superstructure, they argue. Its biases reflect those of the prevailing productive system, a productive system that serves the interest of a particular dominant class. In late medieval Europe, the small but growing bourgeoisie struggled against the forces of feudalism. Because Roman Catholicism was the ally of feudalism, the class interest of the urban bourgeoisie could only be advanced by undermining Catholic authority. Luther pierced the Church's armor, but it was Calvin who provided an ideological structure highly accommodating to the class interests of the bourgeoisie. Does the rapid spread of Calvinism through the urban centers of France, the Low Countries, and England not suggest a convergence of interests? A bourgeoisie that was already engaged in the systematic accumulation of capital was naturally attracted to Calvinism, and Calvinist divines, eager to please their audiences, shaped their messages in a language the bourgeoisie was pleased to hear.

WEBER ANSWERS HIS CRITICS

Weber was not chastened by early criticism of his work. When his essay was republished in 1920, he changed nothing of substance and added a hundred pages of densely argued notes responding point by point to his numerous critics. Neither side in the controversy could generate absolute empirical proof, nor could the matter be resolved easily by routine causal analysis. In determining historical causation, historians attempt to evaluate the importance of forces that bear upon a particular event by asking: if A had not occurred, would B have happened anyway? Or, if A had not occurred, would something akin to B have happened, albeit in significantly modified form?[23] In the case of Weber's thesis, if condition A (the Protestant Reformation) had not occurred, would result B (capitalism) have come about anyway?

Demonstrating the causal relationship between two events is less problematic than ascertaining the causal relationship between belief and action.[24] To achieve the latter, historians require evidence of the independent existence of a belief prior to its implementation in action. This is rarely possible. Normally, we observe actions; we assume the existence of the beliefs that motivate those actions; then we verify the motive power of the beliefs by referring to actions that are consistent with them. The explanation becomes circular, and the further we retreat in historical time, the more we are compelled to rely on actions to provide insight into attitudes.

At no point did Weber declare that capitalism could only have arisen as a result of the Reformation. Nor did he consider religious factors exclusively responsible for the capitalist spirit. But he did contend that in the experience of Europe, Protestant religious forces powerfully affected the "qualitative formation and the quantitative expansion" of the capitalist spirit.[25] In the absence of Protestantism, capitalism would have been delayed, altered, or possibly even precluded, Weber thought. Shortly before he died, he commented on the relative role of material interests (economic forces) and ideas in historical causation: "Interests (material and ideal) not ideas directly determine man's action. But the world views, which were created by ideas, have very often acted as the switches that channeled the dynamics of the interests."[26] Weber always gave precedence to the switches. In so doing, he took the most difficult historiographical approach.

History, Weber knew, was infinitely multidimensional and complex. In searching for the causes of an event, historians identify critical antecedent factors related to that event. Those factors are integrated into an organic formula that weighs the importance of each factor in relation to others and ascertains when various factors entered the process and at what velocity they achieved an impact. Too much of one factor, too little of another, or a different velocity of impact would alter the formula and produce a different historical outcome. Considering the numerous factors at play in the rise of capitalism, how could any scholar hope to get it right? The historian's only recourse, thought Weber, was to seek a higher level of insight.

For him, that higher level involved religion. Before the onset of modern industrial capitalism, religion provided the pervasive medium through which all institutions received validation. This was as true of the Occident as the Orient. Even Tawney readily admitted that medieval Europe was a Church-civilization, that until the sixteenth century religion enveloped all forms of human activity and that governance, law, social comportment, and transactions in the marketplace had to be justified "at the bar of religion."[27] During most of Western history, the Church was better organized for the conduct of politics than secular governments. The Church first developed bureaucratic institutions of government, and the Church set down the model for courtly life.[28] Before the advent of modernity, the forces producing change in society were critically linked to religion, Weber contended.

But how could he confirm his thesis? Only, he thought, by comparative study of other great civilizations. It was only through comparative analysis that one could discover the truly distinctive attributes of Western culture that might have triggered (or, at least, not have impeded) the rise of rational capitalism. Those who asserted that Western capitalism arose naturally through the progressive action of material forces invariably assigned special causal significance to specific factors: to the rise of markets, to the growth of state power, to technical innovation, and so forth. All such material forces were at work in other great world civilizations. Yet those civilizations did not develop rational capitalism. Until Western scholars undertook systematic comparisons of Western and non-Western cultures, they could not know what experiences those cultures shared, what they did not share, and what weight should be given to their differences. Causal analysis of the rise of European capitalism that excluded the comparative dimension was purely speculative.

Weber responded to his own mandate. Suspecting that the chief obstacle to rational capitalism in non-Western cultures was ideological, he pursued a daunting program of research in comparative religious sociology,
studying Judaism, Hinduism, Buddhism, Confucianism, Taoism, and
Islam.[29] He found what he was looking for, as historians generally do.
Having examined the interaction of non-Western religions and non-
Western cultures, Weber concluded that the chief impediment that those
civilizations encountered in achieving rational capitalism lay in the realm
of religion. In India, for example, the caste restrictions of Hinduism
restricted gain-seeking for millions of people. Caste has imposed monumental obstacles to the free and open interaction of peoples in the work-
place or the market. In the West, a religiously inspired worldview
conducive to rational capitalism arose. Outside the West, it did not.[30]

CONCLUSION

Both Sombart and Weber placed highest priority on the formative influence of religious ideas. Sombart considered Weber's concentration on
Calvinism entirely myopic, and this aspect of Weber's work continues to
evoke heaviest criticism. One of his most sympathetic latter-day defenders, Randall Collins, excuses his "error." Having died prematurely,
Collins noted, Weber was never able to complete his studies. The last stop
on his projected intellectual journey through the world's great religions
was to have been ancient and medieval Christianity. Had Weber concluded that enterprise or had he had access to the works of the professional medievalists in the twentieth century, he would have discovered the
revolutionary and rationalizing forces at work in the late-medieval Roman
Church.[31]

Weber always contended that capitalism could not emerge until critical
structural supports were in place: rationalizing technology, free labor,
unrestricted markets, entrepreneurial use of capital. Equally, Weber
acknowledged the importance of the bureaucratic state as the preserver of
order and the provider of legal security to merchants. These preconditions
were in place in the High Middle Ages, writes Collins, and the institution
most responsible for advancing them was the Roman Catholic Church.
The Papacy was the first bureaucratic state. It operated under formal rules,
kept careful records, separated individuals from offices, and instituted
recruitment on the basis of talent. Also, it advanced the concept of citizenship. The Pope was chosen by election; cathedral chapters elected their
own bishops, monasteries their abbots. The concept of citizenship within

a community offset the Church's authoritarian tendencies, fostered calculable law, and provided the clergy with rights from below as well as rights from above.

In economic matters, the Church fostered rationality and entrepreneurial behavior. With the onset of a second wave of monastic orders in the twelfth century—Cistercians, Augustinians, and various crusading orders—monasteries became the most efficient economic units ever to have existed in Europe. Cistercian monasteries maintained factories, often hydraulically powered; they used their capital assets with entrepreneurial aplomb; and they plowed their profits back into the institution. In the secular economy, capital was immobilized for want of promising areas for investment, but among the religious orders capital moved freely. The Roman Church possessed up to a third of the property in Europe. It was clearly the most dynamic, most modernizing sector of the medieval economy. Collins contends, rather dubiously one might argue, that the premodern merchant capitalism of Venice, Genoa, and Florence left no lasting impact on European institutions, whereas the capitalistic practices of the monastic orders laid the groundwork for rational capitalism in Northern Europe.[32]

Weber would have come to this view had he lived longer, Collins believes. Already, at the end of his life, he was gravitating in this direction. Collins thinks that too much attention has been bestowed on *The Protestant Ethic and the Spirit of Capitalism,* Weber's first and most dramatic work, and too little on his last, *General Economic History,* which brings together a full theory of the rise of capitalism. There, Weber remained committed to the proposition that religious ideas were critical in the emergence of rational capitalism in the West. However, at no point in the latter work did he refer to the doctrine of predestination, which figured so heavily in his *Protestant Ethic.* Weber, it seems, was migrating toward the position held by Sombart, Tawney, and many others, that the Church of Rome foretokened the rationalizing impulse that the *Protestant Ethic* had attributed specifically to Calvinism.

Whether a longer-lived Max Weber would have modified his thesis, adopting a more broadly Christian explanation for the spirit of capitalism, we will never know. Nor is it that important. Although Weber may have explained the rise of rational capitalism too exclusively in terms of one Christian sect, he—and to a lesser degree, Sombart—remained committed to the proposition that the roots of Western capitalism must be sought in the realm of religious ideas. Weber did more than intensify debate on the origins of capitalism, he raised the question beyond the confines of Western Europe, challenging serious scholars to view the issue not merely as a problem for European history but as a problem in world history.

NOTES

1. These theoretical disagreements are well presented in Gordon Marshall, *In Search of the Spirit of Capitalism: An Essay on Max Weber's Protestant Ethic Thesis* (New York, 1982), pp. 25–30.

2. Although this work has not been translated into English, a book-length synthesis of it was written by Frederick L. Nussbaum, *A History of the Economic Institutions of Modern Europe: An Introduction to Der Moderne Kapitalismus of Werner Sombart* (New York, 1935).

3. Matthew 19:24.

4. Werner Sombart, *The Quintessence of Capitalism* (New York, 1967), p. 217.

5. Ibid., p. 181.

6. In 1934, one year after the Nazis came to power, Sombart published *Deutscher Socialismus,* a stridently anti-liberal, anti-capitalist, anti-Marxist appeal for collective German national socialist renewal. His work was academic and sophisticated, by no means a piece of party propaganda, but his worldview was, by 1934, largely in harmony with the philosophical orientations of the Nazi regime. The work was translated into English by Karl F. Geiser as *A New Social Philosophy* (Princeton, 1937).

7. Arthur Mitzman, *Sociology and Estrangement: Three Sociologists of Imperial Germany* (New York, 1973), p. 136. As early as 1902, Sombart began to feel estrangement from the Germany that embraced capitalism. In his youth, Sombart had supported the German Historical School's concern to preserve the artisan class and to forestall social revolution within the growing urban proletariat. His early work reflected the School's rejection of British economic models and its desire to achieve German solutions to German problems. By 1890, Sombart had changed his mind. Renouncing the sentimental conservatism of the Historical School, he declared himself in favor of the factory system. Any attempt to save cottage industries and the artisan class was futile and backward-looking, he argued. Industrial capitalism and the factory system would generate wealth in far greater abundance than older productive processes, thereby permitting the lower orders—if they were politically organized—to achieve higher incomes and better public health and education. Capitalism should be seen as a positive force in European history, albeit not a permanent force. With Marx, Sombart argued that socialism would follow capitalism, but he resisted Marx's materialism. Material forces were moving society toward socialism. But human beings, by the exercise of their collective will, were also moving society toward a new, progressive order.

It was during his social democratic phase, the 1890s, that Sombart developed supreme confidence in voluntarism, in the collective will, in the "spirit" that directed human affairs. His confidence deepened over time. Concurrently, however, his faith in the utility of industrial capitalism as a vehicle for uplifting the people diminished. At the end of his life, Sombart had come to share much common ground with the Nazis.

8. Weber's views on this were tightly summed up in his *General Economic History* (New York, 1927), pp. 358–361.

9. Max Weber, *The Protestant Ethic and the Spirit of Capitalism,* trans. Talcott Parsons (1904–1905; New York, 1958), p. 30.

10. Weber, *General Economic History,* p. 356.

11. Weber, *The Protestant Ethic,* pp. 48–50.

12. For example, the rationalization of private law reached its apogee in late Roman antiquity, and its medieval renaissance was most successful in the Catholic countries of Southern Europe, not in the North where capitalism took hold.

13. Weber, *The Protestant Ethic,* pp. 80–81. Even the least capitalistic of the Protestant sects made some contribution in this regard. Luther was conservative, authoritarian, and unsympathetic to capitalist conduct. He condemned usury, material acquisitiveness, and social climbing, yet Lutheranism, like other Protestant persuasions, adopted the concept of the Calling.

14. Weber, *The Protestant Ethic,* p. 115.

15. Matthew 25:14–30.

16. Weber, *The Protestant Ethic,* p. 177.

17. Ephraim Fischoff, "The Protestant Ethic and the Spirit of Capitalism: The History of a Controversy," in S. N. Eisenstadt, ed., *The Protestant Ethic and Modernization: A Comparative View* (New York, 1968), pp. 77–78.

18. Perhaps the most stinging rebuke of Weber's methodology and use of statistics is by a Swedish scholar, Kurt Samuelsson. See Kurt Samuelsson, *Religion and Economic Action,* trans. E. G. French (London, 1961). A segment of Samuelsson's work appears in Robert W. Green, ed., *The Weber Thesis Controversy* (Lexington, 1973), pp. 106–136, a book designed to provide students with the main lines of the Weber debate.

19. Theodore K. Rabb, "The Expansion of Europe and the Spirit of Capitalism," *Historical Journal* 17 (1974): 675–689.

20. Werner Sombart, *The Quintessence of Capitalism: A Study of the History and Psychology of the Modern Business Man,* trans. M. Epstein (1915; New York, 1967), pp. 238–248, 269.

21. Sombart, *The Quintessence of Capitalism,* p. 116.

22. R. H. Tawney, *Religion and the Rise of Capitalism* (New York, 1926).

23. Reinhard Bendix makes this point in the context of Weber's work. See Reinhard Bendix, *Max Weber: An Intellectual Portrait* (New York, 1960), p. 103.

24. For an engaging discussion of methodological issues, see Marshall, *In Search of the Spirit of Capitalism,* pp. 65–68, 149–150. See also Elias H. Tuma, *Economic History and the Social Sciences: Problems of Methodology* (Berkeley, 1971), pp. 117, 176, 204–207.

25. Weber, *The Protestant Ethic,* p. 91.

26. Quoted in Wolfgang Schluchter, *The Rise of Western Rationalism: Max Weber's Developmental History,* trans. Guenther Roth (Berkeley, 1981), p. 25.

27. Tawney, *Religion and the Rise of Capitalism,* p. 4.

28. This argument was made early by Sombart in *Luxury and Capitalism* (1913; Ann Arbor, 1967), pp. 2–4.

29. This enterprise was not entirely completed. Works on Judaism, the religions of India, and the religions of China have been published separately in English. They were

incorporated, with his essays on the Protestant ethic, in his *Gesammelte Aufsätze zur Religionssoziologie* (Tübingen, 1920–1921), 3 vols. Weber did not complete his work on Islam.

30. Weber, *General Economic History*, pp. 313–314, 356–369.

31. Randall Collins, *Weberian Sociological Theory* (New York, 1986), p. 9.

32. Ibid., pp. 45–48.

Part III

The Dynamics of Historical Change: World History

Introduction:
The Global Perspective

In the 1970s, two distinct but highly compatible approaches to the study of history came to maturity: world-system analysis and environmental history. The first of these offered an explicit model that explained the rise and development of capitalism through exploitative relationships established between Western Europe and the wider world during the sixteenth century. World-system analysis was a logical extension of dependency theory, a theory that emerged after World War II in Latin America among development specialists who were disillusioned by the growing disparity between rich nations and poor and by the universal failure of modernization strategies. The second approach, environmental history, received powerful impetus from a United Nations Conference on the Human Environment held in Stockholm in 1971. The report of that conference, *Only One Earth,*[1] grimly alerted readers to the abuse that humans had wrought upon their environment, poisoning air and sea, destroying tens of thousands of species, depleting fisheries, laying waste the forests, encouraging the deserts, and generally endangering the long-term survival of human life on this planet.

Unlike world-system analysis, environmental history offered no over-arching theory of change; rather, it united under one umbrella a host of specialties concerned with climate, population, disease, food, fuel, natural resources, and natural disasters. Environmentalists expressed concern that conventional history, being preoccupied with human affairs, considered nature a constant, a vast and stable theatrical stage upon which human actors played out their drama. This was not the case, they argued. Natural forces are perpetually changing; man and nature have always interacted. If twentieth-century man is capable of devastating nature to such an extent that human life on this planet might become unsustainable, earlier man was a prisoner of changing natural forces, and much of his history was determined by them.

World-system analysis and environmental history are global in scope. The world-system integrates continents through economic interdependence. Environmental historians demonstrate that pollutants observe no frontiers, that the destruction of tropical forest has serious implications for people in temperate countries, that global cooling or global warming affects everyone, and that human or animal diseases that arise in one sector of the globe generally spread to others. Both modes of analysis consider the discovery of America and the biological and botanical merger of hemispheres watershed events of the first magnitude. A leading environmental historian, Donald Worster, urges that Columbus's landfall in the Bahamas and Neal Armstrong's landing on the moon mark off a distinct era in world history.[2]

World-system historians and environmental historians are either openly hostile to capitalism or exceedingly wary of it. With their intellectual roots embedded in Marxism, world-system theorists deplore the unequal distribution of wealth occasioned by capitalism. Environmentalists are alarmed by capitalism's reckless obsession with economic growth and by the extravagant rate at which capitalist societies have consumed the world's resources. Raymond Dasmann divides the world's inhabitants into ecosphere people and biosphere people. The former have the capacity to survive for centuries or longer on the resources of a single ecosystem or on adjacent or related ecosystems. They sustain life without seriously depleting the biological context of the environment upon which they depend. Biosphere people—those deemed more civilized, more sophisticated, more involved in complex divisions of labor—are dependent on world trade, a trade that widely distributes resources drawn from innumerable regional ecosystems.[3] Despite the laying waste (or, perhaps, because of the laying waste) of one regional ecosystem after another, the most powerful biosphere people may, for a time, achieve a very high material standard of living. But persistent and improvident extraction will eventually deplete the world's resources and its biological variety to the extent that the rich and powerful will be unable to sustain their extravagance and the poor will be condemned to wretchedness and desolation.

Historians of both orientations focus heavily on extraction. Environmental historians are alarmed by the growing extractive impulse of powerful biosphere peoples; world-system scholars have attempted to identify the economic linkages through which that extractive process has evolved. There is little doubt, argue the environmentalists, that population pressure and industrial capitalism have rendered thousands of regional ecosystems vulnerable to destruction. This development has been fueled primarily by Western capitalism. Almost every innovation in production, every sophisticated technology, and every development in transportation during the last century or more has been inspired by the demands of capitalist economic culture.[4]

The impulse behind the development of environmental history is clear. Our world is in crisis. If humankind is to survive on this planet, men and women must become conscious of the complex natural and biological relationships that shape the biosphere upon which our future depends. To appreciate our present difficulties and to map coherent strategies for survival, we must understand more about mankind's earlier interactions—for good and for evil—with the natural world. The impulse underlying the development of world-system analysis is less obvious. Therefore, the remainder of this introduction will focus on the changing worldviews and political and economic conditions that gave rise to what is clearly the fastest-growing and most fashionable theory of history treated in this book.

As power relationships change, so do historical orientations. In the early twentieth century, Western historians assumed that Europe would continue to shape the world in its own image, exercising hegemonic power in accordance with the balance of forces prevailing in the North Atlantic. Today, this attitude seems outrageously arrogant. In the context of the time, it was by no means unreasonable.

European power reached its zenith in 1914. All of Africa, save Ethiopia and Liberia, had been absorbed into European empires.[5] The Red Sea and the Persian Gulf were British lakes. Except for Siam (Thailand), all of southern Asia from Aden to Singapore answered to British power. Indonesia was Dutch; Indo-China was French; the Philippines were American; Central Asia and Siberia were Russian; China, while preserving a tenuous independence, had been dissected by Europeans into economic spheres of influence. In the East, only Japan enjoyed real independence.

Australia and New Zealand were self-governing dominions of the British Empire, and the islands of the Pacific, like those of the Atlantic and Indian oceans, were administered by Europeans.[6] Although formally independent states occupied most of Latin America, those states were economic dependencies—"informal colonies"—of the United States and Great Britain. The United States, a transatlantic extension of European material and intellectual culture, had taken its place among the great powers at the end of the nineteenth century. In a famous poem in 1898, Rudyard Kipling welcomed Americans to the inner circle, urging them to "Take up the White Man's burden," to share with Europeans the responsibility to lead the "silent sullen peoples" slowly "toward the light." It was a world ordered and ruled by Europeans and their American offspring, and it was perfectly natural for historians to conclude that any culture capable of exercising such universal predominance was intrinsically superior to those over which it held sway. There was every reason to assume that European culture, in its several variants, would gradually, systematically, subvert all others.

History was written accordingly. Africans, Native Americans, and Aboriginals were considered "people without history."[7] For example, what passed for the history of Africa was the history of European conquest, European competition, and European enterprise in "the Dark Continent." Builders of empire—Prince Henry the Navigator, Columbus, Cortez, Robert Clive, and the American pioneers—were lionized in Western historical literature and fiction.

World War II ended the European era. European countries suffered massive physical damage and unprecedented loss of life. Germany was subdivided; European Russia was devastated; France was humiliated; Britain, although victorious, was exhausted. Having sustained no domestic destruction and having suffered relatively few casualties, the United states of America, still a stronghold of Western culture, emerged as world hegemon. Yet in spite of its position as nucleus of world capitalism, America's hegemony was not deemed secure. Americans believed themselves and their Western capitalist allies imperiled by revolutionary communism, an ideology sustained and promoted in Moscow.

The Cold War, begun in 1947, was an intense ideological struggle fought throughout Eurasia, Africa, and Latin America. It coincided in time with the reluctant, often forced, withdrawal of war-worn European states from their overseas colonies. Beginning with Britain's necessitous grant of independence to India in 1947, the pace of decolonization exceeded anything the Europeans could have imagined. France was driven from Indo-China in 1954; Britain granted independence to Ghana in 1957, and this act was followed throughout French, British, and Belgian Africa by a rush of successful independence movements. European officers who had enrolled in their colonial services at the end of World War II expecting to pursue lifetime careers in African or Asian administration had, by the mid-1960s, returned to Europe to seek other careers. The colonial world had become the Third World, and in the context of the Cold War, the Third World had become an extended battleground for the conflicting ideologies of East and West.

New political circumstances demanded new historical orientations. Prewar assumptions were in tatters. It was no longer useful to focus on Europe's gifts to the world. Alas, the history of Africa had to be a history of Africans, not the history of Europeans in Africa. If the West was to appeal to Third World peoples, it must know them for what they were; it must attempt to comprehend their aspirations and appreciate their historical and cultural contributions. Decades earlier, Max Weber had been a lonely voice urging greater attention to world history. Now, new voices, beginning with William McNeill and L. S. Stavrianos, pioneered the study of world history, deliberately broadening our historical canvas beyond its traditional cultural-centric focus on Western civilization.[8] We live in a "global village," they argued, and our ability to function effectively with our neighbors depends in large measure upon our ability to understand their history and to appreciate our mutual interdependence.

The writers of world history founded their work on an old intellectual abstraction—the distinct and autonomous "civilization." Their chief engine of change was "diffusion," a process by which great autonomous civilizations dispersed their special skills, products, organization, and culture, like the concentric outward movement of ripples created by pebbles tossed into placid water. Such diffusion, they argued, compromised and seduced barbaric peoples on the periphery of the great civilizations. Converging cultural ripples emanating from various distinct civilizations generated action and reaction, borrowing, change, and adjustment between civilizations.[9]

Diffusion became a guiding principle in reshaping the postwar world. In the global village, few countries were rich; many were poor. The poor were considered particularly vulnerable to communist penetration, to political attachment to Moscow, and to permanent alienation from the capitalist West. In the interest of capitalism as well as in the interest of humanity, it was deemed imperative that the rich nations assist the poor in achieving economic development. All regions of the world had been underdeveloped at one time or another, it was argued. It was only in modern times that the West had outdistanced other regions in terms of industrial production, communications, education, political sophistication, public health, and a host of other attributes. The waning European empires had devised strategies for the development of their colonies, but those strategies were set for the long term, and they were predicated on the assumption that colonies should, for the most part, generate whatever income was necessary to underwrite their own development. The Cold War and decolonization created a new sense of urgency about development. If development was to be accelerated, it would require the rapid diffusion of modernism from advanced societies to backward areas. But what strategies, what plans, what theoretical models were to be employed?

The first wave of theorists to attack the postwar development problem, social scientists of the modernization school, were grounded in functionalist theory. Devised by the American sociologist Talcott Parsons, functionalist theory regarded human society as similar to a biological organism. All parts were interdependent, and each part contributed a special function vital to the survival of the whole. In human society, there were four vital functions. The first, the adaptation of society to its environment, was performed by the economy. Goal attainment, the second function, was undertaken by government. The third, the integration of key institutions, was provided through religious and legal structure. The fourth, the preservation of social values over time (what Parsons labeled "latency") was performed by the family and by educational institutions. Functioning together, these vital parts achieved "homeostatic equilibrium," a balanced and uniform state. If change occurred in one social institution, other institutions would change in response to it, thereby reducing tension and preserving equilibrium. Such a system was constantly moving, constantly accommodating, constantly adjusting.[10]

Members of the modernization school were equally attracted to evolutionary theory. Like nineteenth-century Positivists, they believed that human society was perpetually and irreversibly moving from a primitive to an advanced condition. Because Western culture represented the highest state of social and material development, backward societies were bound to emulate it. They could not resist it. Pockets of modernism already existed throughout the Third World, particularly in the cities, yet the countryside in most underdeveloped countries remained bound to tradition, sometimes in quasi-subsistence agricultural villages, sometimes on feudal-type latifundia. The goal of most modernization theorists was to integrate divergent social sectors of the same underdeveloped polity so that the process of homeostatic equilibrium could more rapidly achieve an evolutionary upward adjustment. This, they assumed, would be accomplished most swiftly by the emergence of a commercial and industrial bourgeoisie, a class that would diffuse the cultural requisites of modernism among fellow nationals.

Different theorists offered different formulas for modernization depending upon their personal orientations, their academic disciplines, and the geographical regions they studied.[11] One notable prescription was that of W. W. Rostow.[12] An economist, Rostow discerned five distinct stages in economic development. In ascending order, they were traditional society, precondition for takeoff, takeoff, drive to maturity, and mass-consumption society. A country entered the second stage, precondition for takeoff, when capitalist activity had initiated new industries and expanded domestic markets. Notwithstanding such progress, however, an underdeveloped country could not achieve takeoff into sustained economic growth until it raised its annual rate of productive investment to at least 10 percent of national income. Without it, Rostow argued, annual surpluses would be soaked up by population growth. Investment capital could come from a variety of sources: from redistribution of national income through taxation or confiscation; from borrowing; from foreign trade that paid for the importation of essential technology; or from direct foreign investment. There was at least one other source: foreign aid from the industrialized nations. Recognizing the importance of a high reinvestment rate in underdeveloped countries, the United States and other Western governments contributed millions of dollars and thousands of technicians to enhance Third World infrastructures and establish local industries.

Among Third World peoples, Latin Americans have produced a particularly large and creative literature on development. The problem of underdevelopment has especially rankled intellectuals and nationalists in Latin America because their countries, having been politically independent since the early nineteenth century, have made relatively little economic progress compared to the nations of North America. These matters were addressed in a manifesto by the United Nations Economic Commission for Latin America (ECLA) in 1950.[13] The Commission identified a growing structural problem in the world economy. An international division of labor had arisen between the industrialized countries of the North Atlantic and non-industrialized states elsewhere in the world. The industrial nations formed the center, or nucleus, of the world economy, while the rest constituted a dispersed periphery engaged in the production of primary goods—food and raw materials. The terms of trade were highly unfavorable to the periphery. Although, ideally, all parties would benefit from maximizing production and consumption, unrestrained competition in world markets would occasion a dramatic shift of income to the industrialized center. The Commission determined that Latin American countries, in their earlier history, had unwisely foregone the opportunity to establish manufactures capable of satisfying domestic needs. Instead, they chose to rely on the export of primary products, thereby perpetuating, even enhancing, the social influence and political power of feudal oligarchies. The time had come to redeem that error.

ECLA proposed a comprehensive strategy to encourage the development of industries in Latin America that would supply domestic consumer needs without attempting to compete in overseas markets, at least not right away. This import substitution strategy required that fledgling local industries receive tariff protection until they were fully competitive with foreign importers. While this was happening, the usual export of primary products would supply some of the income needed to pay for the importation of industrial machinery and other capital goods. Latin American governments were urged to support this program in the expectation that it would produce a larger, more powerful and progressive nationalist bourgeoisie, which would not only combat feudalism and traditionalism but encourage democracy.

The ECLA strategy failed. Import substitution did not eliminate Latin America's dependency on foreign industrial suppliers. It simply shifted that dependency from consumer goods to capital goods. Moreover, local markets for manufactured goods did not expand once basic needs were satisfied. Primary exports had fallen off in the excitement over industrialization, and by the 1960s Latin American countries were suffering severe balance-of-payments problems and pervasive economic stagnation.

Modernization theory, the optimistic intellectual product of the world's wealthy societies, had been discredited. Diffusion had not worked—indeed, despite external influences and assistance, the gap between rich and poor nations everywhere was widening, not closing. By the 1960s, modernization theory was being upstaged by a more pessimistic and radical attitude toward Third World development: dependency theory.

The most radical, influential, and controversial dependency theorist was the American-educated German national, André Gunder Frank.[14] In 1967 he combined several powerful essays into a single book, *Capitalism and Underdevelopment in Latin America*, challenging every precept, principle, and presumption of the modernization school. According to Frank, ECLA got one thing right. The world was structurally divided into a capitalist center and a dependent periphery. But this division was much older than ECLA had presumed, and it was not subject to reform by the strategies ECLA had proposed. In fact, it was not subject to reform at all. At no time in their history had Latin American states had the opportunity to industrialize, as ECLA had supposed. The structural division of the world into center and periphery began in the sixteenth century when Europeans initiated the expropriation of surplus from their far-flung colonies. Colonial surplus had helped to generate economic development in Europe while, simultaneously, it had created underdevelopment in the periphery. By placing innumerable restrictions upon manufacture and trade, European metropoles acquired monopoly rights over vital economic functions. Key manufactures and services were preserved for metropolitan businesses while the colonies were deliberately restricted to the production of raw materials.

The development of the center and the underdevelopment of the periphery were two sides of the same coin, argued Frank. It is futile to contend, as members of the modernization school have done, that development and underdevelopment are relative conditions, that one merely represents more development than the other. Development and underdevelopment are not products of different economic systems; they do not represent different stages of economic growth within the same system. Although they have distinct forms, those distinctions must persist because the very existence of underdevelopment derives from the existence of development.

One by one, Frank dismissed the premises of the modernization school. Functionalist theory presumed the existence of homeostatic equilibrium, the tendency of a social system to strive for balance between separate elements of the same social structure. Frank's center-periphery concept presumed a world-scale social structure that was predicated on the permanent existence of disequilibrium between the developed metropole and the underdeveloped periphery. Evolutionary theory was a fiction. The Third World, Frank contended, was stuck in permanent subjection to the industrialized nations. Moreover, the inclination of modernization theorists to focus their analyses on individual national units was myopic, Frank thought. Underdevelopment was a global problem. All nations of the Third World suffered from the same general condition. They were all structurally tied to the developed, metropolitan center. Well-meaning modernization programs that tinkered with social and economic problems within the separate underdeveloped states had no chance of success because they did not address the universal structural condition that produced underdevelopment.

Issues that concerned members of the modernization school were often trivial, Frank thought. How much could it matter whether a country in Latin America or Africa divided its politicians into parties and held free elections? What difference could it make in the overall scheme of things if there was less rather than more political instability in peripheral states?

Frank denied the claim of sociologists that countries in Latin America were backward because they had dual social and economic systems: feudalism in the countryside and capitalism in the cities. The villain of the modernization school, feudalism, was not feudalism at all! What passed for feudalism in a country like Brazil was, in reality, a product of world capitalism, Frank wrote. No part of any Latin American economy was feudal: all of it—right down to the smallest Indian village—was integrated into a single world system of capitalism. As for the hopes that modernizers placed on the development of a national bourgeoisie, Frank demurred. There was no possibility that a national bourgeoisie would be "independent enough" to lead a real national liberation movement or "progressive enough to destroy the capitalist structure of underdevelopment at home."[15] The Latin American bourgeoisie remained a thoroughly compromised tool of foreign industry, he argued. Its interests were shaped by its relations with foreign economic forces, and its members used high government office to spawn policies that perpetuated social, political, and economic underdevelopment.

This was not new. In its earliest days, the independence movement in Latin America was advanced by exporters of raw materials who sought to increase their exports to the British industrial market. Political independence only intensified economic dependency. During the nineteenth century, sectors of the Latin American bourgeoisie involved in marketing raw materials challenged and defeated the more industrial-oriented bourgeoisie in a series of civil wars. Liberal reforms in the nineteenth century were not simply a result of ideological enlightenment: they permitted an increase in the production and export of primary products. Even in the late twentieth century, the Latin American bourgeoisie links itself to the metropole as a junior partner, endorsing policies that increase the economic subjugation of their nations.[16]

In Frank's opinion, the strategies of the modernization school almost always left countries worse off than before. Rostow's concept of stages of economic growth had no bearing on realities in the Third World. It was futile to expect peripheral countries to repeat the growth experience of modern developed nations. Having achieved development by exploiting a colonial periphery, countries of the center continued to prosper by prolonging their exploitative advantage. In a complex global system in which development and underdevelopment, dominance and dependency, were integral elements of a single historical process, dependent communities could not expect benignly to repeat the development experience of the central dominant states. The system required a center and a periphery. The center already existed, and it jealously guarded its privileges. Rostow's formula for modernization would only compound the problems of the Third World. If peripheral countries obtained the means to reinvest more than 10 percent of their national income by borrowing money from great metropolitan financial institutions or by encouraging private investment by large metropolitan corporations, they would only be transferring more surplus from the periphery to the center and thereby increasing the level of their dependency. The only way to change the system was to get rid of it. The only way to get rid of it was through armed revolution.

Frank's theory provoked criticism from both right and left. The right, highly ill-disposed to revolution, accused him of indulging too much in ideology and too little in empirical research. Marxists were mortified. Frank was a proponent of revolution, and he worked within an intellectual context—dependency—that had acquired strong Marxist associations. But he violated the most sacred principles of Marxism. His motor of history was not conflict between classes. Although class was not unimportant, class struggles were integrated in and subsumed by a conflict between geographical regions of the world, between center and periphery. Frank's economic structure was not fundamentally defined by mode of production. Production was meaningful only in the context of exchange relations. In fact, Frank disregarded what Marxist scholars had identified as numerous pre-capitalist modes of production in Latin America. Although such modes might appear to exist, he argued, all productive structures in the region were enveloped by capitalism.

Frank's orientation was particularly disturbing to conventional Marxists who adhered to the proposition that society must evolve through successive economic stages based on mode of production. For them, historical theory served a specific teleological purpose: to provide a guide to revolutionary action. Frank advocated revolution. But, in the absence of class analysis, who did Frank presume would form his revolutionary cadre? Who would serve as his rank and file?[17]

In spite of, perhaps because of, the controversial nature of his views, Frank raised the level and the range of debate. Latin American Marxists, like members of the modernization school, had focused their efforts on individual polities. Frank concentrated upon a world-scale economic system, arguing that underdevelopment is the product of a long historical process. No progress in modernization could be made, he argued, until the historical and structural character of underdevelopment was understood.

Although Frank rooted his theory in history, he made no claim to be a historian, and he readily admitted to the empirical thinness of his historical work. His first concern was Third World development; his intended audience was the people who were striving to achieve it. Still, his concept of the "development of underdevelopment" immediately aroused interest among historians, particularly radical Third World historians for whom similar ideas had been gestating for several decades.[18] In 1972, the radical West Indian scholar Walter Rodney published *How Europe Underdeveloped Africa*, transferring some of the themes of dependency analysis to Africa, where it has since taken root.[19] The ultimate payoff emerged two years later in Immanuel Wallerstein's *Modern World System*, a comprehensive historical theory of the emergence and development of the modern capitalist world.[20] Wallerstein's world-system analysis, an elaboration of Frank's theory, quickly took large sectors of the history profession by storm.

NOTES

1. Barbara Ward and René Dubos, *Only One Earth: The Care and Maintenance of a Small Planet* (New York, 1972).

2. Donald Worster, "The Vulnerable Earth: Toward a Planetary History," in Donald Worster, ed., *The Ends of the Earth: Perspectives on Modern Environmental History* (New York, 1988), p. 4.

3. Raymond F. Dasmann, "Toward a Biosphere Consciousness," in Worster, ed., *The Ends of the Earth*, pp. 277–278.

4. Worster, "The Vulnerable Earth," p. 15.

5. Having barely escaped Italian conquest in the 1890s, Ethiopia succumbed to Mussolini's invasion in 1935; Liberia was, in reality, an economic colony of the United States.

6. In purely territorial terms, the European sway was extended by the defeat of the Ottoman Empire in World War I. Britain and France assumed imperial control over all Arab lands between the Mediterranean and the Persian Gulf.

7. With some sarcasm, Eric Wolf titled his book on the interaction of Europeans with peoples of the wider world as follows: *Europe and the People without History* (Berkeley, 1982).

8. William H. McNeill, *The Rise of the West: A History of the Human Community* (Chicago, 1963); L. S. Stavrianos, *A Global History of Man* (Boston, 1962).

9. William H. McNeill, "Organizing Concepts for World History," *Review* 10 (1986): 211–229.

10. For an overview of the theories adopted by the modernization school, see Alvin Y. So, *Social Change and Development: Modernization, Dependency, and World-System Theories* (Newbury Park, 1990), pp. 17–37.

11. Political scientists emphasized the values of Western democracy—constitutional legitimacy, multiparty systems, and competitive electoral politics. Sociologists, being concerned about political instability, sought to reduce the stress of adjusting from tradi-

tional to modern cultural norms. Economists proposed various strategies to stimulate capital accumulation and market development.

12. W. W. Rostow, *The Stages of Economic Growth: A Non-Communist Manifesto* (Cambridge, 1960).

13. The Commission operated under leadership of Raul Prebisch, an economist, academic, and former director-general of the Central Bank of Argentina. Raul Prebisch, *The Economic Development of Latin America and Its Principal Problems* (New York, 1950).

14. For an introduction to the extensive literature on dependency, see Roland H. Chilcote, "Dependency: A Critical Synthesis of the Literature," *Latin American Perspectives* 1 (1974): 3–29. His edited work, *Dependency and Marxism: Toward a Resolution of the Debate* (Boulder, 1982) brings analysis of the literature further. Also see So, *Social Change and Development*, pp. 91–165.

15. André Gunder Frank, *Capitalism and Underdevelopment in Latin America: Historical Studies of Chile and Brazil* (New York, 1967), xii.

16. André Gunder Frank, *Lumpenbourgeoisie: Lumpendevelopment, Dependence, Class and Politics in Latin America* (New York, 1972), pp. 3–16.

17. Among Marxists, Frank's greatest sin was his effect upon the revolutionary movement. He has been accused of confusing and dividing Marxists across the southern continent. In Marxist theory, class interest should provide the medium through which revolutionary sentiment is galvanized. For example, a class-based revolutionary strategy could set peasants, workers, the petite bourgeoisie, and the industrial bourgeoisie against feudal interests as a preliminary step toward the ultimate socialist revolution. In this context, conventional Marxists might, as an interim step, support the development of a national bourgeoisie. But Frank confounded such class-based strategies, arguing that the structure of dependency had penetrated to the core of Latin American society, corrupting local interests, distorting class interests, and inspiring complicity with foreign capitalist forces at every level.

18. At a December 1986 conference, "South Asia and World Capitalism," held at Tufts University and attended by many of the world's leading South Asian historians, I was astonished by the degree to which the idiom of world-system analysis had penetrated the Asian field.

19. For a striking example of the influence of dependency analysis in African history, see Joseph Inikori's "Introduction" in Inikori, ed., *Forced Migration: The Impact of the Export Slave Trade on African Societies* (New York, 1982).

20. Immanuel Wallerstein, *The Modern World-System I: Capitalist Agriculture and the Origins of the European World-Economy in the Sixteenth Century* (New York, 1974). This is the first of four volumes treating the course of modern history.

7

World-System Analysis

World-system analysis links the rise of capitalism to Europe's overseas expansion in the sixteenth century. It approaches history from the outside in, from the periphery to the center, demonstrating the momentous effect that frontier lands have had on the development of wealth and culture in the metropolis. It is new to the extent that it consolidates within a single comprehensive historical formulation a number of theories that have accumulated in historical literature over many decades.

Americans were the first modern scholars earnestly to address their history from the outside in. A century ago, American history was written from the perspective of the eastern seaboard. Emphasis was placed upon the impact of European influences on the original colonies and the outward dispersal of those influences toward the frontier. In 1893, Frederick Jackson Turner delivered a paper before the American Historical Association revolutionizing historical orientations in the United States. His essay, "The Significance of the Frontier in American History," scorned the "exclusive attention" paid by American historians to

European influences, arguing instead that the frontier, not the Atlantic coast, had "furnished the forces dominating American character."[1] The advance of the frontier had reduced dependence on Britain; it had nurtured "the formation of a composite nationality" among ethnically diverse European immigrants; and most important, the frontier had encouraged individualism and promoted democracy. It was the frontier that shaped the American personality, its coarseness, its inquisitiveness, its inventiveness, its capacity to find expedients, its restless energy, its firm grasp of material things. As well, it discouraged artistic accomplishments, permitted lax business honor, and gave rise to a comparatively low civic spirit, which manifested itself in the spoils system, disreputable currency schemes, and wildcat banking. The underlying dynamic of American history was to be found on the periphery. Initiatives arose there. The frontier generated its own momentum, and that momentum was unstoppable. No treaties, no administrative regulation, no Washington politicians could halt the inexorable march of the westward migrants. The frontier acted; the center reacted.

EUROPE'S GREAT FRONTIER

Considered the most influential thesis in American history, the Turner thesis has had detractors as well as defenders.[2] Among its most ardent defenders was Walter Prescott Webb, a distinguished historian of the American West, who in the years following World War II expanded Turner's thesis to embrace the entire Atlantic basin. Webb lamented that the frontier thesis had been confined to the history of North America. European and Latin American historians had all but ignored it. Yet Europe, too, had had its frontier, wrote Webb. Not only was it a much larger frontier than that of the United States, it was the greatest frontier in history, almost as influential in forming the institutions of Europe as the American frontier had been in shaping those of the United States. Opened by Columbus and the explorers who followed him, it encompassed the entire Western hemisphere in the sixteenth century, expanding thereafter to include Australia, New Zealand, and other regions of the Eastern hemisphere.

Webb used the word "metropolis" to define Europe—a densely populated, small region, a "cultural center holding within it everything pertaining to Western civilization."[3] The Americas, Europe's initial frontier, were a "vast and vacant land without culture,"[4] five to six times the size of the metropolis and capable of producing every conceivable material asset.

European exploitation of these assets gave rise to modern capitalism and precipitated a four-century economic boom unprecedented in human history .

America was a one-time windfall. There are no more Americas left, no more rich and vacant lands. By 1950, Europe's 450-year frontier had closed. The experience of that frontier constituted an utterly abnormal phase in the regular course of historical development. The modern age, beginning with Columbus, did not flow from preceding history as a natural evolution. It emerged boldly under the conditions of economic boom generated by unparalleled and unexpected territorial acquisition.

Advocating what he called the boom hypothesis—"the most naked reality of the modern age"—Webb examined the three classic ingredients of economic productivity—land, labor, and capital—in the context of Europe's frontier experience. He accepted William Graham Sumner's contention that the "ratio of population to land . . . determines what are the possibilities of human development or the limits of what men can attain in civilization and comfort."[5] When Columbus set sail, the population/land ratio in the European metropolis was 26.7 people per square mile. With the addition of 20 million square miles of "fabulously rich [American] land practically devoid of population," that ratio fell to less than 5 persons per square mile. Not until the 1930s would the population/land ratio for Europe and its "great frontier" return to that of Columbus's day.[6]

The metropolis fully exploited the capital assets of its frontier. Between 1492 and 1930, the value of gold and silver in the metropolis rose by over 18,000 percent.[7] The frontier "hung like a horn of plenty over the Metropolis," emptying upon it "an avalanche of wealth beyond human comprehension": coffee, cocoa, sugar, forest products, furs, cotton, maize, hides, tobacco, rubber—not to mention quinine, a drug derived from Peruvian bark that protected Europeans from malaria and enabled them to conquer sub-Saharan Africa.[8]

Webb's simplistic concept of capitalism would have chagrined Max Weber. He defined capitalism merely as a cultural complex involving a striving for profit. Because there was so little wealth for Europeans to strive for, capitalism did not emerge as a general cultural phenomenon before the sixteenth century, he thought. The great frontier changed all that, supplying the gold, silver, and space necessary for a capitalist economy. No one benefitted more than businessmen, Webb contended. Pursuing the arguments of Earl J. Hamilton,[9] Webb observed that bullion flows from the frontier to the metropolis produced price inflation in the sixteenth century. In Europe, commodity prices rose at a much sharper rate than rents or wages, giving advantage to the sellers of "things." Between 1500 and 1700, prices in France increased by 101 percent, wages by only 35.8 percent. A similar situation prevailed in England. Landlords and laborers were losing advantage; entrepreneurs were gaining. There was never a time in history so accommodating to the businessman, the speculator, and the profiteer. The century from 1550 to 1650 was a golden age, declared John Maynard Keynes: it was the time when modern capitalism was born.[10] Capitalism had waited upon opportunity. When the great frontier provided that opportunity, capitalism took hold.

The frontier imposed its stamp upon human values and public institutions as well. If the frontier inculcated in North Americans a strong sense of individualism and a predisposition for democracy, it also inspired a respect for hard work. Walter Prescott Webb may never have read Max Weber, but like Weber, he seized upon Benjamin Franklin as the human embodiment of a particular set of values—the values of the frontier, not the values of European-based Calvinism, as Weber had contended. When Franklin addressed his American audience through *Poor Richard's Almanack,* delivering homely maxims like "God helps them that help themselves" or "God gives all things to industry" or "Early to bed and early to rise makes a man healthy, wealthy, and wise," he was expressing the folk wisdom of a people who had learned such lessons through prolonged encounter with the frontier. Although metropolitan governments and metropolitan peoples may have been the main beneficiaries of the opening of the great frontier, the dynamic forces that drove the historical process and shaped the character of Western civilization after 1500 emerged on the periphery.

Webb's orientation was reinforced by an Oxford-educated Trinidadian scholar, Eric Eustace Williams, who shocked his English mentors and aroused intense controversy by contending, most persuasively, that plantation colonies in the British West Indies generated the capital that underwrote the English Industrial Revolution. His book, *Capitalism and Slavery* (1944), offered the quintessential outside-in argument. It rooted the origins of one of the two most significant events in human history (the other being the Agricultural Revolution, B.C. 8000–3500) on the colonial periphery of Europe's world economy.

Williams defied conventional historical wisdom. The Industrial Revolution began in England in the eighteenth century, spread to Belgium and northern France in the early nineteenth century, thence to Central Europe and the United States. Since Arnold Toynbee first gave expression to the abstraction, "the Industrial Revolution," historians have sought its origins in the special conditions of Europe and the particular genius of Europeans. Because Britain experienced the only unassisted industrial revolution (all follower states had a British model to emulate), the tendency of historians has been to ask "Why was England first?" and to seek the particular combination of forces within England that propelled the nation's economy toward industrialization.[11] Economic historians generally recognize the importance of colonial trade in the evolution of the British economy, but as a rule they consider internal trade to have been more important than overseas trade in the eighteenth century. Even the late Ralph Davis, a specialist in early English trade and author of *The Rise of the Atlantic Economies,* concluded that colonial economies were merely "subsidiary to" and an "enhancement of" the internal economies of the individual European states.[12]

At the time of its publication, *Capitalism and Slavery* received little attention from scholars. What attention it did get was mainly hostile. In the 1950s, however, colonial independence movements produced a highly receptive audience for Williams's point of view. His work embraced the salient historical issues of the postwar world: racism, slavery, the origins of industrialization, and the evolution of a world order divided between rich and poor.[13]

Williams observed that the opening of the Americas vastly increased world trade. For Britain, that trade was chiefly triangular, linking Africa and plantation America with the Mother Country. Trade in African slaves was "the mainspring" that set "every wheel in motion."[14] By 1750, there was hardly a trading or manufacturing town not connected with the slave trade. The British West India colonies, alone, represented nearly one-seventh of Britain's total overseas trade between 1714 and 1773.[15] Every Englishman with ten slaves in the West Indies gave employment to four workers in England; moreover, the West Indies were the commercial partners of North American colonists who exported fish, timber, grains, farm animals, vegetables, and assorted other primary products to the plantations to sustain the slaves. At home, Bristol's trade with the West Indies was worth double that of its other overseas commerce. Liverpool owed its success as a port to the slave trade. Lodged in Lancashire, the nuclear region of the Industrial Revolution, Liverpool called the industry of Lancashire into existence, not the reverse. Williams gave numerous examples of individual entrepreneurs who, having accumulated capital in the slave trade, in slave holding, in ship building, or in industries supplying the slave trade and the slave plantations, invested their earnings in Britain's infant industries. It was capital earned from the West Indian trade, he noted, that financed James Watt and the steam engine.[16]

In the 1960s, Williams's argument garnered powerful support from Richard Sheridan, an assiduous American economic historian who demonstrated that tropical American plantations yielded large capital surpluses for investment in Britain.[17] In the final years of the eighteenth century, West Indian property earned between 8 and 10 percent of the income of Great Britain, Sheridan argued.[18] Like Williams, he used selected examples to show that the richest colonial planters invested enormous sums in British government securities, the factorage business, shipping, and industry.[19] In the main, however, Sheridan, like Williams, offered little comparative data on the relative importance of West Indian capital in stimulating particular areas of British industry. Both have relied on the general argument that trade begets trade, that earnings produce investment, and that the slave colonies, as a center of trade and a source of savings, provided the necessary impetus to launch the English Industrial Revolution.[20] Scholars in the Third World have embraced the Williams-Sheridan position. In the First World, most historians have continued to seek the origins of modern industrialization in forces internal to Europe.[21]

THE WORLD-SYSTEM

The most expansive history from the outside-in, a work that integrates provocative studies like those of Webb and Williams with modern dependency theory, is Immanuel Wallerstein's multi-volume treatise on the modern world-system. Wallerstein's model is the most influential to appear in recent decades. It is certainly among the most controversial. A sociologist by training, Wallerstein has founded a "school" of history, a scholarly journal, and an institute to facilitate world-system research.[22] His historical orientation, like that of Eric Williams, has been most warmly embraced in the Third World. Third World scholars continue to seek explanations for their dependency, for their poverty, for the decimation of local institutions, traditional values, and collective self-esteem. The world-system model identifies a long-standing exploitative relationship that assigns moral culpability to the West and sanctions righteous indignation in the wider world. It appeals, therefore, at both polemical and professional levels.

In the remainder of this chapter, it will be possible only to present Wallerstein's general theory, the main lines of his analysis, and a brief critique of his work. I will focus exclusively on his first volume, *The Modern World-System I: Capitalist Agriculture and the Origins of the European World-Economy in the Sixteenth Century* (1974). Here, in dealing with the transition from the medieval to the modern world, Wallerstein offers an explicit presentation of theory and a systematic response to key historical questions.

What is the subject to be studied? The creation of the modern world, a complex process involving the rise of capitalism. How important is it? Wallerstein considers it equivalent in importance to the Agricultural Revolution. How should such a study be organized? Not country by country, but as a comprehensive, integrated historical experience involving Europe and the entire Western hemisphere. Social change can be fathomed only in social systems, Wallerstein argues. National states do not constitute social systems, even though they may be important components of social systems. To understand the rise and development of the capitalist world, one must study the capitalist social system as a whole—the modern world-system.

How do we define the modern world-system? It is an economic, not a political, phenomenon. Historically, it functioned through an exploitative division of labor that permitted West Europeans to extract surplus wealth from Eastern Europe and America to fuel their breakthrough to capitalism. Systemically, it involved a division of the Atlantic basin into three concentric hierarchical tiers distinguished by their products and by their modes of production: northwestern Europe was the commercial and industrial core; central and southern Europe constituted a dependent semiperiphery; Europe east of the River Elbe and most of the American colonies formed a dependent periphery engaged in the production of primary products. The system was driven by the desire for profit. Its efficient functioning required the use of free wage labor at the core, tenantry and share-cropping in the semiperiphery, and coerced labor in the periphery. All three zones were integrated through trade, and trade was dominated by merchants of the core. These are the main elements of the world-system. Each will be treated in greater detail later.

Wallerstein chose the term "world-system" because it transcended any juridically defined political unit. As his title indicates, he also used the term "world-economy" to refer specifically to economic aspects of the world-system.[23] The modern world-system encompassed a congeries of nations, city-states, and empires bound together by economic forces. Before the advent of modern world-economy, there were others—Roman, Persian, Chinese—but each of these became coequal with a political empire. Although such empires were capable of guaranteeing economic flows from the periphery to the center through the regulation of trade and tribute, they required bureaucracies at the center and repressive military forces at the perimeter. Both absorbed profits. The distinguishing characteristic of the modern world-system is that it thrived and expanded in the Atlantic basin without a central political structure. In fact, argues Wallerstein, it thrived and expanded *because* it lacked a central political structure. Capitalism and modern science provided the structure.

Capitalism did not impel Europeans to launch their overseas empires. *Capitalism was a product of European expansion.* It was the discovery and colonization of the New World, writes Wallerstein, that saved Europe from collapsing into anarchy. Late-medieval Europe was in crisis. In the three centuries before 1300, the continent had experienced geographic, commercial, and demographic expansion. Between 1300 and 1450, what had expanded contracted. To explain this contraction, Wallerstein combines three theoretical lines of argument. First, he accepts the neo-Malthusian theory of cyclical economic trends treated in Chapter 4 of this book, arguing that population, having grown beyond the capacity of land and technology to sustain it, suffered decline. Second, he takes up the Marxist argument, examined in Chapter 5, that a thousand years of surplus extraction in the feudal mode of production had produced impasse. The lords wanted more, but the peasants were unwilling and unable to produce more. Third, he accepts the climatic argument that a fall in average temperatures reduced soil productivity in Europe. The crisis of feudalism, he argues, resulted from a conjuncture of these three conditions. There was only one way for Europe to escape economic contraction and social chaos: to expand overseas.[24]

Expansion was the first and most critical requirement for the formation of a capitalist world-system. There were two others: (1) the establishment of differing methods of production in the three zones of the world-economy; (2) the development of strong state machineries in the European core states.

The first of these insured greater efficiency in the production of staple foods and minerals across several climatic zones. In much of tropical and subtropical America where native populations were thin or nonexistent, European masters imposed slave labor.[25] Slave labor was needed in situations where open land resources required a rigid disciplining of workers to achieve efficient plantation production. Slave labor was possible in America because Africa was willing to supply the slaves. East of the Elbe, the capitalist world-economy called into being a "second serfdom," what Wallerstein prefers to call coerced cash-crop labor. In the semiperiphery, share-cropping was widely adopted. Because population/land ratios in Southern Europe were generally higher than in Eastern Europe, the amount of coercion required to stimulate agricultural production there was lower. In the northwest European core, high population density, intensive farming practices, and urban manufacturing all conspired to encourage the use of competitive free labor.

In describing the effect of capital transfers between the New World and the Old, Wallerstein uses the same sources[26] and much the same argument as Walter Prescott Webb. American bullion stimulated inflation, and inflation, unaccompanied by a comparable rise in real wages, generated a profit windfall for the manufacturers and sellers of "things." Wallerstein takes Webb's argument a step further. Different European workers responded differently to inflation. In old industrial centers where workers enjoyed strength (e.g., Flanders and northern Italy), wages tended to keep pace with inflation. Where workers possessed little power or solidarity (e.g., Spain) wages lagged far behind prices. In Holland and England, a middle position prevailed: relative wages fell, but not catastrophically. On balance, the sixteenth century witnessed both a reduction of income for workers and a redistribution of manufacturing investment within Europe. Manufacturers were ill-disposed to invest in low-wage countries like Spain because low wages impaired purchasing power and thereby depressed regional markets. Entrepreneurs steered away from high-wage areas like Venice because wages absorbed too much of their profits. It was the mid-range countries, notably England and Holland, that offered optimal conditions for industrial investment. During the sixteenth century, it was these countries that established their position at the core of the capitalist world-economy.

Despite differences in labor control and apparent differences in modes of production across the several tiers of the capitalist world-economy, the whole system was capitalist, argues Wallerstein. The argument is identical to the one advocated by André Gunder Frank for twentieth-century Latin America. No large region produced exclusively for a local economy. All labor forms were calculated to produce the largest quantity of goods in the most efficient manner for a world market, and the governing principle of that market was capitalist.[27] The Caribbean slave holder, the Polish seigneur, and the Dutch manufacturer were all capitalists, for the exploitative pressures that each of them exerted upon their laborers were dictated by the demand-supply curve of the world market. There is little doubt, adds Wallerstein, that the capitalist world-economy had established a unified market: in 1500, the price gap between the Christian Mediterranean and Eastern Europe was around 6 to 1; by 1750, it was 2 to 1.[28]

THE WORLD-SYSTEM AND THE STATES SYSTEM

The rise of capitalism and the development of powerful states at the European core were mutually reinforcing phenomena. Strong states were necessary to ensure the preservation of order, control of the seas, and efficient exploitation of colonial lands. A plurality of states at the core was equally important; otherwise, the world-economy might become a world-empire. The principal preoccupation of any state is self-preservation. In the case of empire states, self-preservation involves either the repression or the accommodation of all sectors of the imperial polity. Both are expensive. The latter is generally achieved by insuring that the wealth of the empire is dispersed with some degree of equity to all parts of the imperial community. Economic efficiency is thereby sacrificed to political necessity. In the case of the capitalist world-system, a plurality of strong states at the core of the world-economy insured inter-state competition at the core. This competition promoted more efficient distribution of production functions and capital flows throughout the system, and it inspired a more thorough exploitation of the periphery in the interest of preserving the competitive edge of the core states. Capitalism has flourished, writes Wallerstein, "precisely because the world-economy has had within its bounds not one but a multiplicity of political systems.[29]

For Wallerstein, that which determined whether a country would become a powerful core state was its ability to establish a secure bourgeoisie dedicated to commercial and industrial enterprise. England and Holland did it. Spain did not. France held a middle ground. Geography as well as politics (one might even say, politics as a function of geography) played a decisive role. The overriding political issue of the sixteenth century was the conflict for imperial pre-eminence in Europe between the houses of Habsburg (Spain, Austria) and Valois (France). They competed for the title of Holy Roman Emperor; they fought numerous wars for control of Italy; and they remained hostile and belligerent well into the seventeenth century, mutually exhausting one another while succumbing to a succession of royal bankruptcies. The Spanish government paid out its American silver to support war and to purchase the manufactures of the Low Countries, offering little inducement for the development of its own domestic industries. When, in the interest of imperial religious solidarity, Catholic Spain attempted to discipline its Calvinist-ridden estates in the Low Countries, rebellion erupted there, destroying the prosperity of Flanders and establishing an independent economic power of the first magnitude in the Netherlands. The United Netherlands became the quintessentially bourgeois state.

England outdistanced France as a core state. The reason lies partly in geography. With no part of the country more than 75 miles from the sea, England was decidedly maritime. She enjoyed the benefits of cheap water transport. Like the Netherlands, the country could serve as a half-way station for trades linking the Baltic and Mediterranean; and, of course, England stood opposite the great river estuaries of the Meuse and the Rhine, which carried trade goods to and from the continental interior. With the growth of New World trades, England and the Netherlands concentrated on the sea. By contrast, France was both a maritime and a continental state. The kingdom had three natural geopolitical zones: the northwest, looking outward to the Atlantic; the northeastern Rhenish area; and the south. In the great imperial struggle with Spain, the latter two took precedence. The French nobility preserved its pre-eminence while the French bourgeoisie was seduced into seeking status enhancement through the purchase of royal offices. In England the aristocracy and gentry readily took to commerce, occasioning the embourgeoisement of power. In France, on the other hand, the bourgeoisie was feudalized. Dutch and English capitalists undersold French competitors in domestic as well as foreign markets. French shipbuilding and French trade fell behind, and the country relied increasingly on the production of goods for which it held a historic edge—luxuries, especially silk—when the sale of cheaper goods in wider markets would have provided a firmer industrial base. In the new capitalist world-economy, France was able to preserve advantage over Spain and Germany, but the English and Dutch achieved advantage over all.

HOW THE WORLD-SYSTEM FUNCTIONED

The sixteenth-century capitalist world-system had a specific geographical dimension. Its size was limited principally by the speed at which communication could occur between its most widely separated components.[30] Whenever technological developments increased the speed of communications, the world-system was capable of expanding. As Wallerstein conceived it, the world-system was highly self-contained. If the sixteenth-century capitalist world-system had been cut off from all external regions of the world, it would have continued to function in essentially the same way.[31]

In response to changing geopolitical and resource factors, the relative position of all entities within the capitalist world-system was subject to change. Individual components were able to rise in status, say from peripheral to semiperipheral status, or to fall a notch. Wallerstein's concept of a semiperiphery, a third tier in the world hierarchy, is a major innovation upon Frank's bimodal (metropolis-satellite) theory of dependency. While each tier is only an abstract category—a convenient mental vehicle—the concept of the semiperiphery offers slack to the world-system and facilitates our understanding of how structural change occurs. The middle layer interacted with both core and periphery; it considered itself superior to the periphery; and it indulged (albeit less fully than the core) in the exploitation of the periphery. Consequently, the semiperiphery deflected some of the political heat that peripheral communities would otherwise have directed exclusively upon the core.

Although Wallerstein suggests several ways in which states can rise within the world-system,[32] his system is biased in favor of stability. Division of labor within the world-system is both functional and geographical. The most complex tasks requiring the highest skill levels and the heaviest capitalization have been reserved for the core. Because the system rewards these tasks at a higher rate than the less skilled tasks performed in the periphery, the tendency of the system has been to perpetuate the prevailing geographical maldistribution of wealth—indeed, to intensify it.[33]

Wallerstein has produced an elaborate division of labor model, although it is one that differs in subtlety and complexity from that of Adam Smith and later-day historians of the commercial school. Wallerstein does not assume that commercial growth and an expanding international division of labor will uniformly generate higher levels of economic prosperity and greater cultural enrichment. The world-system division of labor may have multiplied the world's wealth, but it distributed it unequally. In Poland and other regions east of the Elbe, for example, the advent of large-scale international trade led to a monocultural economy based on grain exports to the West, the demise of the regional bourgeoisie, the decline of handicrafts, the withering of towns, the impoverishment of cultural life, and the growth of serfdom—the "second serfdom." Having consolidated their land holdings and intensified their exploitation of labor, Polish lords aggrandized in their own behalf the profits of international trade. Meanwhile, Poland became a peripheral country from which surplus was drained to the northwest European core.

Like André Gunder Frank, Wallerstein challenged conventional Marxist analysis. Marxists generally attempt to explain the transition from feudalism to capitalism within the geographical confines of Western Europe, ordinarily focusing on the operation of historical forces within single sovereign states. Class differentiation was thought to be dictated by local productive forces, and differing modes of production—whether feudal or capitalist—represented different stages of development toward socialism. Wallerstein subsumes all such differences within a single vast world-system, declaring the whole enterprise to be capitalist. As an engine of change, class struggle has been replaced by interaction and struggle between geographical regions of the world-system.

Wallerstein devotes little attention to demographic forces, except as a partial explanation for the crisis of the late Middle Ages. Although he recognizes that the core states were Protestant and the semiperipheral states Catholic, he dismisses Weber's theory of the Calvinist roots of capitalism without engaging it. In his view, religious ideas are highly malleable and, in the sixteenth century, they were marshalled to reinforce specific social and economic interests. Along with many of Weber's critics, Wallerstein thinks the great German sociologist could just as easily have written a book entitled "The Catholic Ethic and the Spirit of Capitalism."

CHALLENGES TO THE WORLD-SYSTEM MODEL

The world-system model may be weakest at its point of inception. Wallerstein provides an eclectic blending of the arguments of neo-Malthusians, Marxists, and a noted climatic determinist to explain why Europeans expanded overseas and established the capitalist world-system. Late medieval Europe was in crisis, he says, and that crisis was the result of three conditions: a Malthusian demographic crisis; a crisis in the feudal mode of production; and a climatic reversal. Since the issue of climate will be addressed in the next chapter, we need only consider the former two explanations here.

How grave was the crisis in Europe when overseas expansion came to the continent's rescue? Plague had swept away up to 33 percent of the population in the years around 1350, and recurring epidemics had kept the population well below its late-thirteenth-century level until the sixteenth century. By the time Prince Henry the Navigator launched the Portuguese overseas explorations, population pressure had eased all across Europe. As for the Marxist contention that class conflict between lords and serfs had reached an impasse, that too had subsided with the demographic blowout of the plague. If there was a feudal crisis after 1450, it involved the decline of the lords' bargaining power and the consequent emancipation of the serfs. Population decline might have occasioned a fall in the volume of international trade, with the effect that some commercial towns were weakened, but per capita income for working people—and that represents the vast majority of Europeans—rose in the fifteenth century.[34]

By presenting an unduly gloomy picture of the state of Europe in 1450 and by urging that without overseas expansion the continent would have succumbed to anarchy and fratricidal war, Wallerstein is guilty of highly tactical argumentation. Because he exaggerates the peril of Europe's situation, he unduly enhances the importance of the remedy employed to escape it—the discovery and colonization of America.

Explaining Europe's thrust overseas, Wallerstein contends that above all, Europeans needed more abundant food supplies (calories) and fuel. This has become a popular line of argument, and it would be futile to contend that Europeans—or anyone else in the fifteenth century—would not have benefited from greater food. But were Europeans driven by the exigencies of hunger into overseas exploration and colonization? Falling population since 1350 had reduced pressure on the land. The least productive lands had been taken out of cultivation; Baltic grain was beginning to arrive in northwestern Europe in sufficient quantity to permit English landlords to transform arable land into grazing land; and increasing numbers of workers in the Lowlands were leaving agriculture in favor of industry. Even after the Americas were discovered, there was no inordinant rush to bring the new lands into cultivation. North America lay vacant for a century. The Portuguese held a claim to Brazil for over thirty years before they initiated formal settlement there.[35] When settlement was undertaken, the reason was not to supply food to European markets but to prevent another European power from claiming the region.

Having exaggerated the ills of Europe in the fifteenth century, Wallerstein is compelled to ask why Portugal was the agent that extricated Christendom from want and chaos. Why would one of the weakest, poorest, and most peripheral kingdoms step forward to save the continent? Because, argues Wallerstein, Portugal's location adjacent to vital ocean currents made it easier for her to undertake exploration and because "she alone of the European states maximized will and possibility."[36] The currents had always been there, even in 1300 when population pressure was at its peak and the need for new lands was greatest. As for maximizing will and possibility, that may be a clever turn of phrase, but it is not an explanation.

The problem is that Wallerstein cannot draw a logical connection between his analysis of Europe's needs and Portugal's action. The question "Why Portugal?" is not new. It has long perplexed historians and given rise to elaborate myths about a far-sighted royal prince, Henry the Navigator, who steered his tiny impoverished country along a steady course of Atlantic exploration. It is more probable that Henry and his compatriots took greater interest in Morocco than the Atlantic, in knight-errantry and plundering Moors than commerce, and in personal conquest rather than the satisfaction of Europe's broad social needs.[37] In sum, Wallerstein does not offer a convincing argument about the historical forces that initiated the capitalist world-system.

In fairness, however, the central importance of Wallerstein's work rests on the operation of the world-system, not on its inception. The strength of the model hinges on two overriding hypotheses: (1) that American wealth was a necessary prerequisite for the breakthrough to capitalism in Europe; (2) that division of labor in the world-economy consistently favored the core at the expense of the periphery. If the first of these propositions is true, why did American metals circulate so quickly to parts of Europe beyond Spain unless, of course, they were attracted there by production? In the main, America's precious metals were converted to coin, not hoarded or used for religious ornamentation. The latter usage would have been consistent with the priorities of a precapitalist economy in which the volume of commercial exchange was limited. Since the highest priority for silver and gold in Europe was for use as a circulating medium, would that not imply that the society exercising that priority possessed an active exchange economy?

When does an exchange economy become active enough to be declared capitalist? Wallerstein does not say. In fact, he does not define capitalism as an economic phenomenon, institution, or way of life apart from his world-system. Like Webb, Wallerstein sees capitalism as a striving for profit within a cultural complex; unlike Webb, he provides elaborate definition of that complex. Yet the world-system did not take shape immediately upon the opening of the Americas. It was a half-century from the first settlements in Hispaniola to the discovery of silver loads in Mexico and Peru. The major American plantation crops were not developed until the late sixteenth and seventeenth centuries.[38] Are we to assume that the advent of capitalism awaited the slow consolidation of the Atlantic system of trade and empire?

Fernand Braudel thought not. The great distance between Europe and America and the long turnaround time for investors meant that only large-scale capitalists could have managed trade with America.[39] If America's precious metals were an important factor in European development, it was because Europe was ready to exploit them.[40] Had America offered no bullion, Europe would have discovered other outlets and secured other spoils, Braudel argued.[41] Ironically, Europeans may have been better off focusing on the East, where complex commercial networks and sophisticated infrastructures rendered wealth more accessible.[42] Many of Wallerstein's critics would reverse his outside-in ordering of history: it was not the exploitation of American bullion that created a vibrant European exchange economy; it was a vibrant European exchange economy that gave rise to a particular exploitation of America's resources.

There is no point in denying that American bullion oiled the productive process and accelerated the rate of circulation in Europe. But who benefited from it, and by how much? Spain, the immediate imperial profiteer of American mineral wealth, derived very little long-term economic benefit. In fact, it has been repeatedly argued that American bullion was the undoing of the Spanish economy. It permitted the Spanish to purchase desired manufactures from the northwest European countries while neglecting the development of the country's domestic industries. A Venetian ambassador to Madrid once observed that American treasure fell on Spain like rain on a roof—"it poures on her and it flows away."[43] Since most of it flowed to the manufacturing economies of the Northwest, it has been assumed that the Dutch and English were the real beneficiaries of Spain's American mines.

This assumption ignores one of the principal uses to which Spain's American bullion was put. Silver enabled Spain to pursue a century of warfare, much of it against the Protestant states of northwestern Europe. Warfare is a form of negative productivity. If, in the sixteenth century, warfare obliged the so-called core states, in their defense, to expend a large portion of their resources unproductively, should it not be concluded that one of the principal contributions of American bullion to the European world-economy was that it permitted a semiperipheral country, Spain, to misappropriate the continent's human and physical resources? The capitalist states of the core, against whom Spain directed its attacks, may have become capitalist not because of surplus extraction from America, but in spite of it.[44]

Did a world-scale division of labor consistently favor the core? Was the capitalist world-system enhanced by using free labor at the core and coerced labor in the periphery? Robert Brenner, a Marxist critic of world-system analysis, thinks not. In both cases, he uses Poland to illustrate his point. The imposition of an oppressive coerced labor regime in Poland, he argues, did not enhance the long-term growth of the core states. Nor can

Poland's feudal mode of production be considered an integral part of the capitalist system. It was because Polish lords persisted in a feudal mode and resisted capitalist development that Poland impeded rather than advanced economic growth in the core. In a manner typical of the feudal mode, Polish nobles made no effort to improve productive processes or to maximize their profits. They merely sustained their dominance and acquired Western luxuries by squeezing increasing levels of absolute surplus labor from the serfs. Without technical innovation, the non-capitalist Polish economy was unable to export more than 7 percent of its total grain product. When a genuine capitalist agriculture arose in the West, Polish grain became increasingly uncompetitive; exports from the Baltic fell; and the terms of trade began to run against the core and in favor of the periphery.[45]

Poland constitutes a problem for all the models treated in this book. The trade-based division-of-labor model assumes that increasing commercial exchange and international division of labor will, of necessity, generate higher levels of prosperity, social diversity, and human freedom. That happened in the West; it did not happen in Poland. According to demographic theorists, the fifteenth century should have been a favorable time for peasants, a period of trial for landowners. This was not the case in Poland. Moreover, the Polish experience does not fulfill the expectations of conventional Marxist analysis. Internal inconsistencies and class struggle within the feudal mode of production in Poland did not unhinge the oppressive system there in spite of a low population/land ratio. In Poland, the feudal system gathered strength from the same forces that are supposed to have destroyed it in the West. If Brenner's attack on Wallerstein's analysis of the East European periphery is reliable, then none of the models presented in this book satisfactorily explain why East Elbian Europe developed in the manner that it did.

Many historians bristle at Wallerstein's methodology. Even those with a high tolerance for grand social-science theorizing are frequently irritated by Wallerstein's penchant for reification and his tendency to engage in teleological explanation. There is little sense of contingency in his history, little coincidence, little blind luck, no accidents that send events lurching in unexpected directions. All things are linked and everything happens purposefully, as in the case of Portugal's rescue of a hungry and fratricidal Europe. The world-system is an abstract organizing concept, as are each of the hierarchical tiers within it; yet at one point or another Wallerstein affords them a conscious and deliberate will of their own. In summing up his world-system, he declares: "the capitalist world-economy was built on a worldwide division of labor in which various zones of this economy . . . were assigned specific economic roles, developed different class structures, used consequently different modes of labor control, and profited unequally from the workings of the system."[46] Did the capitalist world-system "assign" economic roles to the zones? Because states, zones, continents, and social classes are among the chief actors in Wallerstein's history, reification is difficult to avoid. Usually, Wallerstein keeps his language in check, but the abiding impression one garners from repeated readings of his work is that the world-system is not simply an organizing abstraction that reflects reality but a reality with a capacity for organization.

CONCLUSION

Wallerstein lifts the rise of capitalist modernity out of the parochial context of Western Europe. Employing the dependency theory of André Gunder Frank and building upon the historical insight of scholars like Webb and Williams, he has conceived a highly useful model to explain the organic relationship between diverse political and geographical entities in the modern world. Although the world-system he describes is conflictive and exploitative, the dynamic he employs is not Marxist. It is an elaborate division-of-labor model, driven by commerce and the desire for profit. Divisions within the model are determined by geography and resources, not by social class. If there is abiding tension within the system, it is an inter-regional, not inter-class, tension. Production distinctions are not ignored. They are critical to the operation of the model insofar as the world-system demands the use of free labor in the core and coerced labor in the periphery. Distinctions between the slave, the feudal, and the capitalist modes of production are acknowledged, but they are not given central importance because the whole system is defined by its dominant mode: capitalism.

Because the world-system is three-tiered, it has considerable flexibility. Peripheral countries can ascend to the semiperiphery, core countries can fall to the semiperiphery, and so on. The original structure was set in place by the exploitation of America's alluvial wealth. Bullion flows from America stimulated a price revolution in Europe, triggering a geographical division of labor that determined which states became the core, which the semiperiphery, and which the periphery. A plurality of sovereign states in the industrial core kept the system competitive and efficient, precluding the merger of the world-economy with a world-empire.

The model is more successful in explaining how early modern capitalism functioned over time and space than it is in explaining how capitalism came into being. Having followed Webb's lead in linking the advent of capitalism to the discovery and exploitation of America, Wallerstein drew too sharp a distinction between Europe, desperate and hungry, in the fifteenth century and Europe, saved by overseas expansion, in the later sixteenth. Virtually all scholars agree that the colonization of America significantly advanced the economic prospects of Europe, but many would deny that Europe's rapid economic and demographic growth during the sixteenth century—or for that matter, its transition to capitalism—hinged so profoundly upon the exploitation of the New World.

NOTES

1. Printed in Turner's *The Frontier in American History* (New York, 1920).

2. The debate on the Turner thesis has been the subject of two compilations for use in American history courses. See Ray Billington, ed., *The Frontier Thesis: Valid Interpretation of American History?* (Huntington, 1977) and George Roger Taylor, *The Turner Thesis Concerning the Role of the Frontier in American History* (Boston, 1956).

3. Walter Prescott Webb, *The Great Frontier* (Boston, 1952), p. 8.

4. Webb's language and orientation would give great offense in the 1990s. For him, the Americas and Australia were "the empty lands" without culture. Native populations were disregarded.

5. William Graham Sumner, "Earth-Hunger or the Philosophy of Land Grabbing," in Albert G. Keller, ed., *Earth-Hunger and Other Essays* (New Haven, 1913), p. 31, quoted in Webb, *The Great Frontier*, p. 17.

6. Webb, *The Great Frontier*, pp. 17–18. Webb was a woefully imprecise statistician. It must be granted that the discovery of the New World favorably altered the population/land ratio for Europeans, but Webb calculated the whole of the Western hemisphere as an immediate windfall. In fact, the windfall was realized one region at a time as Indian empires were subdued or European settlements pressed upon the wilderness. At no point did Webb include the native population of the Western hemisphere in his calculations. A great portion of the Americas (North America, Brazil, the Argentine) were sparsely populated. Very little of America was vacant; some of it— Central America and Peru—was rather densely inhabited. Despite the crude character of his calculations, his overall point is not invalidated by these statistical deficiencies.

7. Webb used the figures of Michel Chevalier, *Remarks on the Production of the Precious Metals and on the Depreciation of Gold* (London, 1853). Values would have been estimated in nineteenth-century American dollars.

8. Webb, *The Great Frontier*, p. 20.

9. Earl J. Hamilton, "American Treasure and the Rise of Capitalism (1500–1700)," *Economica* 9 (1929): 338–357.

10. Webb quotes Keynes to this effect; see *The Great Frontier*, p. 177.

11. N. F. R. Crafts, "Industrial Revolution in England and France: Some Thoughts on the Question, 'Why was England First?' " *Economic History Review* 30 (1977): 429–441. Special attention has been paid to technological innovation, to the substitution of inorganic (coal) for organic (wood) sources of energy, to trade and to capital accumulation, to demographic growth and the pressure of demand in the marketplace, to government institutions, to the degree of state regulation of industry, to guild structures, to the particular character of English society, to the flexibility of English law, and to the special advantages of England's geography. For a review of the historiography of the Industrial Revolution, see R. M. Hartwell, ed., *The Causes of the Industrial Revolution in England* (London, 1967).

12. Ralph Davis, *The Rise of the Atlantic Economies* (Ithaca, 1973), xiii.

13. There were, in fact, several theses lodged in *Capitalism and Slavery*: that black slavery generated racism, not the reverse; that slavery, the slave trade, and the slave plantations produced the capital that financed the Industrial Revolution; and that mature industrial capitalism, having arisen through the suffering of slaves, turned on slavery and destroyed it when the interests of capitalism were best served by free labor and free trade. Economic necessity produced slavery; economic necessity, not Christian philanthropy, ended it. In all their dealings in the wider world, Williams thought, the metropolitan peoples have consistently served themselves at the expense of others. Each of Williams's theses has been the subject of intense controversy, none more than his claim that the slave system underwrote the Industrial Revolution. For the most recent compilation of scholarly exchanges on Williams's work, see Barbara L. Solow and Stanley L. Engerman, eds., *British Capitalism and Caribbean Slavery: The Legacy of Eric Williams* (Cambridge, 1987).

14. Eric Williams, *Capitalism and Slavery* (Chapel Hill, 1944), p. 51.

15. Ibid., p. 58.

16. Ibid., pp. 102, 126–127.

17. Richard B. Sheridan, *Sugar and Slavery: An Economic History of the British West Indies, 1623–1775* (Baltimore, 1974) and "The Plantation Revolution and the Industrial Revolution, 1625–1775," *Caribbean Studies* 9 (1969): 5–25. Recent support has been forthcoming from Barbara Solow, "Caribbean Slavery and British Growth: The Eric Williams Hypothesis," *Journal of Development Economics* 17 (1985): 99–115.

18. Richard B. Sheridan, "The Wealth of Jamaica in the Eighteenth Century," *Economic History Review* 18 (1965): 292–311.

19. Richard B. Sheridan, "Simon Taylor, Sugar Tycoon of Jamaica, 1740–1813," *Agricultural History* 45 (1971): 285–296; "Planters and Merchants: The Oliver Family of Antigua and London, 1716–1784," *Business History* 13 (1971): 104–116.

20. Sheridan's conclusions on the profitability of the colonies were challenged by Robert Paul Thomas, who, through cost-benefit analysis of data generated largely by Sheridan, concluded that the eighteenth-century West India colonies were not profitable and that Britain would have gained more by investing its wealth elsewhere. Philip Coelho reached a similar conclusion. See Robert Paul Thomas, "The Sugar Colonies of the Old Empire: Profit or Loss for Great Britain?" *Economic History Review* 21 (1968): 30–45; Philip Coelho, "The Profitability of Imperialism: The British Experi-

ence in the West Indies, 1768–1772," *Explorations in Economic History* 10 (1973): 253–280. Sheridan responded: "The Wealth of Jamaica in the Eighteenth Century: A Rejoinder," *Economic History Review* 21 (1968): 46–61. Using figures provided in secondary sources, Stanley Engerman determined that the slave trade contributed only about 1 percent to national income in Britain and that the sum of profits from the slave trade and from West Indian plantations—if calculated on the most generous basis— would have been less than 5 percent of British income in an early year of the Industrial Revolution. This is not sufficient to sustain Williams's or Sheridan's conclusions. Stanley L. Engerman, "The Slave Trade and British Capital Formation in the Eighteenth Century: A Comment on the Williams Thesis," *Business History Review* 46 (1972): 430–443.

21. Recent work, whether for England or the continent, has followed true to form. See for example, Rondo Cameron, "A New View of European Industrialization," *Economic History Review* 38 (1985): 1–23; A. E. Musson, "Industrial Motive Power in the United Kingdom, 1800–70," *Economic History Review* 29 (1976): 415–439; Thomas C. Cochran, "The Business Revolution," *American Historical Review* 79 (1974): 1449–1466; J. F. Gaski, "The Causes of the Industrial Revolution: A Brief 'Single Factor' Argument," *Journal of European Economic History* 11 (1982): 227–233.

22. The Fernand Braudel Center for the Study of Economies, Historical Systems, and Civilization is located at the State University of New York at Binghamton. The Center publishes the quarterly journal, *Review*.

23. The two terms are almost interchangeable. Still, they are not synonymous. Non-economic links between component parts of a world-system, especially cultural links, render a world-system something more than a world-economy.

24. Immanuel Wallerstein, *The Modern World-System I: Capitalist Agriculture and the Origins of the European World-Economy in the Sixteenth Century* (New York, 1974), pp. 37–38.

25. Where Indian labor was available, coercion took the form of *encomienda*, whereby a Spanish settler gained the right to use the services of a prescribed body of Indians who were to provide him personal services, goods, or a combination of these.

26. Earl J. Hamilton, "American Treasure and Andalusian Prices, 1503–1660," *Journal of Economic and Business History* 1 (1928): 1–35; "American Treasure and the Rise of Capitalism," *Economica* 9 (1929): 338–357; "Prices and Progress: Prices as a Factor in Business Growth," *Journal of Economic History* 12 (1952): 325–349. John Maynard Keynes, *A Treatise on Money*, vol. 2 (New York, 1930), pp. 154–164.

27. Wallerstein, *World-System I*, pp. 92–93.

28. Ibid., p. 70.

29. Ibid., p. 348.

30. Wallerstein argued that a world-system would not be larger than the distance that could be covered in forty to sixty days by the best means of transport. *World-System I*, p. 17.

31. This, of course, is a non-testable, counter-factual hypothesis. It is not possible for historians to separate the sixteenth-century world-system from regions external to it—in effect, to remove all consideration of contacts between Asia, the Middle East, Africa (except for a few coastal enclaves), and the capitalist world-system in order to determine whether that system could have operated in much the same fashion.

32. For a brief exposition of this, see Alvin Y. So, *Social Change and Development,* pp. 180–184.

33. Wallerstein, *World-System I,* p. 350.

34. Wallerstein recognizes this elsewhere in his book; see *World-System I,* p. 80.

35. Davis, *The Rise of the Atlantic Economies,* p. 172.

36. Wallerstein, *World-System I,* p. 51.

37. Among the leading scholars of the age of discovery, J. H. Parry argued that Portugal had desperate need of gold. Portugal struck no gold coins between 1383 and 1435. Even silver coinage was uncommon. The kingdom's copper coinage was seriously debased, and inflation raged. Parry also emphasized the knight-errantry of the Portuguese. See his *Discovery of the Sea* (Berkeley and Los Angeles, 1981), pp. 84, 90–94. Vitorino Magálhaes Godino, like Wallerstein, presents a shopping-basket approach to Portuguese motives for discovery. But gold stands at the top of his list and receives primary emphasis in his analysis. See his *L'économie de l'empire portugais aux XVe et XVIe siècles* (Paris, 1969).

38. Chief among them was sugar. In 1570, there were only 60 sugar mills in Brazil; this rose to about 120 by 1585. Alexander Marchant, *From Barter to Slavery: The Economic Relations of Portuguese and Indians in the Settlement of Brazil, 1500–1580* (Baltimore, 1942), p. 125. Frédéric Mauro claims that there were 235 mills in Brazil by 1628. See his *Le Portugal et L'Atlantique au XVIIe siècle, 1570–1670* (Paris, 1960), p. 195. A plantation economy in sugar was not launched in the Caribbean until the 1640s. Tobacco took hold in North America around 1620.

39. Fernand Braudel, *The Mediterranean and the Mediterranean World in the Age of Philip II,* vol. 1 (New York, 1972), p. 377.

40. Pierre Vilar observed that strong money (gold and silver) never streams into a system unless it is attracted there by production. Money is a commodity, exchanged in the marketplace for other commodities. Vilar is highly critical of the Hamilton-Keynes thesis upon which Wallerstein rests his argument for capital accumulation in Europe. Pierre Vilar, "Problems of the Formation of Capitalism," *Past and Present* 10 (1956): 15–38.

41. It would have exploited more fully its own silver loads. John Davy contends that by 1460 the European bullion famine had run its course. Hitherto intractable European silver deposits had become commercially exploitable in the fifteenth century by the introduction of new technology, and between 1450 and 1530 European silver output may have increased fivefold. John Davy, "The Great Bullion Famine of the Fifteenth Century," *Past and Present* 79 (1978): 3–54.

42. Braudel, *The Mediterranean,* vol. 2, p. 679. The single decisive factor in Europe's swift development was not American silver, argued Braudel. It was "the restless energy of the West."

43. Carlo M. Cipolla, *Guns, Sails and Empires: Technological Innovation and the Early Phases of European Expansion 1400–1700* (New York, 1965), p. 36.

44. Analyzing the silver question in terms of a Marxian concept of surplus value, Dennis Flynn observes that Marx considered surplus value to be created in the process of production, not circulation. The surplus that accrued to Spain from its control of American mines must be measured in terms of the differential between the value expended in producing bullion and the value obtained from the bullion when it was exchanged for commodities or services in the European marketplace. When an exchange occurred between Spaniards and members of another community in which silver was

traded for industrial manufactures, that exchange was voluntary and, one must presume, in the interest of both parties. The surplus value that accrued to the Spanish because they controlled the production of American silver was not attached to the silver itself, an object of exchange. Consequently, surplus value was not passed on to Spain's trading partners in the process of circulation. It was retained by the Spanish, who acquired it in the original act of production. The Spanish chose to use it to sustain a century of warfare. Dennis Flynn, "Early Capitalism Despite New World Bullion: An Anti-Wallerstein Interpretation of Imperial Spain," paper delivered at meetings of the Social Science Historical Association, Washington, D.C., 1983.

45. Robert Brenner, "The Origins of Capitalist Development: A Critique of Neo-Smithian Marxism," *New Left Review* 104 (1977): 68–73. Brenner's criticism, whatever its merits, does not challenge Wallerstein's proposition that Western Europe needed foodstuffs from the East to release its own productive forces and that Polish grain imports permitted the launching of a modern capitalist economy in the sixteenth century. In response to Brenner's criticism, it could be argued that the introduction of capitalism into sixteenth-century Poland was altogether unlikely and that without coercion peasants would have eaten up their surpluses, allowing for no important export of grain.

46. Wallerstein, *World-System I*, p. 162.

8

Environmental History

Environmental history has flourished under crisis. During the century before World War II, scattered voices warned that the earth's resources were being despoiled, that greater efforts at conservation and greater caution in the use of toxic substances were essential if humankind was to preserve its natural heritage. Hiroshima demonstrated the ability of humans to destroy as well as to befoul their habitat, and nuclear contamination was added to a growing list of perils. In 1948, two American environmentalists issued sober judgments on past and present behavior. Fairfield Osborn declared that over the last century, the story of the United States regarding "the use of forests, grasslands, wildlife and water sources [was] the most violent and most destructive of any . . . in the long history of civilization."[1] William Vogt concurred: "By excessive breeding and abuse of the land mankind has backed itself into an ecological trap. By a lopsided use of applied science it has been living on promissory notes. Now, all over the world, the notes are falling due."[2]

Rachel Carson argued that the promissory notes of applied science often promised nothing short of ecological cataclysm. In its attempt to enhance the quality of human life through the production of synthetic insecticides, the chemical industry had poisoned animal, bird, and marine life and was endangering humans through the progressive accumulation of toxic substances in the food chain. While insect pests were quickly developing resistance to one chemical agent after another, other forms of life were being jeopardized so seriously that we could, in the not too distant future, witness a "silent spring" in which birds no longer sang, bees no longer pollinated the apple blossoms, and fishermen, themselves grown weak, no longer waded into fishless streams.[3]

A report on world environment commissioned by the secretary-general of the United Nations in 1971 gave every indication that a doomsday scenario was entirely possible if humankind did not exercise more "careful husbandry" of its "thin and fragile" environment.[4] The 152 experts[5] who advised Barbara Ward and René Dubos, the report's authors, had little difficulty agreeing on factual evidence relating to the global environment, but their opinions diverged widely on how those facts should be interpreted, what priorities should be established, and where the burden of ecological probity must rest. Can that burden be shared without prejudice? Having done most to create an environmental crisis, will the industrialized nations try to impede industrialization among the poor nations? At the same time, can industrialization proceed in the Third World without causing irreversible ecological damage? All agree that environmental degradation is a global problem that must be addressed globally.

At the root of the environmental controversy is the conflict over first principles. What is humankind's role in the natural order? Genesis informs us that God gave man "dominion over the fish of the sea, the birds of the air, and the cattle, and over all the wild animals and all the creatures that crawl on the ground." Man has behaved accordingly, striding the earth as its landlord, determining where to till and where to drill, which landscapes to protect, which to transform, what forms of life to preserve, what forms to sacrifice, and in whose interest the tilling, the drilling, and the preserving are to be undertaken. Ward and Dubos do not deny humans their proprietary function; rather, they urge upon them the burden of stewardship, the responsibility to serve as trustees, to protect and preserve our natural patrimony for generations unborn. Most theoretical ecologists hold a different view. For them, humankind is the most elevated of the species, but no more significant than other elements of our natural ecosystem. Some favor a systematic process of deindustrialization to save the planet; others fear that no measures sufficient to save the earth are likely to be taken in a world suffused with greed.

James Lovelock, a British scientist, disagrees with both orientations. Stewardship is important, he declares, but if the survival of intelligent life on this planet were to depend solely upon the benevolent trusteeship of human beings, our situation would surely be lost. At the same time, there is no need for panic, no need to deindustrialize, no need to despair. Instead, Lovelock offers the Gaia hypothesis. Gaia, mother earth, is perceived as a complex and self-regulating organism that reacts to chemical and other threats to its well-being in compensatory ways that preserve homeostatic equilibrium and ensure that life is sustained. Lovelock states the concept graphically: "the entire range of living matter on Earth, from whales to viruses, and from oaks to algae, could be regarded as constituting a single living entity, capable of manipulating the Earth's atmosphere to suit its overall needs and endowed with faculties and powers far beyond those of its constituent parts."[6]

Life began on earth about 3.5 billion years ago. Yet despite the changing output of heat from the sun and changing surface properties of the earth, the planet's climate has remained remarkably stable. The earth's atmosphere continues to give evidence of extraordinary homeostasis.[7] We need not ban aerosol sprays in a frenzy of fear over a depleted ozone layer. When Krakatoa erupted in 1895, the volcanic effluent spewed into the stratosphere was sufficient to deplete the ozone by 30 percent. This amounts to twice the depletion that might occur if the 1979 rate of chlorofluorocarbon emissions were continued to the year 2010. Although numerous natural forces have continually filled the stratosphere with ozone-depleting chemicals, natural compensation has been achieved through the self-regulating capabilities of the earth. In light of modern industrial growth and the rise of population, human vigilance has become increasingly important. The earth's vital organs reside between latitudes 45 degrees north and 45 degrees south, especially in the tropical forests and the inshore waters of the continental shelves. It is here that reckless human action could do irremediable damage.[8] Humans must be the stewards of their environment, but their stewardship is merely a complement to the natural, self-regulating properties of Gaia. Humans cannot destroy the life-sustaining capability of the earth, argues Lovelock, but they can render the planet incapable of supporting their own form of life.[9]

Whatever views diverse groups of environmentalists may take of man's role in the natural order, all of them concur that humans are integral elements of the ecosystem, reactive to modifications within it and capable of dramatically altering its character. Mankind's planetary environment should no longer be viewed as a stable backdrop against which the drama of human history is played. The environment is and always has been a major player. Sadly, it is only the surging crisis of the twentieth century that alerts us, as historians, to the pervasive importance of environmental factors in the human experience.

Environmental history is distinguished by a particular orientation to the past, an orientation that integrates people with nature and exposes the impact upon human affairs of numerous forces that are beyond the control or beyond the immediate understanding of men and women. It encompasses climate, disease, natural disaster, and the ecological effects of displaced plants and animals. It treats the ecological implications of various forms of agriculture and industry; it examines the altering ratios of humans to the land and of humans to other species, and it considers the effect of these changing ratios upon all forms of life in the ecosystem. Environmental history catalogues our judicious exploitation and our reckless befouling of the global habitat. It informs us of our place within the natural order; it alerts us to the precarious state of our existence; and it identifies the tortured and tortuous roadways that have brought us to our current predicament.

Many older works of scholarship anticipate the concerns of modern environmental historians. Among them are the writings of Frederick Jackson Turner and Walter Prescott Webb, scholars mentioned in the previous chapter. These frontier historians identified the changes wrought by humans in a vast continental ecosphere.[10] French historians of the *Annales* school were the first well-defined body of scholars who self-consciously affirmed the significance of mankind's dynamic encounter with its environment. The signature, *Annales*, derives from the title of a scholarly journal founded in 1929 by Marc Bloch and Lucien Febvre in protest against the prevailing orthodoxy of event-oriented narrative history that focused almost exclusively on political, diplomatic, and military topics.[11] *Annalistes* advocated "total history," a more comprehensive and human history that would study societies as wholes, eliminating barriers between academic disciplines while creating a single "science of man."[12] *Annales* historians are noted for their creative methodologies, not for any overriding theory of change. Working generally in the pre-industrial era, they have concentrated on underlying structures, the great institutions and social formations that have stabilized the human condition. In the process, they have demonstrated considerable concern for the interplay between customs, values, and the material environment. In this regard, they have foretokened the work of environmental historians.[13]

The most ambitious venture by an *Annaliste* into environmental history is Fernand Braudel's luxuriant work, *The Mediterranean and the Mediterranean World in the Age of Philip II* (1946). This triumph in "total history" is divided into three parts, each part being concerned with different structural phenomena and different rates of change. The first examines structures of great duration—the *longue durée*—in which change occurs almost imperceptibly over as much as a thousand years. Topics include geography, climate, and the interaction of humans with both. Part two concerns trends, cycles, and rhythms of medium duration—say, fifty or a hundred years—involving such matters as economic systems, demography, and modes of warfare. Part three treats events of short duration, *l'histoire événementielle*—what Braudel disdainfully described as brief, rapid fluctuations, momentary outbursts, mere surface disturbances that are explicable only in terms of the deeper forces of medium or long duration.[14]

The most persistent criticism of Braudel's work is that he was not able to achieve harmonious integration between the three planes of his study, between durable phenomena and rapidly changing human events.[15] The most persistent criticism of *Annales* scholars in general is their tendency to view history as a natural science in which vast impersonal forces of long and medium duration rule out the possibility that individual human beings make their own history.

Environmental historians confront similar problems. They too work with vast, impersonal, often inanimate forces, and they do it, very often, in the more complex context of modern times. Equally committed to holism, they must penetrate numerous disciplines: geology (the aging of the planet), climatology, soil chemistry, plant biology, geography (the restructuring of past landscapes), and ecology (the interaction between different organisms and between organisms and their physical environment). In its human dimension, environmental history is intimately linked to anthropology, to the role of nature in shaping culture (and vice versa), as well as to aesthetics, ethics, and religion, fields that shed light on the way in which humans perceive and value nature.[16] Despite the formidable range of their interests, environmental historians are less inclined than *Annalistes* to dismiss the importance of the history of events (*l'histoire événementielle*) or to deny individual human beings a role in deciding their own destiny. Much of the impetus for the development of environmental history derives from the gathering crisis over human survival. Without intelligent human stewardship at the everyday level of politics, diplomacy, and military affairs, the men and women of planet earth may be approaching the end of their history.

It is one thing to know what must be done to achieve holistic environmental history. It is another thing to do it—to master and reconcile so many diverse historical forces. The field is relatively young. Environmental history has produced no single study of Braudelian scale and no universal theoretical model that accommodates all past experience. It may never do so. Yet a number of theoretical models have been proposed for various segments of the field,[17] and scholars working in those areas have produced important hypotheses concerning the forces that promote change. This chapter will concentrate on two environmental factors—climate and disease—indicating the extent to which they may have influenced historical development on a macrohistorical scale.

CLIMATE AND HISTORY

Some of the most distinguished historians of our time have made farreaching claims concerning the importance of climate. Having observed the similarity of long-term demographic rhythm in regions as widely separated as Europe and China, Braudel declared that in all probability the universal factor providing unity to world history was climate.[18] In *Commercial Revolution of the Middle Ages, 950–1350* (1971), Yale University historian Robert Lopez suggested that climatic variation was a primary cause of major developments in the ancient world.

> The cyclical flows and ebbs of disease and famine, which can be observed over multisecular periods, seem to be connected with certain "pulsations" of climate. . . . Less long and sharp than the great prehistoric alterations of glacial and interglacial periods, these pulsations have brought about, in historical time, slow yet telling changes in the average temperature and humidity of the earth. Scattered but consistent evidence indicates that the last centuries of antiquity and the first ones of the early Middle Ages were especially cold and wet. This might not in itself have been disastrous for the normally warm and dry Mediterranean world, but it made the traditional techniques of dry farming less successful and accelerated the already advanced process of erosion. It was a great shock for Rome, in the fifth century, to be sacked by the Ostrogoths, but the slow degradation of the surrounding countryside, which preceded those dramatic events, was a greater economic catastrophe. Campania was turning into a stony wilderness, Etruria into a malarial swampland. Some other regions were less affected by soil exhaustion and endemic disease, but none was spared by the dramatic succession of "pestilences" which ravaged the Greco-Roman world over and again, from the year 180 to the mid-sixth century. These periodical epidemic out-

bursts were probably caused by several agents, but the greatest killer undoubtedly was the bubonic plague. There have been only two multisecular periods in recorded history when the plague, normally confined to some pockets in the Far East, repeatedly spread over the Eurasian continent: the one we have just mentioned, and the stretch between the mid-fourteenth century and the mid-seventeenth. It is probably not an accident that both periods coincided with a cold and wet pulsation of the climate.[19]

The pulsations of climate to which Lopez refers are associated in Europe with westerly winds that encircle polar regions of the globe. When the westerlies extend into lower latitudes, cold years become colder and harvest failures occur with greater frequency. The final centuries of the ancient period were relatively cold, as Lopez contended, but at the beginning of the ninth century, Europe experienced a warming trend that lasted about four hundred years. The fourteenth century opened wet and cool, and for about two hundred years thereafter weather appears to have been highly variant. By the sixteenth century, Europe was sliding into an extended cold phase, the Little Ice Age, circa 1550–circa 1850.

Climate does not change abruptly, nor do changes occur simultaneously in all regions of a large country or continent. During the Ice Age when glaciers up to two miles thick covered much of North America, average annual temperatures were only five degrees centigrade lower than they are today and, according to some climatologists, winters were no more severe.[20] In the last five thousand years, the earth's climate has remained remarkably constant. It is probable that world temperature has fluctuated within a range of plus or minus two degrees centigrade and that rainfall fluctuations have not exceeded 5 percent.[21] Nevertheless, small changes in mean temperature can have significant impact along the climatic margins, the cold and dry limits of agriculture, if those changes are extended over a considerable period of time. A decrease of one degree centigrade (1.8 degrees fahrenheit) in average temperature in Iceland reduces growing degree days by 27 percent.[22] In the warm years of the late ninth and tenth centuries, Vikings settled Iceland and Greenland. Eric the Red's Greenland colony numbered 3,000 people working 280 farms. With a shift of the westerlies in the twelfth and thirteenth centuries, the Greenland settlements had to be abandoned, and Icelandic sagas, which for centuries had made no mention of pack ice, began recording massive ice flows that gripped the island in winter. Farms retreated lower into the valleys of Norway, and by the fifteenth century dozens of vineyards that had flourished in England were given up.[23]

Two types of evidence permit us to reconstruct climate history. One is derived from natural materials, field data; the other is the human record. Among the former, tree rings, ice cores from glaciers and from arctic ice-sheets, and cores of sediment from ancient lake beds provide year-by-year weather information. The analysis of marine organisms buried in the ocean floor, the layering of stalagmites, and radiocarbon dating provide further information. Records 125,000 years old can be gathered from pollen fossils in lake beds or peat deposits. Most of our knowledge of post–Ice Age climatic history before 1950 was derived from pollen analy-sis. This type of evidence can be correlated with data gathered from human sources. Although readings from meteorological instruments (if only crude ones) provide the most reliable information, sagas, chronicles, and diaries frequently offer direct observations of meteorological events. Finally, "proxy data" provides weather-related information from continu-ous records of such things as price series for grains and other vital food-stuffs, crop-yield ratios, and the dates when harvests were taken.[24]

In relating climate and history, we must distinguish between random and non-random phenomena. The random intervention of weather in human affairs (e.g., the "Protestant winds" that dispersed the Spanish Armada) may be important, but such intervention is unpredictable and un-sustained. Climatic explanation at a deeper level requires that we correlate long-term climatic shifts with significant human developments: demo-graphic changes, modifications in economic behavior, crises of disease, or the rise and fall of great states—the type of phenomena treated in the foregoing quotation from Lopez.

Climatic shifts occur on varying scales. The coming of the Ice Age was an event of enormous proportion; the Little Ice Age, although significant for human history, was comparatively minor. There are even lesser "trends"—warm or cool phases lasting ten to fifty years—and, of course, there are random climatic episodes that obscure definitional distinctions between "climate" and "weather." This group includes volcanic eruptions that distribute sun-shielding dust throughout the stratosphere, lowering temperatures at the earth's surface and reducing crop yields for two or three years.

John Post studied such an episode, the explosion in 1815 of the East Indian volcano Tomboro, which in combination with other volcanic activ-ity precipitated what he called the last great subsistence crisis in the West-ern world, 1816–1817. Summer temperatures were among the lowest in recorded history; crops failed; hunger and disease, vagrancy and social disorder increased; and European governments responded with repressive measures. Historians have commonly explained the distress of these years by reference to economic dislocations occasioned by the Napoleonic wars, but Post emphasizes the environmental variable. Further, he encourages scholars to take account of similar climatic episodes for eight other three- to five-year periods in modern European history when veils of volcanic dust and economic depression coincided.[25]

Consideration of climate as the critical engine of historical change began in earnest with the work of Gustaf Utterström. In a celebrated article, Utterström declared that over the last millennium periods of prosperity and population growth in Europe occurred during warm climatic intervals. Furthermore, the late medieval crisis and the crisis of the seventeenth century could be explained in large part, he thought, by climatic change.[26] Utterström's argument is circumstantial. In pre-modern Europe, most people were engaged in agriculture, and agriculture was fundamentally dependent upon weather. Braudel made the same point: 80 to 95 percent of people in pre-industrial European societies "lived from the land and from nothing else. The rhythm, quality and deficiency of harvests ordered all material life."[27] These arguments were sufficient to convince Wallerstein. Citing Utterström, he declared climatic change to be one of the three forces that impelled fifteenth- and sixteenth-century Europeans to surmount their difficulties through overseas colonization.

In 1979, conferences of scholars were held in Britain and the United States to explore the relationship between climate and history. Each conference inspired the publication of a scholarly volume. [28] The tone of both volumes is cautious. The greatest problem for climate history, it was determined, is the shortage of precise evidence. There can be no substitute for abundant and reliable instrumental records, and these are unavailable before the nineteenth century. One cannot use instrumental readings taken in England or Holland in the seventeenth century to draw conclusions about Germany or Scandinavia. Ambiguities inevitably emerge. Climate historians agree that there was a Little Ice Age, but there is considerable disagreement over its dates.[29] For all the shortcomings of data on Western Europe, it is the best documented region of the world since 1500. English experts argue that there will never be enough reliable evidence for most areas of the globe to permit precise evaluations of the relationship between climate and human society.[30]

Historians require evidence on climate that can be dated with precision. Field data may yield valuable information, particularly for ancient periods, but some of it is difficult to date precisely. As one scholar observed, "approximate dating of plus or minus fifty years, although marvelously precise on the scale of geological time, does not satisfy the needs of most historians."[31] Even chronicles, diaries, and journals that allude to weather episodes with precise dating tend to focus on specific events, usually disastrous ones, and offer little information about routine weather conditions.[32] A serious danger for climate historians, M. L. Parry observes, is that in their frustration over the shortage of precise and reliable evidence they are tempted to draw conclusions from the mere synchronism of climatic and economic events. Such arguments establish no more than a time-space coincidence.[33]

A deleterious shift in climate that shortened the growing season and created food shortages for humans and their animals would require adjustments at many levels. But people do adjust. The historian should no more assume that society is a constant to be impacted by climatic change than that climate itself is a constant. Jan de Vries stresses human adaptability in past times, noting that Dutch farmers substantially increased the planting of buckwheat, a hardy crop with a short growing season, during the cool sixteenth century. Other farmers in Europe substituted barley, oats, and rye for wheat during the Little Ice Age.[34] Acknowledging mankind's extraordinary adaptability, Le Roy Ladurie, who reconstructed French climate history from the timing of annual grape harvests, concluded that "in the long term the human consequences of climate seem to be slight, perhaps negligible, and certainly difficult to detect."[35]

Some historians of climate object to Le Roy Ladurie's minimalist conclusions, but few of them advocate grand climatic determinism.[36] Recent scholarship has deflated Braudel's hopeful supposition, uttered in 1967, that climate might provide the key to understanding universal trends in world history. At the same time, research has demonstrated the importance of climatic variables on a modest scale. On some issues, the jury is still out. We do not know for certain the extent to which cold phases— either during the last centuries of antiquity or the Little Ice Age—may have influenced human demography, nor do we fully understand the relation between meteorological stress and epidemic disease.

EPIDEMIC DISEASE AS AN ENGINE OF CHANGE

As an independent variable, disease may provide a better vehicle than climate for explaining universal rhythms in world history. For this insight we are indebted to William H. McNeill, a pioneer world historian who, among his many provocative and perceptive contributions to the field, has shown that epidemic disease operates in predictable patterns and that those patterns provide discernable contours for much of world history. His book, *Plagues and Peoples* (1976), forms the basis for much of the following discussion.[37]

All living organisms are parasites. As humans devour plants and beasts, so viruses, bacteria, and multi-celled creatures attach themselves to human tissue as a source of food. Some microparasitic organisms reside in their human host and cause no apparent damage. Some produce infections that diminish vigor without endangering the life of their host. Still others provoke acute disease that either kills their human host or induces an immunity reaction.[38] A disease organism that quickly kills its host must confront its own crisis of survival: unless it can find another host who will provide it nourishment and keep its reproductive chain intact, the organism may perish. Therefore, disease organisms and human or animal hosts commonly achieve a level of mutual adaptation that permits both to survive.

Viral and bacterial infections can achieve stable accommodation in human hosts only when the human population is fairly dense. Measles provides an example. In modern urban communities, measles propagates in a wave-like pattern that crests at roughly two-year intervals. To sustain this pattern, there must always be seven thousand persons susceptible to the disease. In light of modern birth rates and socialization practices, the minimal population required to sustain measles in a modern urban complex is around half a million.[39] Other diseases require different densities. It was not, however, until circa B.C. 3000 when stable, relatively sophisticated agricultural communities were established in the river valleys of Asia that human society provided the required population density to sustain many forms of epidemic disease.

Each of the widely separated civilizations that arose throughout Eurasia after circa B.C. 3000 was attacked by different diseases. Each achieved its particular adaptation to them. Diseases that arrived with lethal force were accommodated, in time, by immunity reactions. They became the "childhood diseases" of the stable civilizations, serious but only occasionally fatal. Because these diseases retained their full destructive power when introduced to unexposed populations, civilized societies with their acquired immunities possessed a potent weapon in dealing with alien peoples on their frontiers who lacked those immunities. The expansion of early civilized states is intelligible only in light of these epidemiological realities, McNeill argues.[40]

By the beginning of the Christian era, four "divergent civilized disease pools" had come into being—one in the Roman Mediterranean, others in the Middle East, India, and China. When trade and travel between these civilizations became regular and organized, as it did in the centuries from

B.C. 200 to A.D. 200, the interpenetration of disease from one pool to another was inescapable. The Antonine Plague, A.D. 165–180 took a heavy toll in Rome, as did a succeeding epidemic in 251–266. McNeill speculates that these episodes marked the entry of measles and smallpox to Europe, precipitating secular demographic decline in the Roman Empire. We have less specific knowledge of epidemics in other civilizations, although severe die-offs are known to have occurred in China after 161 and 310. Bubonic plague descended upon the Mediterranean in 541, upon China in 610. In both places, it cut recurring swaths of death for about two hundred years.

The tenth century was a watershed in the disease history of the Eastern hemisphere. By then, plague had disappeared, and people from Europe to China finally achieved what McNeill describes as a "successful biological accommodation" to the infections that had assailed their forefathers.[41] A homogeneous disease pool had been established across the hemisphere. As a result, population growth resumed everywhere. Economies expanded, and in succeeding centuries Europeans, in particular, would experience the cultural efflorescence of the High Middle Ages.

How might the disease patterns mentioned thus far have specifically affected historical developments? McNeill thinks the impact of new infections upon a Roman population that lacked established immunities contributed to civil disorder as well as to secular population decline in the second and third centuries. Agreements permitting German tribesmen to settle inside the Roman frontier as well as the laws of Diocletian (285–305) forbidding cultivators from leaving the land suggest that Roman population was falling sharply. Such a fall would have affected the volume of commerce throughout the Empire and the flow of tribute to the imperial treasury. Epidemic disease may also have assisted the rise and consolidation of Christianity. Care of the sick was for Christians an established religious duty. When normal social services broke down in periods of heavy die-off, the provision of nursing—even such simple practices as distributing food and water—would likely have endeared survivors to Christianity.

The plague of Justinian that struck Constantinople in 542 prevented the emperor from pursuing his plan to restore imperial unity. Recurrences of bubonic plague through the seventh and eighth centuries help to explain why Roman and Persian armies were ineffectual in resisting the advance of Moslem forces that erupted out of Arabia after 634. Pirenne argued that the shift of Christian civilization away from the Mediterranean was a result of Moslem conquests and political fragmentation around the inland sea. Is it not equally plausible that the shift was a deliberate turning from bubonic plague, which remained confined to the Mediterranean and its immediate hinterland?

McNeill is swift to point out parallels in China. Population fell sharply after the second century. Imperial administration faltered with the end of the Han Dynasty in A.D. 220. Invasions from the steppes followed, and the country was fragmented into as many as sixteen rival states. The height of this fragmentation coincided with the arrival of either measles or smallpox. Buddhism, an import from India in the first century, offered the type of care and comfort associated in the West with Christianity. It too taught that death was a release from pain and that believers could be reunited with loved ones in a sublime afterlife. Buddhism gained official dominance at court in the third century. While no cause-effect relationship between disease and these developments can be proven, McNeill finds them "intrinsically persuasive."[42]

After the tenth century, two major disease crises occurred that require attention: (1) the Black Death, and (2) the epidemiological decimation of the American Indian population. Both demonstrate how a severe disease episode triggers reaction and change across the spectrum of human activity. Both had an effect upon the growth of capitalism, and both were significant in the rise of Europe to world hegemony.

The Black Death

The Black Death has been treated in some detail in Chapter 4. There it was observed that bubonic plague erupted all across the Eastern hemisphere in the fourteenth century. If, as I have argued, there was no necessary connection between prevailing population pressure in Europe and the onset of plague, then the Black Death constitutes a thoroughly exogenous force. Nothing specific to European society triggered the disease. There was nothing that Europeans could have done to prevent it, and there was nothing they could have known that would have moderated its impact.[43] No prior trends in Christian civilization—economic, social, or demographic—significantly weakened or intensified the plague's depradations.

All societies invaded by plague—Egyptian, Chinese, European— suffered many of the same social consequences. At the same time, each culture responded to aspects of the crisis somewhat differently as its particular material and cultural circumstances dictated.[44] Everywhere, the price of foodstuffs fell (depopulation reduced demand) and the price of manufactures rose (labor costs increased). Landowners suffered losses of income. Merchants died in large numbers; cities wilted; and the volume of commerce fell. Still, if the demographic blowout of the fourteenth and fifteenth centuries reduced commercial activity in Europe, it accelerated social changes that facilitated the growth of capitalism by undermining what Marxists have defined as the feudal mode of production.

Fourteenth- and fifteenth-century die-offs in Europe are an important element in both the demographic and Marxian analyses examined in Part I of this book. In both cases, the fourteenth century was a time of crisis, and population pressure was central to that crisis. For neo-Malthusians, excessive population was expected to trigger a Malthusian check. That check, by reducing population, would have restored balance between land and people. Marxists considered the crisis a result of an exploitative social system that extracted surplus from serfs but discouraged production efficiencies that would have increased food production and sustained a larger population. Logically, a stand-off between classes would have produced class warfare.

Several things could have happened in fourteenth-century Europe. A Malthusian check, however unpleasant, could have improved the land/labor ratio and permitted peasants to subsist more easily despite continuing demands by their lords. Class warfare could have erupted, or significant technical innovations could have increased agricultural productivity, permitting the conflictive lord-peasant relationship to persist at a somewhat higher material level. Conceivably, the lords could have eased their extractive pressure to a level commensurate with the ability of the serfs to survive.

Any of these was possible. Only one, class warfare, would have posed an immediate threat to the prevailing feudal order. Yet none of these possibilities materialized. At least, none of them fully ran its course. Instead, Europe was "blind-sided" by an exogenous biological force, the Black Death, that hastened the dissolution of the feudal mode of production. As we have seen, massive die-offs altered bargaining power between peasants and lords, permitting the former to escape serfdom throughout Western Europe. Altered demographic conditions and the manifold dislocations caused by recurring pestilence provided opportunities for the most ambitious and long-lived peasant families to accumulate lands and local influence—to become "kulaks" or "cocks" of the villages. Their successes in acquiring rights to the land displaced other peasants, transforming the latter into landless (or virtually landless) wage workers available for hire in agriculture or manufacturing. The new organization of land was considerably more conducive to agricultural innovation. If, as Marxists argue, the structural adjustments required to produce capitalism were first

achieved in the countryside, it was the awesome depradations of plague
that promoted those adjustments.

Epidemic Disease and the Native American

The impact of epidemic disease upon the American Indian population
may be likened to the first encounters of early civilizations with epidemic
scourges or to the interpenetration of diseases between major civilizations
in Eurasia at the beginning of the Christian era. It is probably the most
devastating disease experience on historical record. Native Americans
migrated to the New World during the Ice Age when the formation of
glaciers had lowered sea levels and exposed a land bridge between Siberia
and Alaska. Global warming restored the Bering Straits by B.C. 10,000,
permanently separating the continents. By B.C. 9000 scattered bands of
hunters had occupied the Americas from the extreme north to Tierra del
Fuego. In the millennia that followed, they became more isolated from the
rest of humanity than any other population except aboriginal Australians,
who also walked to their new continent during the Ice Age. Genetically,
Amerindians were exceptionally uniform. From southern Canada to the tip
of South America, over 90 percent of the population carried blood type O.
By contrast, blood types in the Eastern hemisphere are highly variant.[45]

The disease history of the Native American was also different. America
was not a disease-free paradise. Pre-Columbian skeletal and mummified
remains and studies of fossilized fecal matter from archaeological sites
give evidence of infectious diseases such as pneumonia and tuberculosis
as well as the presence of intestinal parasitic infestations. Still, the initial
passage of Old World migrants through Siberia and across the Bering land
bridge probably provided a "cold filter" that prevented the survival of
many disease organisms that thrive in warm climates.[46] It stands to reason
that Native Americans had no experience of and no immunity to the
epidemic diseases that became endemic in settled Eurasian societies during
the four millennia after B.C. 3000.

They paid heavily for their epidemiological innocence. After Columbus
united the hemispheres, contact between Europeans and Native Americans
commonly exposed the latter to epidemic disease. The English settlement
at Roanoke generated pestilence among natives. Disease, probably contracted from European fishermen and fur traders, swept through New
England in 1616–1617, clearing the way for the early Massachusetts
settlements. The most monumental depradations of epidemic disease
occurred in territories occupied by the Spanish. Historians have been all

too inclined to attribute demographic devastation among the Indians to the cruelty of conquistadors. Cruelty there was. The Bahamas and many of the Lesser Antilles were stripped of their populations to feed the mines of Hispaniola and the pearl fisheries of Venezuela. On Hispaniola, the site of Columbus's first settlement, natives were brutalized and enslaved, but their precipitous decline was accelerated by disease. With the limited evidence at our disposal, it is impossible to offer precise numerical estimates for the Amerindian "contact" population of Hispaniola. Although scholarly estimates for the island range from 100,000 to eight million, most scholars consider one million an entirely reasonable, if not modest, figure.[47] By 1548, just a half-century after the Spanish landings, Gonzala Fernandez Oviedo, a contemporary historian, asserted that surviving descendants of the original population numbered about 500.

Smallpox was not among the early killers of Hispaniola Indians. It arrived in epidemic form in 1519 and finished off a thoroughly weakened population. The disease invaded Puerto Rico and Cuba with similar effects, then vaulted to the mainland with or before Cortez's hardy band of conquistadors. That the mighty Aztec Empire of Central Mexico should fall to several hundred Spaniards in two years is attributable more to disease than to valor. Smallpox raged in the Aztec capital for sixty days before Cortez launched his final successful attack. A similar fate would befall the Inca Empire of upland Peru.[48]

All through tropical and subtropical America, Indian populations were decimated, authority structures were dissolved, and native confidence was broken as Americans repeatedly witnessed the agonizing deaths of their fellows while Europeans, protected by their immunities, survived unscathed. Although estimates of the contact population are highly speculative, all the figures offered by scholars bear grisly witness to the tragedy. Focusing on Central Mexico, William Sanders estimated the Indian population in 1520 to have been 11.4 million. Sherburne Cook and Woodrow Borah, spokesmen of the California school of historical demographers, argued for 25–28 million, Henry Dobyns for 30 million.[49] What we know with some certainty is that the native population of Central Mexico in 1600, eighty years after the conquest, was scarcely above one million. If we adopt Sanders's comparatively low estimate, the demographic collapse in Central Mexico exceeded 85 percent.

There is little doubt that Europeans would have overcome the resistance of Amerindians even if the latter had not been decimated by diseases of the Eastern hemisphere.[50] European penetration of the densely populated and culturally more developed East Indies and India testifies to that. White men had weapons of steel and cannons that wrought terror and destruction. They had horses for mobility, sailing ships to deliver soldiers along the coast, and technical skills that awed primitive opponents who faced their assailants with little more than obsidian-tipped spears, arrows, and clubs. Yet who would deny the tenacity or ferocity of healthy Iroquois, Sioux, or Apache warriors? Against a healthy native population, European conquest would have been long and arduous. Charles I (1516–1556), Cortez's sovereign lord, had no troops to spare for America. His reign and that of his son, Philip II (1556–1598), were consumed by struggles with the French, Turks, and Protestants. Even with so formidable an ally as disease, Europeans did not swarm to the open spaces of the New World before the nineteenth century. In 1800, North America, the most hospitable region for European settlement, had only five million whites. Central America, South America, and the West Indian islands contained far fewer.

Without the social, demographic, and psychological ruination caused by disease, Native Americans would not have surrendered their gold and silver so readily, nor would they have permitted, without heavy casualties, great tracts of tropical and semi-tropical land to be absorbed by plantations of sugar, coffee, tobacco, and rice. Europe's "windfall" in America would have been much more painfully earned, much more costly in manpower and money, and much slower to materialize. The timing and the contours of Western capitalism would have been different. Certainly, Professor Wallerstein would have had fewer reasons to contemplate a capitalist world-system in the sixteenth century.

Disease in Animals

Animal disease, though rarely treated by historians, has exercised important influence in human affairs. One example will suffice. In 1889, on the eve of European conquest in East Africa, rinderpest, an alien cattle disease, was introduced to the region with animals brought from Asia to provision Italian soldiers. Rinderpest spread quickly to all parts of East Africa, killing up to 90 percent of the herds of pastoral peoples. Starvation followed. As many as two-thirds of the Masai died of famine, and great tracts of grazing land lay vacant. The ecological balance was disturbed, and the range of the tsetse fly, carrier of deadly sleeping sickness, expanded in the region. Authority structures collapsed, and regional political balances were altered. As for the political balance between Africans and Europeans, Lord Lugard, speaking for the British, drew these conclusions: "Powerful and warlike as the pastoral tribes are, their pride has been humbled and our progress facilitated by this awful visitation. The advent of the white man had else not been so peaceful."[51]

ECOLOGICAL IMPERIALISM

The overseas expansion of European animal species—vermin, domesticated animals, and the diseases of both—constitutes a further dimension of environmental history. Alfred Crosby has documented what he calls ecological imperialism, the invasion of Australia, New Zealand, Southern Africa, and the Americas by Europe's fauna and flora as well as its people. Prior to Columbus, there were no cattle, horses, pigs, goats, or sheep in the Americas. There were no sheep in Australia or New Zealand, although by 1974 New Zealanders were grazing 55 million sheep. Rabbits did not arrive in Australia until 1859. Less than a century later, the rabbit population was estimated at around 500 million, and rabbits had become serious competitors with cattle and sheep—both European imports—for the continent's natural grasses. To everyone's dismay, Europe has exported its weeds—notably, for the suburban lawn-keeper, the dandelion and the plantain. Across the pampas of Argentina, only about a quarter of the grasses now growing are native to America. The intercontinental transfer of plants is an important element of environmental history, one that has direct bearing on the modern explosion of population. If Europeans introduced wheat, wine grapes, sugar cane, olives, the banana, and various fruits to America, they received, in return, maize, potatoes, tomatoes, peanuts, manioc, cacao, various types of beans, pumpkins, and squashes. Maize and potatoes provide comparatively high caloric output per acre, the latter being particularly suited to the cool, often damp climate of the North European plain extending from Germany to the Urals. When the potato was introduced to this region, it generated four times the caloric value per acre of rye, the only reliable grain crop in that climate. Because it could be planted on fallowed fields needed for the successful cultivation of rye, the potato supplemented without reducing the production of grain.[52] During Europe's nineteenth-century population explosion, the potato dominated the diet of the poor.[53]

CONCLUSION

Among the topics treated in this chapter, disease provides a better prospect for understanding universal developments than climate, although the secular rhythms of climate and disease exhibit considerable similarity in pre-modern European history. The ebb and flow that demographic historians have attributed to Malthusian forces coincides with the patterning of epidemic disease in Europe. Falling population in the latter centuries of the ancient world can be attributed to the interpenetration of Eurasian disease pools, compounded in the sixth century by plague. The consolidation of a homogeneous pool across the Eastern hemisphere by the year 1000 permitted a general resumption of population growth until the second universal assault of plague arrived in the fourteenth century. Growth returned everywhere in the sixteenth century—except in America, where European conquest and Indian collapse were largely a function of disease. Demographic and economic decline in the final centuries of the ancient world coincided with a cool climatic phase. The period of growth from the tenth to the fourteenth century occurred in a warm phase. The fourteenth-century crisis was experienced during a period of climatic variability that led, by the sixteenth century, to the Little Ice Age. The extent to which all these phenomena may be linked is, as yet, undetermined.

Environmental history is all-embracing. No single historian can possibly master every aspect of the field, and apart from sweeping (albeit unverifiable) hypotheses like Lovelock's Gaia hypothesis, it is difficult to comprehend how anyone or any group could generate a governing model that would effectively encompass climate, disease, demography, culture, and everyday politics. Yet, as inhabitants of an endangered planet, we can no longer ignore the environmental implications of everyday politics, nor can we dismiss the political implications of population pressure, infectious disease, or global warming. No orientation to history is more sensitive to human interdependence in the global village than environmental history, nor is any more conscious of the mutual dependence of humans and other creatures—whether wild or tame, of land or of sea. Environmental history raises our sights to another level—beyond commercial, class, or demographic analysis. It does not supplant these forms of analysis. It enlarges them. It alters our perspective and compels us to seek creative methodologies that will enable us to integrate more effectively the *longue durée* and *l'histoire événementielle*.

NOTES

1. Fairfield Osborn, *Our Plundered Planet* (Boston, 1948).
2. William Vogt, *Road to Survival* (New York, 1948), p. 28.
3. Rachel Carson, *Silent Spring* (Boston, 1962), pp. 2, 16–17, 263–275.

4. Barbara Ward and René Dubos, *Only One Earth: The Care and Maintenance of a Small Planet* (New York, 1972), xviii.

5. A distinguished body of scientific and intellectual leaders from 58 countries served as consultants to Ward and Dubos, who had been commissioned to prepare a report on the United Nations Conference on the Human Environment, May 1971.

6. J. E. Lovelock, *Gaia: A New Look at Life on Earth* (New York, 1979), p. 9.

7. Lovelock observed: "The chemical composition of the atmosphere bears no relation to the expectations of steady-state chemical equilibrium. The presence of methane, nitrous oxide, and even nitrogen in our present oxidizing atmosphere represents violation of the rules of chemistry to be measured in tens of orders of magnitude." Ibid., p. 10.

8. Ibid., pp. 120–121.

9. This argument was affirmed by a group of Russian scholars who adopted a position not unlike that of Lovelock. N. N. Moisseiev, Yu. M. Svirezhev, V. F. Krapivin, and A. M. Tarko, "Biosphere Models," in Robert W. Kates, Jesse Ausubel, and Mimi Berberian, eds., *Climate Impact Assessment: Studies of the Interaction of Climate and Society* (New York, 1985), p. 494.

10. In particular, see Frederick Jackson Turner, *The Frontier in American History* (New York, 1920), and Walter Prescott Webb, *The Great Plains* (Boston, 1952).

11. First entitled *Annales d'histoire économique et sociale*, the journal's name was changed in 1946 to *Annales, Economies, Sociétés, Civilisations*. It is closely linked to the Sixth Section of the Ecole Practique des Hautes Etudes, founded in 1947 in Paris as an interdisciplinary center for scholarship in the social sciences.

12. George Iggers, *New Directions in European Historiography* (Middletown, 1975), p. 57. Iggers offers a comprehensive treatment of the *Annales* tradition.

13. There are numerous historiographical analyses of the *Annales* tradition. See Maurice Aymard, "The *Annales* and French Historiography (1929–72)," *Journal of European Economic History* 1 (1972): 491–511; Robert Forster, "Achievements of the *Annales* School," *Journal of Economic History* 38 (1978): 58–75; J. H. Hexter, "Fernand Braudel and the *Monde Braudelien* . . . ," *Journal of Modern History* 44 (1972): 480–539; Lynn Hunt, "French History in the Last Twenty Years: The Rise and Fall of the *Annales* Paradigm," *Journal of Contemporary History* 21 (1986): 209–224; Samuel Kinser, "*Annaliste* Paradigm? Geohistorical Structuralism of Fernand Braudel," *American Historical Review* 86 (1981): 63–105; H. R. Trevor-Roper, "Fernand Braudel, the *Annales*, and the Mediterranean," *Journal of Modern History* 44 (1972): 468–479; Traian Stoianovich, *French Historical Method: The Annales Paradigm* (Ithaca, 1976).

14. Fernand Braudel, *The Mediterranean and the Mediterranean World in the Age of Philip II*, vol. 1, trans. Sian Reynolds (New York, 1972), p. 21.

15. This weakness may explain the reluctance of other Annalistes to work on so vast a scale. Most of Braudel's successors have focused on individual regions, provinces, or cities.

16. For a detailed statement of historiographical architecture of environmental history, see Donald Worster, "Doing Environmental History," in Worster, ed., *The Ends of the Earth* (Cambridge, 1988), pp. 289–307.

17. See, for example, Jennifer Robinson, "Global Modeling and Simulations," in Kates, Ausubel, and Berberian, eds., *Climate Impact Assessment*, pp. 469–492. Cultural anthropologists have provided environmental historians a reservoir of engaging

theoretical formulations about man and nature that serve as interesting points of departure. For example, Marvin Harris employs a model he calls "cultural materialism" to explain similarities and differences in the thought and behavior of diverse human groups. All groups of people are constrained by the need to produce food, shelter, and tools, and by the necessity to reproduce their numbers. The parameters within which humans struggle to satisfy these basic requirements are dictated by environment. "For cultural materialists," writes Harris, "the most likely causes of variation in the mental or spiritual aspects of human life are the variations in the material constraints affecting the way people cope with the problems of satisfying basic needs in a particular habitat." In effect, aesthetics; moral values; religious beliefs; political, legal, and social institutions—however important—are largely derivative of humans' encounter with the material and biological realities of their environment. Marvin Harris, *Culture, People, Nature: An Introduction to General Anthropology,* 3d ed. (New York, 1980), pp. 5, 116–119. For a full elaboration of this thesis, see Marvin Harris, *Cultural Materialism: The Struggle for a Science of Culture* (New York, 1979).

18. Braudel wrote:

The 'little ice age' . . . during Louis XIV's reign was more of a tyrant than the Sun King. Everything moved to its rhythm: cereal-growing in Europe and the rice fields and steppes of Asia; the olive groves of Provence and the Scandinavian countries where snow and ice, slow to disappear in normal circumstances, no longer left the corn sufficient time to ripen. . . . Natural disasters also multiplied in China in the middle of the seventeenth century—disastrous droughts, plagues of locusts—and a succession of peasant uprisings occurred in the interior provinces, as in France under Louis XIII. All this gives additional meaning to the fluctuations in material life, and possibly explains their simultaneity.

Fernand Braudel, *Capitalism and Material Life 1400–1800,* trans. Miriam Kochan (New York, 1975), p. 19.

19. Robert S. Lopez, *The Commercial Revolution of the Middle Ages, 950–1350* (Englewood Cliffs, 1971), p. 12.

20. Reid A. Bryson and Thomas J. Murray, *Climates of Hunger: Mankind and the World's Changing Weather* (Madison, 1977), p. 64.

21. F. Kenneth Hare, "Climatic Variability and Change," in Kates, Ausubel, and Berberian, eds., *Climatic Impact Assessment,* p. 63.

22. Reid A. Bryson and Christine Padoch, "On the Climates of History," *Journal of Interdisciplinary History* 10 (1980): 589.

23. Bryson and Murray, *Climates of Hunger,* pp. 49–55, 67.

24. For a discussion of the methods mentioned in this paragraph, see H. H. Lamb, *Climate, History and the Modern World* (London, 1982), pp. 67–100.

25. John D. Post, *The Last Great Subsistence Crisis in the Western World* (Baltimore, 1977), xii.

26. M. M. Postan, leading scholar of the demographic school, had acknowledged that famines in early fourteenth-century England were touched off by heavy rains and cold weather, but Postan preferred a Malthusian to a climatic explanation. Utterström tied population movements directly to climatic fluctuations, and he chastised the demographic school for failing to do the same. Gustaf Utterström, "Climatic Fluctuations and Population Problems in Early Modern History," *Scandinavian History Review* 3 (1955), reprinted in Worster, *The Ends of the Earth,* pp. 39–79. Utterström's position

is forcefully argued in H. H. Lamb, *Climate, History and the Modern World*, pp. 6, 187.

27. Braudel, *Capitalism and Material Life*, p. 18.

28. Theodore K. Rabb and Robert I. Rotberg, eds., *Climate and History: Studies in Interdisciplinary History* (Princeton, 1981). Papers presented in this book first appeared in the *Journal of Interdisciplinary History* 10 (1980). Thomas M. L. Wrigley, Martin J. Ingram, and Graham Farmer, eds., *Climate and History: Studies in Past Climates and Their Impact on Man* (Cambridge, 1981).

29. H. H. Lamb, who uses the most conventional dating, 1550–1850, notes that other scholars do employ other dates: 1300–1900, 1430–1850, 1550–1700. Lamb, *Climate, History and the Modern World*, p. 276. See also Lamb and Ingram, "Climate and History," p. 138.

30. H. H. Lamb and M. J. Ingram, "Climate and History," *Past and Present* 89 (1980): 138. This article was a report on the International Conference on Climate and History, Norwich, England, July 1979.

31. David Herlihy, "Climate and Documentary Sources: A Comment," *Journal of Interdisciplinary History* 10 (1980): 713.

32. Proxy evidence may also be fraught with imprecision. Le Roy Ladurie and Christian Pfister have compiled long runs of the dates when grape harvests were initiated in France and Switzerland. The earlier the start of harvest, the warmer the summer season, it is assumed. But the process of selecting the day to begin harvesting did not lie exclusively with the growers, nor was it based entirely upon when the grapes were mature. The decision was taken by government authorities in order to regulate economic enterprise and to prevent one group of growers from gaining comparative advantage over others by harvesting their crops early. Political influences must have penetrated the process as upland growers whose grapes would have ripened more slowly vied for influence against lowland growers who might have sought an early beginning of harvest. Herlihy, "Climate and Documentary Sources," pp. 716–717.

33. M. L. Parry, "Climatic Change and the Agricultural Frontier: A Research Strategy," in Wrigley, Ingram, and Farmer, eds., *Climate and History*, p. 321.

34. Jan de Vries, "Measuring the Impact of Climate on History: The Search for Appropriate Methodologies," *Journal of Interdisciplinary History* 10 (1980): 625.

35. Emmanuel Le Roy Ladurie, *Histoire du climat depuis l'an mil* (Paris, 1967), revised and translated into English as *Time of Feast, Time of Famine: A History of Climate since the Year 1000* (New York, 1971), p. 119. For strong confirmation of this, see J. L. Anderson, "Climatic Change in European Economic History," *Research in Economic History* 6 (1981): 1–34.

36. For an excellent overview of the state of climatic history from someone who is more optimistic than Le Roy Ladurie, see Robert H. Claxton, "Climate and History: From Speculation to Systematic Study," *The Historian* 45 (1983): 220–236.

37. For an abbreviated but highly stimulating presentation of many of the arguments lodged in *Plagues and Peoples*, see McNeill's *The Human Condition: An Ecological and Historical View* (Princeton, 1980).

38. William H. McNeill, *Plagues and Peoples* (Garden City, 1976).

39. Ibid., p. 60.

40. Ibid., p. 73.

41. Ibid., p. 137.

42. Ibid., p. 123.

43. The plague bacillus, *Pasteurella pestis*, was not discovered until 1894. Under pressure of an outbreak of plague in the Far East and India (six million deaths occurred in India in a decade), teams of scientists working at the beginning of the twentieth century gradually revealed the etiology of bubonic plague.

44. For a comparison of Christian and Moslem religious reactions, see Michael Dols, *The Black Death in the Middle East* (Princeton, 1977), pp. 122–124, 297.

45. Alfred W. Crosby, Jr., *The Columbian Exchange: Biological and Cultural Consequences of 1492* (Westport, 1972), pp. 2–29.

46. John W. Verano and Douglas H. Ubelaker, "Health and Disease in the Pre-Columbian World," in Herman J. Viola and Carolyn Margolis, eds., *Seeds of Change* (Washington, 1991), pp. 210–215.

47. See, for example, David Henige, "On the Contact Population of Hispaniola: History as High Mathematics," *Hispanic American Historical Review* 58 (1978): 217–237; R. A. Zambardino, "Critique of David Henige's 'On the Contact Population of Hispaniola,' " ibid., 700–708; Henige, "David Henige's Reply," ibid., 709–712.

48. For a thorough account of the disease exchanges occasioned by the merger of hemispheres, see Crosby's *The Columbian Exchange*, pp. 35–63, 122–164.

49. Woodrow Borah and Sherburne F. Cook, *The Aboriginal Population of Central Mexico on the Eve of the Spanish Conquest* (Berkeley, 1963), pp. 1–5, 88–91; Borah and Cook, *Essays in Population History: Mexico and the Caribbean*, vol. 1 (Berkeley, 1971), p. 115. William T. Sanders, "The Population of the Central Mexican Symbiotic Region, the Basin of Mexico, and the Teotihuacan Valley in the Sixteenth Century," in William M. Denevan, ed., *The Native Population of the Americas in 1492* (Madison, 1976), pp. 85–150. Denevan's book incorporates numerous articles and statistics dealing with all areas of the Americas.

50. Smallpox, chicken pox, measles, and cholera were brought to America by Europeans. Malaria, yellow fever, typhus, and typhoid may have been of African origin. Murdo J. MacLeod, *Spanish Central America: A Socioeconomic History, 1520–1720* (Berkeley, 1973), p. 16. Of America's native diseases, only venereal syphilis had any profound impact upon the Old World.

51. Quoted in Helge Kjekshus, *Ecology Control and Economic Development in East African History: The Case of Tanganyika, 1850–1950* (Berkeley, 1977), p. 131.

52. William H. McNeill, "American Food Crops in the Old World," in Viola and Margolis, eds., *Seeds of Change*, pp. 46–50.

53. The potato offers adequate nutrition for humans with minimal need of supplement. See William L. Langer, "Europe's Initial Population Explosion," *American Historical Review* 69 (1963): 1–17, and Langer, "American Foods and Europe's Population Growth, 1750–1850," *Journal of Social History* 8 (1975): 51–66.

Part IV

Summation

9

The Continuing Pursuit of Order

I began this book by observing that different people perceive the logic of history in different ways. If this is true of contemporaries, as I have repeatedly stressed, it is doubly the case for historians who have written in different centuries. Medieval writers considered history to be the slow, steady unfolding of God's will. In our time, no historian of renown, whatever his or her religious conviction, explains historical causation by reference to on-going divine intervention. Because we live in a materialist century, we commonly explain the process of change by reference to materialist forces—and these differ.

Our geographic focus has also shifted. In recent centuries, Europe led the world in the arts of civilization. Europe acted, the rest of the world reacted. It appeared entirely logical, therefore, for Western scholars to pursue the inner dynamic of history in the context of European experience. With the waning of European influence and the rise of a "global village" mentality, Western historians have begun to employ models of change that have a more universal application.

In the post-industrial world, change occurs at an alarming rate. Our way of life may be more remote from that of George Washington, Thomas Jefferson, and Andrew Jackson than theirs was from ancient Romans. The dynamics that underlie Western man's transition from a profoundly religious agrarian society regulated by customary practice and personal relationships to a secular, urban, industrial society regulated by bureaucracy are infinitely complex. The models examined in this book represent attempts by historians to fathom that process. Most of the historians treated here identify key changes in Western society between the tenth and eighteenth centuries with the rise and evolution of capitalism. Of course, "capitalism" is an abstraction, an omnibus term that means different things to different people, and the unwary student who stalks "capitalism" through the pages of numerous histories will find himself in pursuit of a perpetually moving target.

HISTORIANS AND THE RISE OF CAPITALISM

How one defines capitalism depends largely on one's theory of change. Still, everyone can agree on certain fundamentals. Capitalism involves the exchange of moveable goods for the purpose of earning profit in markets that employ a money economy. This definition suffices for some, not for others. Marxists contend that capitalism is primarily a mode of production that supports a particular set of class relations. Wallerstein insists that the inception of capitalism required the evolution of a trans-hemispheric world-system. Weber took a less structured view. For him, capitalism was a way of life, an orientation derived from particular religious foundations that inspired rational economic behavior and a dutiful orientation to profit making.

Since capitalism is variously defined, historians offer different timetables for its inception and development. With his relatively uncomplicated market orientation, Henri Pirenne located the origins of capitalism in expanding European towns of the twelfth century. Weber acknowledged the importance of markets, the evolution of an urban proletariat, and the improvement of business techniques in the late Middle Ages, but capitalism as a way of life did not take hold, he thought, until the Protestant Reformation of the sixteenth century. For quite different reasons—notably, the discovery of America and the exploitation of its mineral resources—Wallerstein also assigned a sixteenth-century date to the rise of capitalism. Marxists admit that the feudal mode of production was largely defunct by the sixteenth century. Nevertheless, the class structure of feudalism lingered in Europe during the Age of Absolutism, and the transition to capitalism, achieved in England in the seventeenth century, did not occur on the continent, Marxists argue, until the eighteenth century.

The late Fernand Braudel, possibly the most esteemed historian of the twentieth century, closed the interpretive ring by combining world-system analysis with the old commercial model. In a three-volume masterwork, the luxurious product of a lifetime of scholarship, he scanned the entire range of interpretive opinion from Pirenne through Wallerstein.[1] Although he borrowed Wallerstein's core-periphery concept, he rejected his notion that European capitalism waited upon the exploitation of Peruvian bullion. Braudel challenged every pillar of Marxist explanation except its materialism. Having minimized the importance of agrarian developments in the evolution of capitalism, he recoiled from the Marxist definition of capitalism as a system of production, and he dismissed the proposition that historical time should be or can be measured by successive changes in mode of production. History is too complicated for that, Braudel wrote: every mode of production coexists with every other in ways that enhance the power of the elite at the core. Similarly, Braudel discounted demographic explanations. It was improvements in agricultural technology and the demand pull of the towns that generated demographic change in pre-modern Europe, not the reverse.[2]

Concurring with almost every social-scientific scholar who has pursued these matters, Braudel judged modernity to be synonymous with capitalism. With Adam Smith, he believed that capitalism was rooted in commerce, that the size of the market determines division of labor, and that division of labor has given rise to the modern economy. In effect, Braudel returned to the place where we began, to the commercial division of labor model, but he presented that argument with a different perspective. For him, capitalism was more than large-scale exchange in a market economy. It was the *exclusive* realm of great financiers. Like birds of prey, they hovered above the economic landscape, diving opportunely to swoop up carefully selected rewards. Theirs was the exercise of raw money power.

They moved money freely from trade to state loans to manufacture. They intervened where they chose, how they chose, when they chose, and for as long as they chose, always in the interest of profit. If, as Wallerstein argued, the capitalist world-economy encompassed a spatial hierarchy of economic zones, the economy of the core area was also hierarchically divided. At its top resided the capitalists, and they controlled it all.

While achieving a marriage between the commercial and world-system theories, Braudel imparted a very different emphasis to Wallerstein's model. Where Wallerstein, true to his Marxist origins, concentrated on production, Braudel emphasized commercial forces and focused on circulation. He saw great concentrations of money power reaching out and setting in motion the productive systems of the periphery.[3] Where did this money power come from? From the early trade of towns, Braudel argued. Echoing Pirenne, he agreed that money power achieved its highest level of concentration among long-distance traders who earned extraordinary profits by exploiting the price differentials prevailing in widely separated markets. Europe's political structure did not inhibit the accumulation of great wealth in private family dynasties, and by the thirteenth century significant private holdings had given rise to the mentalities and instrumentalities of capitalism. Everything was in place, he wrote: "bills of exchange, credit, minted coins, banks, forward selling, public finance, loans, . . . colonialism—as well as social disturbances, as a sophisticated labour force, class struggles, social oppression, and political atrocities."[4] Two evolving nodes of capitalist development—one in the Low Countries, the other in northern Italy—were united at the Champagne fairs. Thereafter, Europe was bisected by a Venice-Bruges-London axis. A "string of glittering towns" prospered astride that axis (Augsburg, Nuremberg, Regensburg, Ulm, Basle, Strasbourg, and Cologne, to name a few), and the first capitalist world-economy, a coherent, interdependent, and largely autonomous economic network, came to life.

Where Wallerstein emphasized regions of the world-economy, Braudel concentrated on cities. Each world-economy, he argued, possessed a single urban metropole, and each metropole was distinguished by its command of the money supply, credit, and comprehensive exchange facilities. A capitalist world-economy centering on Venice was in being nearly three centuries before Wallerstein's sixteenth-century Atlantic-oriented model took form. Moreover, the mantle of leadership shifted with some frequency—from Venice to Antwerp around 1500; thence to Genoa after 1568; to Amsterdam after 1627; subsequently to London and New York.[5]

Braudel's emphasis on long-distance trade, a market-determined division of labor, and the vital role of cities—"like yeast in some mighty dough"—has reshaped and revitalized the commercial orientation that dominated historical explanation in the years between the world wars. Like Pirenne, Braudel located the roots of capitalism in early medieval Europe, although Braudel's more refined and hierarchical definition of capitalism confines it to Europe's predatory rich at the summits of economic life. Like earlier proponents of a trade-based model, Braudel is progressivist. Occasional mention is made of a fourteenth-century crisis or a fifteenth-century recession, but such references fail to daunt his upward and onward orientation to European economic history.

The Braudelian interpretation may have closed the interpretive circle, but his model is certain to generate as much skepticism as the other theories examined in this book. Braudel is exceedingly vague about the internal geographical hierarchy of the world-systems he describes. Even though he accepted Wallerstein's contention that the wealth of the core could be achieved only at the expense of the periphery, he made no attempt to specify core-periphery distinctions in terms of the production of primary as opposed to secondary goods. Most important, the internal dynamic that shaped relationships between tiers of the Braudelian world-economy is not clear.

EXPANDING USE OF WORLD-SYSTEM THEORY

Braudel is one of many scholars to embrace the core-periphery concept. André Gunder Frank, having accepted Wallerstein's elaboration upon his own dependency theory, has stridently advocated world-system analysis as a means of structuring world history over the past five thousand years.[6] The dean of world historians, William McNeill, has also offered his blessing. McNeill has reaffirmed his faith in "civilization" as the chief organizing principle in world history, and he continues to defend cultural diffusion as a motor of historical change. But these, he argues, are no longer sufficient. Because advanced civilizations intersected, overlapped, and interpenetrated, historians should employ a higher organizational model to identify and explain significant trans-civilizational developments. After B.C. 1700, McNeill declares, a world-system emerged in the Middle East. For a time, it was "preserved within ever-widening boundaries of a succession of great empires—Egyptian, Hittite, Assyrian, Babylonian, and Persian"; later, it encompassed the entire continental land mass from the Mediterranean to the Pacific.[7] The societies of ancient Greece and India, until now studied as distinct civilizations, should be integrated as elements of an expanding Middle Eastern world system. Special efflorescence passed from region to region within this ancient world system, McNeill asserts: from Hellenic civilization (B.C. 500–A.D. 200) to Indic (200–600), to Muslim (600–1000), to Chinese (1000–1500). Then, with European penetration of America, the mantle of world hegemony passed to the West.

Histories of the kind proposed by McNeill have already begun to appear. In 1989, Janet Abu-Lughod described the complex operation of a thirteenth-century Middle Eastern world-system. Its range extended from northwestern Europe to China.[8] Abu-Lughod is intent to show that Wallerstein's sixteenth-century capitalist world-system was not the first of its kind and that European society had no inherent qualities that rendered it exceptionally capable of achieving the breakthrough to capitalism. Except for the peculiar sequence of events that dissolved the thirteenth-century world-system, writes Abu-Lughod, modern capitalism might have developed outside of Europe. The rise of the West, she concludes, was preceded and facilitated by the fall of the East.

Applying the world-system model before 1500 is problematic. Premodern links between regions of the Afro-Eurasian ecumene were relatively thin, and evidence of them is difficult to unveil. Abu-Lughod's conceptualization of a thirteenth-century world-system is founded on her conclusion that interregional commerce in both primary and manufactured goods increased significantly after 1250. Her world-system comprises an "archipelago of cities"—among them Bruges, Venice, Cairo, Baghdad, Samarkand, Calicut, Canton—where rich merchant communities conducted inter-regional commerce with the aid of sophisticated exchange institutions that involved credit, the pooling of capital, and the sharing of risks.

What Abu-Lughod describes as a "system" has no single hegemon, no central core, no overarching hierarchy, and no clear geographical configuration. There is no explicitly defined interregional division of labor in her thirteenth-century world-system, nor does the "system" appear to require geographically differentiated methods of production for its efficient operation. Abu-Lughod has identified a far-flung network of commercial exchange that affected peoples from Bruges to Canton, but skeptics will ask whether the definition of this network as a system is not a case of academic hyperbole. No one, not even Braudel, has been as rigorous as Wallerstein in defining and integrating the numerous components of the world-system model. For Abu-Lughod, the core-periphery concept is more an organizing principle than a comprehensive theoretical model, and there is every reason to expect that Wallerstein's exacting criteria for what constitutes a legitimate world "system" will be diluted in forthcoming premodern world histories.

Wallerstein's work poses a dilemma for Third World historians as well as for world historians who write about the pre-modern era. His appealing and highly integrated analysis of capitalist development during the sixteenth century links Europe with the Western hemisphere, but it excludes Asia and Africa, thereby leaving three of the world's four great civilizations—China, India, and the Near East—outside of his formulation on the origins of capitalism. Abu-Lughod and others contend that the rise of capitalist modernity need not, as Wallerstein's model suggests, have occurred in the West. The fact remains, however, that capitalism *did* arise in the West. And the most compelling historical question of our time is, why? Why Europe?

COMPARATIVE WORLD HISTORY: WHY EUROPE?

Among the theorists treated in this book, only two, Max Weber and Immanuel Wallerstein (Weber more than Wallerstein), have undertaken the type of comparative analysis needed to address that question. Weber considered it myopic to engage in elaborate causal analysis of the rise of capitalism in Europe before careful study had been undertaken of other great civilizations. For all we know, he insisted, the factors and forces that Eurocentric historians consider to have been evocative of capitalism in Europe could have been amply present in other civilizations as well.

In an exemplary book, Eric Jones addresses the question—why Europe?—through comparative analysis of the four great civilizations. Jones is a world historian, an economic historian, an environmentalist. He is not an exponent of world-system theory, although clearly he has been influenced by Wallerstein. His topic is universal. It requires a universal framework, a common basis upon which to evaluate political, economic, social, and religious developments in four widely separated regions of Eurasia. Ignoring the possibility raised by Sombart that the ability of different peoples to sustain complex forms of civilization is biologically (therefore genetically) determined, Jones concludes that environment—physical habitat, climate, and disease—has been a most formidable influence upon the cultural habits and institutions of human beings. If all peoples encounter their environments with the same biological endowments, then environment itself must constitute the principal variable evoking diverse cultural responses.

By 1500, Jones argues, Europeans had the highest real wages of any of the world's most civilized peoples. Europe ranked third, behind China and India, in aggregate biomass (the total weight of humans and animal livestock), but Europeans had more working capital per head, more meat in their diets, more draught animals, more timber per person, more iron, higher literacy per capita, a more equitable distribution of income, and a better ability to obtain what they lacked through trade.[9] In substantial part, these advantages were the reward of environment. Europe was not troubled by schistosomiasis and worm infestations common to hot climates where irrigation agriculture prevailed and human excrement was used as fertilizer. Endoparasitic infestations that reduced human energy levels narrowed the real manpower gap between Europe and Asia. Watered by rainfall, European soils generally yielded less than the soils of Asia. Still, Europeans did not attempt to maximize crops by sowing all areas in which arable farming was possible. They persistently held population below the maximum and kept land back for livestock husbandry and woodland use.

Population control in Europe was achieved through the nuclear family, a family system that discouraged marriage until a couple could acquire sufficient land or goods to establish an independent household. If Europeans married late, Asians married early, maximizing family size. One effect of maximizing population was the need for irrigation farming. This, in turn, required the construction and coordination of large hydraulic works, projects that promoted the establishment of despotic, authoritarian regimes. Maximization of population in Asia was deliberately calculated to provide families with enough male children to facilitate recovery from environmental disasters. Because the environment of India and China was particularly susceptible to "shocks," males were favored over females and cows were venerated over oxen. Males offered greater physical strength, and cows served as essential breeding stock during post-disaster recovery (also, in a pinch, cows could function as draught animals).

Jones considers risk environment the crucial determinant of social behavior. An Asian was thirty times more likely to die in an earthquake than a European. Floods, drought, and famine were more frequent and more severe in Asia. Locusts were a recurring problem in Asia, not in Europe. Of all shocks, war was the most profound. Jones believes that the human costs of war were higher in Asia and that the loss of capital equipment was heavier still. Capital equipment in Europe was atomistic in nature— fences, roads, houses, livestock. Except in the Netherlands, there was little hydraulic agriculture with costly dykes that were vulnerable to destruction in time of war.[10] Because risks were greater for Asians than Europeans, the former attempted to maximize their numbers as an adaptation to the mortality peaks caused by environmental catastrophes and war. Enjoying a more stable environment, Europeans were able to limit fertility so that despite their lower soil yields, they accumulated capital more rapidly and were "in the *very* long term slightly but significantly better off than their Asian counterparts."[11]

A vital aspect of Europe's evolution toward capitalism, the consistent onward drift of technology, does not lend itself to environmental explanation. Nor can this drift be explained by market forces or by demography alone, since advances in technology often accompanied price recessions and demographic retreat, as in the fifteenth and seventeenth centuries. Europe's propensity to modernize through technology was not occasioned by a shortage of raw materials. In fact, this forward technological drift does not even appear to have been strongly driven by economic forces. Although many of the most important technological innovations embraced by Europeans were borrowed from Asia—the compass, printing, and gunpowder from China; others from the Middle East—Europeans commonly refined those borrowed technologies to a degree beyond that of their Asian originators. This was as true of gunpowder as it was of printing. When the composite effect of these new technologies had ignited "the fires of modernization," those fires "burned quickly to the fringes of this European system," wrote Jones. There they stopped, at the frontiers of Islam. Moslems showed no sign of response and no inclination to emulate the West.[12]

It was advancing technology combined with sheer energy that carried European power to America. What is most important and most characteristic about the exploitation of America is Europe's ability to rationalize and develop New World resources.[13] Like Wallerstein, Jones contends that Europe's ecological windfall in the New World stimulated unprecedented system-wide economic growth. Also like Wallerstein, Jones contends that the most important factor in the rational exploitation of America was Europe's political plurality—a states system that was decentralized, flexible, and intensely competitive.

After Rome, there was no successfully constructed empire across the whole of Europe. Europe developed a system of states that was maintained through balance of power. To some extent at least, political plurality was a product of environment. The core areas around which several of the most important states took their rise—the Paris basin, the Thames basin, the Po valley, and Flanders—were areas of good soil and relatively high productivity. In effect, they were areas that offered a relatively large base for taxation. As late as the fourteenth century, there were up to 1,000 polities in Europe; by the fifteenth century, 500; by the nineteenth century, 25. The core areas of most surviving states are traceable to a fertile heartland that amply supported its occupiers in extending their sway over neighboring lands. Jones is not an environmental determinist, and he acknowledges that environment alone did not dictate the shape of European states. Environment interacted with human personality, dynastic marriage, luck in battle, and other variables, but it was a major factor in the process.[14]

Along with Wallerstein, Jones characterizes large imperial states as economically inefficient, subject to corruption, and prone to taking economic decisions for political reasons. The European states system produced a spirit of competition that encouraged the diffusion of sound economic practices. If one state excluded or expelled disfavored groups of entrepreneurs, other states having different attitudes readily admitted them. The states system, wrote Jones, was "an insurance against economic and technological stagnation."[15] It was not sufficient cause for Europe's extraordinary economic development, but it was a necessary cause of the particular form of development that occurred.[16] The key to the European economic miracle is to be found in politics.

Of the other three great civilizations, only pre-modern China had any prospect of achieving an early breakthrough to capitalism, Jones argues. The Ottoman Empire of the Middle East, with a relatively small population (less than 30 million), was a "plunder machine." It operated an economic system that relied on "confiscation, displacement, and a total, calculated, insecurity of life and property."[17] The Mughal rulers of India were as oppressive and despoiling as the Ottomans. Although taxes were burdensome, taxes secured the people no real help against disasters. As Max Weber had noted, caste imposed endless restrictions on human interaction in the labor market, serving thereby as a formidable impediment to economic development. Hindu religious scruples, including taboos against the killing of rodents and insects, contributed to disease problems. The subcontinent had few navigable rivers, and inland communications were difficult.

China is a more difficult case. The Chinese had the technology, economic sophistication, and infrastructure to upstage the West, but Ming overlords (1368–1644) systematically promoted agriculture at the expense of industry. In the fifteenth century, Chinese armadas ventured as far as Zanzibar, but such seaborne adventurism (as impressive as that of either the Portuguese or Columbus) was abruptly terminated by political authorities in the interest of continental defense. In all the world's great civilizations, kings and emperors were extractive. Asian rulers were especially plunderous and given to arbitrary violence upon their subjects. No Asian civilization experienced an ecological windfall on the scale of America, but Europe's conquest of America did not occur until the sixteenth century, and by then, as Jones has noted, Europeans already enjoyed a higher average standard of wealth than the peoples of China, India, or the Middle East.

Jones's work tackles the most compelling historical issue of our time—why Europe? It is rooted in theory, creative in the questions it asks, and courageous, though not reckless, in the interpretations it offers. Such macrohistory cannot be written without sound, defensible theory. Historians who work within narrow time frames in regional or national histories might question whether comparative history on the scale attempted by Jones is feasible. Certainly, the data available from different cultures, though massive, is uneven. That which merited the attention of record-keepers in one age or one society may have been of little interest in others. Because the documentary record between civilizations is skewed, vast comparative analyses, like that undertaken by Jones, cannot even pretend to be definitive. This caveat does not negate the value of asking big questions. The importance of historical questions bears no necessary relationship to the availability or consistency of historical data, and no history, whatever its scale, can pretend to be entirely definitive. To grapple with big questions, one must often disregard regional experience. But the importance of regional history is not thereby diminished, for the ultimate value of large-scale patterns and of the macrohistorical models they inspire rests upon their ability to accommodate large numbers of diverse regional histories.

In his comparative history, Jones draws upon many of the models examined in this book without formally adhering to any. In fact, he questions whether historians should even seek the breakthrough to capitalist modernity in positive forces such as commercial innovations, demographic behavior, or Protestant ethics. On the contrary, Jones suggests, we should be attentive to negative factors, to the political, economic, religious, and environmental conditions that impeded economic development. Everywhere people tried to maximize material gains, and all the major civilizations exhibited considerable creativity and energy. But some were subject to more stringent constraints than others. Negative environmental constraints do not, in themselves, explain why Europe achieved an economic breakthrough and Asia did not, but they do help us to understand how and why political distinctions arose between the Orient and Occident. In this way, environmental factors provide powerful reinforcement to a theory of comparative history based fundamentally on political criteria.[18]

Jones's book makes comparative judgments that will be tested and retested by scholars working in the several geographical regions he surveyed. Although his work builds on a generation of scholarship in world history, it represents a fresh, almost breathtaking invitation to apply grand theory on a vast scale. If Braudel closed the circle on the theories of change commonly employed to explain historical developments in European history, Jones widens our range of inquiry and deftly employs universal environmental criteria in an attempt to answer universal questions. His work is a prime example of the degree to which both the complexity and the scale of historical inquiry have evolved in this century.

All the great theoreticians studied in this book have attempted to understand the past by discovering the process through which meaningful change occurs. The facts of history have significance only when they are integrated into an organic concept of change. In this regard, the historian's attempt to fathom the mysteries of history may be likened to the mental process of a great chef who is challenged to devine the recipe of an elaborate and many-layered cake by savoring a mere sliver of it. The great chef, his tastes acute, subtle, and refined, might with little difficulty recognize the chief ingredients of the cake, just as a historian might fathom the chief ingredients of a historical situation. But having identified ingredients, neither the chef nor the historian would have proceeded beyond the most preliminary stage of his assignment. If the chef is to reproduce the cake, he must determine how much of each ingredient was used, in what order the ingredients were joined, for how long, and at what temperature they were baked. Then, and only then, can he posit a recipe. Only by a similar endeavor can the historian posit an organic explanation of change, a model. In reality, neither the truly great chef nor the truly great historian is ever likely to get it entirely right.

REVISING THE FRAMEWORK OF HISTORY

In Part I of this book I examined the framework of history, the subdivision of time into historical periods. It was observed that periodization is one of the most pervasive and influential theoretical properties of history, one that determines how we derive images, draw associations, and perceive the beginning, middle, and ending of things. Historical periods, it was noted, assume a life of their own, being nurtured from generation to generation in the structure of university departments, the training of graduate students, the focus of professional journals, and the writing of texts. We continue to use a tripartite division of European historical time—ancient, medieval, modern—with watershed dates around 500 and 1500. These dates reflect concepts of continuity and change embraced by our intellectual forefathers. Not only have historians persisted in them, but they have adopted 1500 as the principal divide for the study of world history. Do the rhythms of world history so conform to those of Europe that the two periodizations actually harmonize? Have our historical priorities and the theoretical concepts we employ to explain historical dynamics not undergone change since tripartite periodization was adopted? Is it time to reconsider periodization?

How do the dynamic models of change that are examined in this book challenge or confirm existing modes of periodization? For the commercial division of labor model, it is partly a question of focus. Should we concentrate on social elites or on the commonalty? In drawing an epochal frontier around 1500, we have subscribed to an elitist position, for in 1500, substantial material change was experienced almost exclusively by people of wealth, education, and influence. As has been noted on several occasions, there was no significant growth in per capita income in Europe until the nineteenth century. Commercial institutions, business techniques, and division of labor were developing (with occasional setbacks) from the twelfth century, but a major change in consumer behavior did not occur until the eighteenth century. Neil McKendrick has shown that in England the consumer revolution of the eighteenth century occasioned a momentous historical discontinuity that sharply interrupted the gradual commercial gestation of earlier centuries:

> The eighteenth century marked a major watershed. Whatever popular metaphor is preferred—whether revolution or lift-off or the achievement of critical mass—the same unmistakable breakthrough occurred in consumption as occurred in production. Just as the Industrial Revolution of the eighteenth century marks one of the great discontinuities in history . . . so . . . does the matching revolution in consumption.[19]

There is little doubt that the Industrial Revolution constitutes one of the great watersheds in human experience. There is equally little doubt that it was vastly more than a revolution in technology. Historians have tended to concentrate on production in the Industrial Revolution. Of late, however, scholarly attention has shifted to the other side of the equation, to demand and to such subjects as consumerism. Although the basic institutions of capitalism (banking, bills of exchange, and the like) were in place by 1500, the trade-based division of labor model more emphatically points to the eighteenth and early nineteenth centuries as the critical time when old continuities were eroded and new continuities established.

The demographic explanation offered by neo-Malthusians achieves comfortable accommodation with standard epochal frontiers. The demographic cycle that commenced in the tenth century reached its apogee in the fourteenth. A Malthusian crisis compounded by the Black Death drove down population for a century and a half, but by 1500 a new growth phase was under way. The moment of transition from one demographic cycle to the other commenced around 1500. However, if demographic shifts, whatever their origins, constitute the main engine of change in history, the eighteenth century offers a much more emphatic point of departure for the modern world than the sixteenth. Figures on population before the industrial age are speculative, and different authors provide different numbers. All demographers agree, however, that European population, followed closely by world population, shot upward at an unprecedented rate after the eighteenth century. In Europe, population rose as much as 80 percent in the century between 1750 and 1850. This rate of growth was more than double that of any preceding hundred-year period, and scholars appropriately identify it as the "vital revolution." Humankind reached the one-billion population mark in 1850. Seventy-five years later it added the second billion; thirty-five years thereafter, the third.[20] Currently, world population stands at around 5 billion. It is expected to reach 6.2 billion by the year 2000 and 8.5 billion by 2025. Before leveling off at the end of the twenty-first century, world population could soar to 10 billion, a 1,000 percent growth in a mere 150 years![21] Whether we are experiencing a third great demographic cycle since the year 1000—and where in that cycle we might be—cannot be said for certain. What can be said is that this unparalleled upward thrust in population, the most remarkable and transforming demographic phenomenon in human history, began in the eighteenth century.

Like the practitioners of other materialist models, Marxists consider capitalism as a distinct morphological category requiring recognition as a separate epoch of history. Explaining the transition between the end of the feudal mode and the beginning of the capitalist mode of production has been a problem for them. Whatever explanation different Marxists have offered, they generally agree that capitalism as a new and dynamic mode of production did not come into being in Europe until the late seventeenth or the eighteenth century.

Surprisingly few historians have directly addressed the issue of periodization in the past half century. Those who have—Dietrich Gerhard, Geoffrey Barraclough, and Herbert Butterfield—have rejected standard tripartite periodization and the period break around 1500. Unlike the theoreticians we have studied, none of these authors has been primarily concerned with materialist phenomena. Barraclough, a medievalist, expressed the common outrage of his colleagues over popular misapprehensions that the Middle Ages was a dark and catastrophic time. He urged the adoption of a four-part periodization for European history after the fall of Rome: (1) European prehistory, to 800 or 900; (2) the age of the formation of European societies, 900–1300; (3) the "Middle Ages" of Europe, 1300–1789; and (4) the modern period from 1789 to the present. What gives coherence to this scheme is Barraclough's personal judgment that each of these four periods possesses continuities in ideas and attitudes. Modern attitudes—what Troeltsch called the modern outlook—did not arrive in Europe, he argues, until the eighteenth-century Enlightenment.[22]

Butterfield agreed that continuity prevailed "in the texture of history" between 1400 and at least 1660. He too rejected 1500 as a meaningful watershed, and he too was interested primarily in ideas. Butterfield considered the Scientific Revolution of the seventeenth century the intellectual progenitor of the Enlightenment and a new beginning for European civilization. While his essay is learned, his advocacy of the Scientific Revolution as a leading sector of historical change is idiosyncratic and episodic, being altogether unattached to any broader argument involving an unfolding intellectual process in history.[23]

Gerhard offers an aggregate view. Before 1000, he writes, "one cannot speak of *European* history."[24] For the centuries after 1000 he posits a perpetual dialectical confrontation between two conflicting orientations to civil life. On one side stood tradition, privilege, social stratification, corporate organization, and regional and local attachments; on the other, the desire for change, for equality, and for centralized power and authority. All European history from 1000 to 1800 is encompassed in this struggle. The forces of change gradually eroded the forces of tradition, and the French Revolution constituted the culminating climactic event in the transition from old Europe to modern Europe.[25] Gerhard's dialectical tension is not driven by an overriding force, as in the case of Marx's class struggle. Nor are his periods distinguished by conditions as specific as modes of production. By coincidence and happenstance, various social and institutional orientations appeared to jell in the eleventh century. In the eighteenth century those orientations were finally overwhelmed by others. The tension between them provided continuity to the interim centuries.

None of these writers employed sophisticated methodology in defining period frontiers. Exercising personal priorities, each identified the existence of significant forms of change, but none probed beneath those forms to determine whether a powerful and pervading undercurrent propels the process of change, thereby creating major transitional moments. Nevertheless, each of them offered important suggestions that resonate well with the process models we have examined.

In forming historical periods, it is imperative that we reject any specific date, whether 1000, 1300, 1500, or 1789, as denoting the end of one epoch and the commencement of another. Major discontinuities involving multiple aspects of civil life do not happen suddenly. Transitional eras must be seen as *eras*, extended periods of time having numerous significant moments when old continuities are displaced and new civil coherencies become established.

Two such eras stand out in post-Roman European history. The first lies between the ninth and eleventh centuries, much as Barraclough and Gerhard have suggested. It is the time when Viking, Saracen, and Magyar invasions ended, permitting greater division of labor, encouraging trade and the formation of towns, and facilitating the consolidation of feudal government. In church, state, and economy, it was an era when new foundations were laid or secured. Historical demographers declare this era the beginning of three centuries of population growth, the first leg in a macrohistorical demographic cycle. Marxist study of the transition from ancient slavery to the feudal mode of production is still in its infancy, but it has a rich beginning in the work of Perry Anderson, who contends that the transition was slow, that it made its way incrementally across the continent, and that it was not solidified until the tenth and eleventh centuries.[26] A period break in the tenth and eleventh centuries is consistent with all the models we have examined, the individual judgment of scholars who have addressed periodization, and the longstanding practice among medievalists of dividing the early from the high Middle Ages roughly at the year 1000.

The second great discontinuity occurs in the eighteenth century. More emphatically than any other division of time, an eighteenth-century period break possesses logical consistency with the models we have considered. Butterfield's advocacy of the Scientific Revolution does not confute this dating. The evolution of Western science was gradual, and the consolidation of what might be called a European scientific community may only have been achieved in the early eighteenth century.

The interim period, as Gerhard has argued, is characterized more by continuity than discontinuity. Our problem with it, for practical historians, is how to accommodate this eight-century span of time to the requirements of academic specialization and to the organization of the history curriculum.

Can a periodization contrived by Europeans for the study of European history provide a meaningful structure for the study of world history? World historians appear to think so. Periodizing on a global scale, they have, ironically, affirmed, not dismissed, epochal divisions created for European regional history. The consensus among world historians is that a major global discontinuity occurred around 1500, and this view is powerfully strengthened by the ecological and epidemiological studies of Alfred Crosby, Jr. Having measured the botanical implications of the merger of the hemispheres after 1492, Crosby offered the following sober conclusion:

> Not for a half a billion years, at least, and probably for long before that, has an extreme or permanent physical change affected the whole earth. The single exception to this generality may be European man and his technologies, agricultural and industrial. He has spread all over the globe, and non-European peoples have adopted his techniques in all but the smallest islets. His effect is comparable to an increase in the influx of cosmic rays or the raising of whole new chains of Andes and Himalayas.[27]

The theoretical requirements of global historians are not identical with those of regional historians. World historians must identify conditions and forces that provide common denominators for all regions of the globe. Regional historians are concerned primarily with continuity and change in a particular region of the world. What is theoretically valid for one may or may not be valid for the other. If the world was integrated (commercially, biologically, and in other ways) as a result of the fifteenth- and sixteenth-century discoveries of Europeans, that integration occurred incrementally in the various regions affected. The great era of discontinuity for Native Americans was the sixteenth century; for Indonesian subjects of the Dutch, the seventeenth century; for the Indians of South Asia, the eighteenth century; for the Chinese and for many African peoples, the nineteenth century. After 1500, all peoples would encounter what McNeill called the "restless, disturbing ways" of the Europeans, but they would encounter them under different timetables. These differing timetables demand different regional periodizations. It is entirely fitting that regional historians of Amerindian civilization acknowledge a major discontinuity around 1500. For reasons that are not dissimilar, Chinese historians consider the Opium War of the 1840s the dawn of their modern era.

For global historians, the advent of world-system analysis has powerfully confirmed the sixteenth-century division between pre-modern and modern epochs. Also, it has intensified contemporary emphasis upon the primacy of materialist forces in driving the historical process.

For European history, a new division of time since the Roman era is needed. I concur with Gerhard and Barraclough, albeit for different reasons, that the tenth and the eighteenth centuries were times of major discontinuity in European society and that the centuries between 1000 and 1800 were distinguished more by their continuities than by their changes. An aggregate, episodic view of the tenth and eighteenth centuries would recommend them as watershed eras; indeed, medievalists and modern historians have traditionally subdivided their epochs at these junctures. More important, the theories of change that historians most commonly employ to explain process in history affirm these centuries as moments of fundamental transition and transformation.

Ironically, then, this study commends for world history the continued use of a period frontier, circa 1500, that was created for European history and the adoption of a different epochal structure for use in European regional history.

History is what we make of the past. It is our means, however feeble, of imposing rational order upon chaos. As our needs, our perceptions, and our priorities change, so must our history. Even if the data of the past were to remain the same—which it does not—the information we would attempt to derive from it would change. What determines the shape of historical knowledge is the questions we ask. Those questions are perpetually changing, and in each new phase of inquiry we must guard against purposeful teleological argumentation and undue subjectivity. At the same time, it is essential that those who write history reconstruct the past with some coherent and consistent theoretical orientation. Likewise, it is important that those who teach history and those who study it remain alert to the theoretical properties of historical literature. Good theory is no guarantee of good history, but bad theory or the contradictory employment of theory is a sure guarantee of bad history. Still, all historical theory has its limitations, as this book has attempted to demonstrate. No theory is gospel, nor is any ever likely to become gospel. We will never escape all the pitfalls that lay in wait for us. We will never entirely avoid teleology. We cannot extinguish our subjectivities, although to the extent that we are able, we should try to acknowledge them. History is not a pursuit of perfection. It is a pursuit of meaning. But the pursuers, if they are worthy, will seek diligently to avoid deceiving themselves as well as others.

NOTES

1. Fernand Braudel, *Civilization and Capitalism, 15th–18th Century:* vol. 1, *The Structures of Everyday Life;* vol. 2, *The Wheels of Commerce;* vol. 3, *The Perspective of the World* (New York, 1981, 1982, 1984).

2. Braudel, *The Perspective of the World,* pp. 94–96.

3. In Poland, Braudel wrote, "the western entrepreneurs first came knocking at their (the noblemens') door," luring them into the web of international capitalism. The

American plantations "were capitalist creations *par excellence*," the progeny of "money, credit, trade, and exchange." Braudel, *The Wheels of Commerce*, p. 272.

4. Braudel, *The Perspective of the World*, p. 91.

5. The shift from Venice was occasioned by the Portuguese discovery of the Atlantic sea route to India. Antwerp was dislodged by the Spanish bankruptcy of 1557, and Genoa's banking families were crippled, though not undone, by the Spanish bankruptcy of 1627.

6. André Gunder Frank, "A Theoretical Introduction to 5,000 Years of World System History," *Review* 13 (1990): 155–248; also (with Barry K. Gills), "The Cumulation of Accumulation: Theses and Research Agenda for 5,000 Years of World System History," *Dialectical Anthropology* 15 (1990): 19–42; and "A Plea for World System History," *Journal of World History* 2 (1991): 1–28.

7. William H. McNeill, "*The Rise of the West* after Twenty-Five Years," *Journal of World History* 1 (1990): 12.

8. Janet L. Abu-Lughod, *Before European Hegemony: The World System, A.D. 1250–1350* (New York, 1989).

9. E. L. Jones, *The European Miracle: Environments, Economies, and Geopolitics in the History of Europe and Asia* (Cambridge, 1981), pp. 3–5.

10. Ibid., pp. 24–41.

11. Ibid., p. 20.

12. Ibid., pp. 45–62.

13. Ibid., p. 80.

14. Ibid., pp. 106–108.

15. Ibid., pp. 118–119.

16. Ibid., p. 124.

17. Ibid., p. 187.

18. For an interesting defense of aspects of his approach, see E. L. Jones, "Disasters and Economic Differentiation across Eurasia: A Reply," *Journal of Economic History* 45 (1985): 675–682.

19. Neil McKendrick, John Brewer, and J. H. Plumb, *The Birth of a Consumer Society: The Commercialization of Eighteenth-Century England* (Bloomington, 1982), p. 9. See also Lorna Weatherhill, *Consumer Behavior and Material Culture in Britain, 1660–1760* (New York, 1988).

20. Philip M. Hauser, "The Population of the World: Recent Trends and Prospects," in Ronald Freedman, ed., *Population: The Vital Revolution* (Garden City, 1964), p. 18.

21. Richard N. Gardner, "Bush, the U.N., and Too Many People," *New York Times,* 22 September 1989.

22. Geoffrey Barraclough, *History in a Changing World* (Oxford, 1955), pp. 54–63.

23. Herbert Butterfield, *Man on His Past* (Cambridge, 1955), pp. 128–136.

24. Dietrich Gerhard, "Periodization in European History," *American Historical Review* 61 (1956): 903.

25. Dietrich Gerhard, *Old Europe: A Study of Continuity, 1000–1800* (New York, 1981), p. 139.

26. Perry Anderson, *Passages from Antiquity to Feudalism* (New York, 1978), pp. 128–172.

27. Alfred W. Crosby, Jr., *The Columbian Exchange* (Westport, 1972), pp. 218–219.

Bibliography

A book presenting macrohistorical theories that sweep across many lands and many centuries may invite interested readers to pursue, in greater detail, aspects of history or historiography that are only briefly touched in the text. This bibliography is designed to facilitate further study of the period from the tenth to the eighteenth century. With rare exception, it does not include titles on the Industrial Revolution or on economic and demographic developments since the eighteenth century. Similarly, it excludes studies using world-system analysis to interpret Western or world history over the last two centuries. The bibliography is divided topically in accord with the theories of change introduced in the chapters. Books and articles that defy easy categorization (e.g., the role of warfare in the process of change, or of printing, law, or concepts of time) are usually entered under the General Works section. In the case of publications that bridge two or more categories, I have attempted to achieve consistency in their placement. Works dealing with the aristocracy appear in the General Works section; those concerned with the rise of towns and the people of the city, the bourgeoisie, are listed in the Commerce, Capitalism, and Expansion section. Considerable attention has been given to publications in environmental history, an area that has received less attention than others in university courses to date, but one that will demand increasing consideration in the future.

HISTORY, THEORY, AND ACADEMICS

Acton, Lord (John Emerich Edward Dalberg Acton). *Essays in the Liberal Interpretation of History.* Chicago: University of Chicago Press, 1967.

Appleby, Joyce Oldham. *Economic Thought and Ideology in Seventeenth-Century England.* Princeton: Princeton University Press, 1978.

Ashplant, T. G., and Adrian Wilson. "Whig History and Present-Centered History." *Historical Journal* 31 (1988): 1–16.

Aymard, Maurice. "The *Annales* and French Historiography (1929–72)." *Journal of European Economic History* 1 (1972): 491–511.

Barraclough, Geoffrey. *History in a Changing World.* Oxford: Blackwell, 1955.

Billington, Ray, ed. *The Frontier Thesis: Valid Interpretation of American History?* New York: Kreiger, 1977.

Birnbaum, Norman. "Conflicting Interpretations of the Rise of Capitalism: Marx and Weber." *British Journal of Sociology* 4 (1953): 125–141.

Black, J. B. *The Art of History. A Study of Four Great Historians of the Eighteenth Century.* New York: F. S. Crofts, 1926.

Bodin, Jean. *Method for the Easy Comprehension of History*, trans. Beatrice Reynolds. New York: Columbia University Press, 1945.

Braudel, Fernand. "Personal Testimony." *Journal of Modern History* 44 (1972): 448–467.

Breisach, Ernst. *Historiography: Ancient Medieval, and Modern*. Chicago: University of Chicago Press, 1983.

Brumfitt, J. H. *Voltaire, Historian*. London: Oxford University Press, 1958.

Burckhardt, Jacob. *The Civilization of the Renaissance in Italy*, trans. S. G. C. Middlemore. London: Allen & Unwin, 1944.

Burr, George L. "How the Middle Ages Got Their Name." *American Historical Review* 20 (1914–1915): 813–814.

Butterfield, Herbert. *Man on His Past: The Study of the History of Historical Scholarship*. Cambridge: Cambridge University Press, 1955.

———. *The Whig Interpretation of History*. London: G. Bell and Sons, 1931.

Cahnman, Werner J., and Alvin Boskoff, eds. *Sociology and History: Theory and Research*. Glencoe: Free Press, 1964.

Cameron, Rondo. "The Logistics of European Economic Growth: A Note on Historical Periodization." *Journal of European Economic History* 2 (1973): 145–148.

Carr, E. H. *What Is History?* Harmondsworth: Penguin, 1970.

Clark, G. Kitson. "A Hundred Years of Teaching History at Cambridge, 1873–1973." *Historical Journal* 16 (1973): 535–553.

Clark, Terry Nichols. *Prophets and Patrons: The French University and the Emergence of the Social Sciences*. Cambridge, Mass.: Harvard University Press, 1973.

Cochrane, Eric. *Historians and Historiography of the Italian Renaissance*. Chicago: University of Chicago Press, 1981.

Cohen, Sande. *Historical Culture: On the Recording of an Academic Discipline*. Berkeley: University of California Press, 1989.

Coleman, D. C. *History and the Economic Past: An Account of the Rise and Decline of Economic History in Britain*. New York: Oxford University Press, 1987.

Cook, Albert. *History/Writing*. New York: Cambridge University Press, 1988.

Crafts, N. F. R. "Industrial Revolution in England and France: Some Thoughts on the Question, 'Why Was England First?' " *Economic History Review*, 2d ser., 30 (1977): 429–441.

Darnton, R. "The History of Mentalities." In R. H. Brown and S. M. Lyman, eds., *Structure, Consciousness and History*. Cambridge: Cambridge University Press, 1978.

de Roover, Raymond. "The Scholastic Attitude towards Trade and Entrepreneurship." *Explorations in Entrepreneurial History* 1 (1963): 76–87.

———. "Scholastic Economics: Survival and Lasting Influence from the Sixteenth Century to Adam Smith." *Quarterly Journal of Economics* 69 (1955): 161–190.

Duby, Georges. "L'histoire des systèmes de valuers." *History and Theory* 11 (1972): 15–25.

Elton, G. R. *The Practice of History*. New York: Crowell, 1967.

Ferguson, W. K. "The Interpretation of the Renaissance: Suggestions for a Synthesis." *Journal of the History of Ideas* 12 (1951): 483–495.

———. *The Renaissance in Historical Thought*. Boston: Houghton Mifflin, 1948.

Field, Alexander James. "What Is Wrong with Neoclassical Institutional Economics: A Critique of the North/Thomas Model of Pre-1500." *Explorations in Economic History* 18 (1981): 174–198.

Foster, Robert. "Achievements of the *Annales* School." *Journal of Economic History* 38 (1978): 58–75.

Frank, André Gunder. "A Plea for World System History." *Journal of World History* 2 (1991): 1–28.

———. "A Theoretical Introduction to 5,000 Years of World System History." *Review* 13 (1990): 155–248.

Frank, André Gunder, and Barry K. Gills. "The Cumulation of Accumulation: Theses and Research Agenda for 5,000 Years of World System History." *Dialectical Anthropology* 15 (1990): 19–42.

Gerhard, Deitrich. "Periodization in European History." *American Historical Review* 61 (1956): 900–913.

Gerschenkron, Alexander. *Economic Backwardness in Historical Perspective.* Cambridge, Mass.: Belknap Press of Harvard University Press, 1962.

Gibbon, Edward. *The Decline and Fall of the Roman Empire,* 7 vols. London: Methuen, 1909.

Giddens, Anthony. *Capitalism and Modern Social Theory: An Analysis of the Writings of Marx, Durkheim and Max Weber.* London: Cambridge University Press, 1971.

———. "Marx, Weber, and the Development of Capitalism." *Sociology* 4 (1970): 289–310.

Goldstein, Doris. "The Organizational Development of the British Historical Profession, 1884–1921." *Bulletin of the Institute of Historical Research* 55 (1982): 180–193.

———. "The Origins and Early Years of *The English Historical Review*." *English Historical Review* 101 (1986): 3–11.

Gooch, G. P. "The Cambridge Chair of Modern History." In G. P. Gooch, ed., *Studies in Modern History.* Freeport: Books for Libraries Press, 1968.

———. *History and Historians in the Nineteenth Century.* London: Longmans, 1913.

Gottschalk, Louis, ed. *Generalization in the Writing of History.* Chicago: University of Chicago Press, 1963.

Green, William A. "Periodization in European and World History." *Journal of World History* 3 (1992): 13–53.

Harris, Marvin. *Cannibals and Kings: The Origins of Cultures.* London: Collins/Fontana, 1978.

———. *Culture, People, Nature: An Introduction to General Anthropology,* 3d ed. New York: Harper and Row, 1980.

Hart, B. H. Liddell. *Why Don't We Learn from History?* New York: Hawthorn, 1971.

Hartwell, R. M. "Economic Growth in England before the Industrial Revolution: Some Methodological Issues." *Journal of Economic History* 29 (1969): 13–31.

Hay, Denys. *Annalists and Historians: Western Historiography from the VIIIth to the XVIIIth Century.* London: Methuen, 1977.

———. "Flavio Biondo and the Middle Ages." *Proceedings of the British Academy* 45 (1959): 97–128.

Hexter, J. H. "Fernand Braudel and the *Monde Braudelien.*" *Journal of Modern History* 44 (1972): 480–539.

————. *Reappraisals in History*. Evanston: Northwestern University Press, 1962.

Hicks, Sir John. *A Theory of Economic History*. London: Oxford University Press, 1969.

Hirschman, Albert O. *The Passions and the Interests: Political Arguments for Capitalism before its Triumph*. Princeton: Princeton University Press, 1977.

Hirst, Paul Q. "The Necessity of Theory." *Economy and Society* 8 (1979): 417–445.

Hodges, Richard, and David Whitehouse. *Mohammad, Charlemagne, and the Origins of Europe: Archaeology and the Pirenne Thesis*. Ithaca: Cornell University Press, 1983.

Hollinger, David. "T. S. Kuhn's Theory of Science and Its Implications for History." *American Historical Review* 78 (1973): 370–393.

Hunt, Lynn. "French History in the Last Twenty Years: The Rise and Fall of the *Annales* Paradigm." *Journal of Contemporary History* 21 (1986): 209–224.

————, ed. *The New Cultural History*. Berkeley: University of California Press, 1989.

Huppert, George. *The Idea of Perfect History: Historical Erudition and Historical Philosophy in Renaissance France*. Urbana: University of Illinois Press, 1970.

————. "The Renaissance Background of Historicism." *History and Theory* 5 (1966): 48–60.

Iggers, George. *New Directions in European Historiography*. Middletown, Conn.: Wesleyan University Press, 1975.

Johnson, E. A. J. *Predecessors of Adam Smith: The Growth of British Economic Thought*. New York: Augustus M. Kelley, 1960.

Jones, Gareth Stedman. "From Historical Sociology to Theoretical History." *British Journal of Sociology* 27 (1976): 295–305.

Jordan, David P. *Gibbon and His Roman Empire*. Urbana: University of Illinois Press, 1971.

Keylor, William R. *Academy and Community: The Foundation of the French Historical Profession*. Cambridge, Mass.: Harvard University Press, 1973.

Kinser, Samuel. "Annaliste Paradigm? Geohistorical Structuralism of Fernand Braudel." *American Historical Review* 86 (1981): 63–105.

Kuhn, T. S. *The Structure of Scientific Revolutions*, 2d ed. Chicago: University of Chicago Press, 1970.

Kurzweil, Edith. *The Age of Structuralism: Levi-Straus to Foucault*. New York: Columbia University Press, 1980.

LaCapra, Dominick. *History and Criticism*. Ithaca: Cornell University Press, 1985.

Ladurie, Emmanuel Le Roy. "Motionless History." *Social Science History* 1 (1977): 115–136.

————. *The Territory of the Historian*. Sussex: Harvester Press, 1962.

Leff, Gordon. *History and Social Theory*. University: University of Alabama Press, 1969.

Link, Arthur J. "The American Historical Association, 1884–1984: Retrospect and Prospect." *American Historical Review* 90 (1985): 1–17.

Lloyd, Christopher. *Explanation in Social History*. New York: Blackwell, 1986.

Lowenthal, David. *The Past Is a Foreign Country*. Cambridge: Cambridge University Press, 1986.

Lyon, Bryce. *Henri Pirenne: A Biographical and Intellectual Study*. Ghent: E. Story-Scienta, 1974.

Malthus, Thomas. *An Essay on the Principle of Population*, ed. Philip Appleman. New York: Norton, 1976.

Marwick, Arthur. *The Nature of History*. London: Macmillan, 1970.

McClelland, Charles E. *State, Society, and University in Germany 1700–1914*. Cambridge: Cambridge University Press, 1980.

McClelland, Peter D. *Causal Explanation and Model Building in History, Economics, and the New Economic History*. Ithaca: Cornell University Press, 1975.

McNeill, William H. *Mythistory and Other Essays*. Chicago: University of Chicago Press, 1986.

———. "Mythistory, or Truth, Myth, History, and Historians." *American Historical Review* 91 (1986): 1–10.

———. "Organizing Concepts for World History." *Review* 10 (1986): 211–229.

———. *"The Rise of the West* after Twenty-Five Years." *Journal of World History* 1 (1990): 1–21.

Moore, Barrington, Jr. *Social Origins of Dictatorship and Democracy*. London: Allen Lane, 1967.

Mosse, George L. "History, Anthropology, and Mass Movements: Review Article." *American Historical Review* 75 (1969): 447–452.

Nisbet, Robert A. *Social Change and History: Aspects of Western Theory of Development*. New York: Oxford University Press, 1969.

North, Douglas C. "The Rise and Fall of the Manorial System: A Theoretical Model." *Journal of Economic History* 31 (1971): 777–803.

———. *Structure and Change in Economic History*. New York: Norton, 1981.

North, Douglas C., and Robert Paul Thomas. "An Economic Theory of the Growth of the Western World." *Economic History Review* 23 (1970): 1–17.

———. *The Rise of the Western World: A New Economic History*. Cambridge: Cambridge University Press, 1973.

Novick, Peter. *That Noble Dream: The "Objectivity Question" and the American Historical Profession*. New York: Cambridge University Press, 1988.

Parker, Harold T., and Georg G. Iggers, eds. *International Handbook of Historical Studies: Contemporary Research and Theory*. Westport, Conn.: Greenwood, 1979.

Pirenne, Henri. *Mohammed and Charlemagne*. New York: Norton, 1939.

Popper, Karl. *The Poverty of Historicism*. London: Routledge and Kegan Paul, 1961.

Poster, Mark. *Foucault, Marxism, and History: Mode of Production versus Mode of Information*. New York: Blackwell, 1984.

Preston, Joseph H. "Was There an Historical Revolution?" *Journal of the History of Ideas* 38 (1977): 353–364.

Reddy, William M. *Money and Liberty in Modern Europe: A Critique of Historical Understanding*. New York: Cambridge University Press, 1986.

Reill, Peter Hans. *The German Enlightenment and the Rise of Historicism*. Berkeley and Los Angeles: University of California Press, 1975.

———. "History and Hermeneutics in the Aufklärung: The Thought of Johann Christof Gatterer." *Journal of Modern History* 45 (1973): 24–51.

Rostow, W. W. *How It All Began: Origins of the Modern Economy*. New York: McGraw-Hill, 1975.

———. *The Stages of Economic Growth: A Non-Communist Manifesto*. Cambridge: Cambridge University Press, 1960.

Salomon, Albert. "German Sociology." In Georges Burvitch and Wilbert E. Moore, eds., *Twentieth Century Sociology*. New York: Philosophical Library, 1945.

Schumpeter, Joseph A. *Capitalism, Socialism, and Democracy*. New York: Harper, 1942.

Sherwood, John M. "Engels, Marx, Malthus, and the Machine." *American Historical Review* 90 (1985): 837–865.

Skocpol, Theda, ed. *Vision and Method in Historical Sociology*. New York: Cambridge University Press, 1984.

Smith, Adam. *An Inquiry into the Nature and Causes of the Wealth of Nations*, eds. R. H. Cambell and A. S. Skinner. Oxford: Clarendon Press, 1976.

Stern, Fritz, ed. *Varieties of History from Voltaire to the Present*. Cleveland: Meridian Books, 1956.

Stoianovich, Traian. *French Historical Method: The Annales Paradigm*. Ithaca: Cornell University Press, 1976.

Stone, Lawrence. "The Revival of Narrative: Reflections on a New Old History." *Past and Present* 85 (1979): 3–24.

Symonds, John Addington. *Renaissance in Italy*, 7 vols. London: Smith and Elder, 1875–1886.

Taylor, A. J. P. "Accident Prone, or What Happened Next." *Journal of Modern History* 49 (1977): 1–18.

Taylor, George Roger. *The Turner Thesis Concerning the Role of the Frontier in American History*. Boston: D. C. Heath, 1956.

Teggart, Frederick J. *Theory and Processes of History*. Berkeley: University of California Press, 1960.

Thompson, E. P. *The Poverty of Theory and Other Essays*. London: Merlin Press, 1978.

Tilly, Charles. *As Sociology Meets History*. New York: Academic Press, 1981.

———. *Big Structures, Large Processes, Huge Comparisons*. New York: Russell Sage Foundation, 1984.

Toews, John E. "Intellectual History after the Linguistic Turn: The Autonomy of Meaning and the Irreducibility of Experience." *American Historical Review* 92 (1987): 879–907.

Trevor-Roper, H. R. "Fernand Braudel, the *Annales* and the Mediterranean." *Journal of Modern History* 44 (1972): 468–479.

Tuma, Elias H. *Economic History and the Social Sciences: Problems of Methodology*. Berkeley and Los Angeles: University of California Press, 1971.

Turner, Frederick Jackson. *The Frontier in American History*. New York: H. Holt, 1920.

———. "The Significance of the Frontier in American History." In Ray Allen Billington, ed., *Frontier and Section: Selected Essays of Frederick Jackson Turner*. Englewood Cliffs, N.J.: Prentice-Hall, 1961.

Van Engen, John. "The Christian Middle Ages as an Historiographical Problem." *American Historical Review* 91 (1986): 519–552.

Wallerstein, Immanuel. "Fernand Braudel, Historian." *Radical History Review* 26 (1982): 105–119.

Webb, Walter Prescott. *The Great Frontier*. Boston: Houghton Mifflin, 1952.

Weeks, Jeffrey. "Foucault for Historians." *History Workshop* 14 (1982): 106–119.

White, Hayden. *The Content of the Form: Narrative Discourse and Historical Representation.* Baltimore: Johns Hopkins University Press, 1987.

———. *Metahistory: The Historical Imagination in Nineteenth-Century Europe.* Baltimore and London: Johns Hopkins University Press, 1973.

Wilcox, Donald J. *The Development of Florentine Humanist Historiography in the Fifteenth Century.* Cambridge, Mass.: Harvard University Press, 1969.

GENERAL WORKS

Abel, Wilhelm. *Agricultural Fluctuations in Europe from the Thirteenth to the Twentieth Centuries.* New York: St. Martin's Press, 1980.

Agnew, Jean-Christophe. *Worlds Apart: The Market and the Theatre in Anglo-American Thought, 1550–1750.* New York: Cambridge University Press, 1986.

Allmand, C. T. *Society at War: The Experience of England and France during the Hundred Years' War.* Edinburgh: Oliver and Boyd, 1973.

Appleby, Andrew B. *Famine in Tudor and Stuart England.* Stanford: Stanford University Press, 1978.

Aston, T. H., ed. *Landlords, Peasants and Politics in Medieval England.* New York: Cambridge University Press, 1988.

Aston, T. S. *Crisis in Europe 1560–1660.* New York: Doubleday, 1967.

Bairoch, Paul. "Europe's Gross National Product: 1800–1975." *Journal of European Economic History* 5 (1976): 273–340.

Baron, Hans. *The Crisis of the Early Italian Renaissance,* 2 vols. Princeton: Princeton University Press, 1955.

Barraclough, Geoffrey. *The Crucible of Europe: The Ninth and Tenth Centuries in European History.* Berkeley: University of California Press, 1976.

Basalla, George. *The Evolution of Technology.* New York: Cambridge University Press, 1988.

Bean, Richard. "War and the Birth of the Nation State." *Journal of Economic History* 33 (1973): 203–221.

Beik, William. *Absolutism and Society in Seventeenth-Century France: State Power and Provincial Aristocracy in Languedoc.* New York: Cambridge University Press, 1985.

Berman, Harold J. *Law and Revolution: The Formation of the Western Legal Tradition.* Cambridge, Mass.: Harvard University Press, 1983.

Bloch, Marc. *Feudal Society.* London: Routledge and Kegan Paul, 1961.

———. *French Rural History: An Essay on Its Basic Characteristics,* trans. Janet Sondheimer. London: Routledge and Kegan Paul, 1966.

Blum, J. *The End of the Old Order in Rural Europe.* Princeton: Princeton University Press, 1978.

Bolton, J. L. *The Medieval English Economy.* London: J. M. Dent and Sons, 1980.

Boorstin, Daniel J. *The Discoverers.* New York: Random House, 1983.

Boserup, Ester. *The Conditions of Agricultural Growth.* London: Allen & Unwin, 1965.

Braudel, Fernand. *The Mediterranean and the Mediterranean World in the Age of Phillip II,* 2 vols., trans. Sian Reynolds. New York: Harper and Row, 1972.

Breisach, Ernst. *Renaissance Europe, 1300–1517*. New York: Macmillan, 1973.

Bridbury, A. R. "Before the Black Death." *Economic History Review*, 2d ser., 30 (1977): 393–410.

———. "The Dark Ages." *Economic History Review*, 2d ser., 26 (1969): 577–592.

Britton, David. *The French Nobility in Crisis, 1560–1640*. Stanford: Stanford University Press, 1969.

Bush, M. L. *The English Aristocracy: A Comparative Synthesis*. Dover: Manchester University Press, 1984.

Cameron, Rondo. "A New View of European Industrialization." *Economic History Review* 38 (1985): 1–23.

Carter, Charles Howard. *The Western European Powers, 1500–1700*. Ithaca: Cornell University Press, 1971.

Chaussinand-Nogaret, Guy. *The French Nobility in the Eighteenth Century: From Feudalism to Enlightenment*. Cambridge: Cambridge University Press, 1985.

Cheyney, Edward P. *The Dawn of a New Era, 1250–1453*. New York: Harper and Row, 1936.

Childs, John. *Armies and Warfare in Europe. 1648–1789*. New York: Holmes and Meier, 1982.

Cipolla, Carlo M. *Before the Industrial Revolution: European Society and Economy, 1000–1700*. New York: Norton, 1976.

———. *Clocks and Culture 1300–1700*. London: Collins, 1967.

Clarkson, L. A. *The Pre-Industrial Economy in England, 1500–1750*. New York: Schocken Books, 1972.

Cochran, Thomas C. "The Business Revolution." *American Historical Review* 79 (1974): 1449–1466.

Coleman, D. C. *The Economy of England, 1450–1750*. New York: Oxford University Press, 1977.

Contamine, Philippe. *War in the Middle Ages*, trans. Michael Jones. New York: Blackwell, 1984.

Corvisier, André. *Armies and Societies in Europe, 1494–1789*, trans. Abigail T. Siddall. Bloomington: Indiana University Press, 1980.

Coulanges, Fustel de. *Histoire des institutions politiques de l'ancienne France*. Paris: Hachette, 1975.

Coulborn, Rushton, ed. *Feudalism in History*. Princeton: Princeton University Press, 1956.

Critchley, J. S. *Feudalism*. London: George Allen and Unwin, 1978.

Dahlman, Carl J. *The Open Field System and Beyond*. Cambridge: Cambridge University Press, 1980.

Davis, Natalie Zemon. *Society and Culture in Early Modern France*. Stanford: Stanford University Press, 1975.

Davis, Ralph. *The Rise of the Atlantic Economies*. Ithaca: Cornell University Press, 1973.

Davy, John. "The Great Bullion Famine of the Fifteenth Century." *Past and Present* 79 (1978): 3–54.

Deane, Phyllis, and W. A. Cole. *British Economic Growth 1688–1959*. Cambridge: Cambridge University Press, 1967.

de Vries, Jan. *The Dutch Rural Economy in the Golden Age, 1500–1700*. New Haven: Yale University Press, 1974.

————. *The Economy of Europe in an Age of Crisis, 1600–1750*. Cambridge and New York: Cambridge University Press, 1976.

Dickens, A. G. *Reformation and Society in Sixteenth-Century Europe*. London: Thames and Hudson, 1971.

Dopsch, Alfons. *The Economic and Social Foundations of European Civilization*. London: K. Paul, Trench, Trubner & Co., 1937.

Duby, George. *The Early Growth of the European Economy: Warriors and Peasants from the Seventh to the Twelfth Century*, trans. Cynthia Postan. London: Weidenfeld and Nicolson, 1974.

Duffy, Christopher. *Siege Warfare: The Fortress in the Early Modern World, 1495–1660*. Boston: Routledge and Kegan Paul, 1979.

Duhem, Pierre. *Medieval Cosmology: Theories of Infinity, Place, Time Void, and the Plurality of Worlds*, trans. Roger Ariew. Chicago: Chicago University Press, 1985.

Dyer, Christopher. *Lords and Peasants in a Changing Society: The Estates of the Bishopric of Worcester, 680–1540*. Cambridge: Cambridge University Press, 1980.

————. *Standards of Living in the Later Middle Ages: Social Change in England c. 1200–1520*. Cambridge: Cambridge University Press, 1989.

Eisenstein, Elizabeth. *The Printing Press as an Agent of Change: Communications and Cultural Transformations in Early Modern Europe*, 2 vols. London: Cambridge University Press, 1979.

Elias, Norbert. *The Civilizing Process: The History of Manners*. New York: Pantheon Books, 1978.

Elliott, J. H. "The Decline of Spain." *Past and Present* 20 (1961): 52–75.

————. *Imperial Spain, 1469–1716*. New York: Mentor, 1966.

————. "Self-Perception and Decline in Early Seventeenth-Century Spain." *Past and Present* 74 (1977): 41–61.

Elton, G. R. *The Tudor Revolution in Government*. Cambridge: Cambridge University Press, 1953.

Febvre, Lucien. *The Coming of the Book: The Impact of Printing 1450–1600*. London: New Left Books, 1976.

Ferguson, Wallace. *Europe in Transition, 1300–1520*. Boston: Houghton Mifflin, 1962.

Ferro, Marc. *The Great War 1914–1918*, trans. Nicole Stone. London: Routledge, 1973.

Flynn, Dennis O. "Fiscal Crisis and the Decline of Spain (Castile)." *Journal of Economic History* 42 (1982): 139–148.

Forster, Robert, and Jack P. Greene, eds. *Pre-Conditions of Revolution in Early Modern Europe*. Baltimore: Johns Hopkins University Press, 1970.

Ganshof, F. L., and A. Verhulst. "Medieval Agrarian Society in Its Prime: France, the Low Countries and Germany." In M. M. Postan, ed., *The Cambridge Economic History of Europe*: vol. 1, *The Agrarian Life of the Middle Ages*, 2d ed. Cambridge: Cambridge University Press, 1966.

Gaski, J. F. "The Causes of the Industrial Revolution: A Brief 'Single Factor' Argument." *Journal of European Economic History* 11 (1982): 227–233.

Gerhard, Dietrich. *Old Europe: A Study of Continuity, 1000–1800*. New York: Academic Press, 1981.

Gimpel, Jean. *The Medieval Machine: The Industrial Revolution of the Middle Ages.* New York: Penguin Books, 1977.

Godino, Vitorino Magãlhaes. *L'économie de l'empire portugais aux XVe et XVIe siècles.* Paris: S.E.V.P.E.N., 1969.

Gottfried, Robert S. *Bury St. Edmunds and the Urban Crisis, 1290–1539.* Princeton: Princeton University Press, 1981.

Goubert, Pierre. *The Ancien Regime: French Society 1600–1750,* trans. Steve Cox. New York: Harper Torchbooks, 1974.

———. *Louis XIV and Twenty Million Frenchmen,* trans. Ann Carter. New York: Pantheon, 1972.

Grigg, David. *Agricultural Systems of the World.* Cambridge: Cambridge University Press, 1974.

———. *The Dynamics of Agricultural Change: The Historical Experience.* New York: St. Martin's Press, 1982.

Guenée, Bernard. *States and Rulers in Later Medieval Europe,* trans. Juliet Vale. New York: Blackwell, 1985.

Haley, K. H. D. *The Dutch in the Seventeenth Century.* New York: Harcourt Brace Jovanovich, 1972.

Hallam, H. E. *Rural England, 1066–1348.* Brighton, Sussex, and Atlantic Highlands, N.J.: Harvester and Humanities Presses, 1981.

———. *Settlement and Society.* Cambridge: Cambridge University Press, 1965.

Hamilton, Earl J. "American Treasure and Andalusian Prices, 1503–1660: A Study in the Spanish Price Revolution." *Journal of Economic and Business History* 1 (1928): 1–35.

———. *American Treasure and the Price Revolution in Spain, 1501–1650.* Cambridge, Mass.: Harvard University Press, 1934.

———. "American Treasure and the Rise of Capitalism." *Economica* 9 (1929): 338–357.

Hartwell, R. M. *The Industrial Revolution and Economic Growth.* London: Methuen, 1971.

———, ed. *The Causes of the Industrial Revolution in England.* London: Methuen, 1967.

Harvey, P. D. A., ed. *The Peasant Land Market in Medieval England.* New York: Oxford University Press, 1984.

Hatcher, John. *Plague, Population and the English Economy, 1348–1530.* New York: Macmillan, 1977.

Hay, Denys. *Europe in the Fourteenth and Fifteenth Centuries,* 2d ed. London/New York: Longman, 1989.

Heaton, Herbert. *Economic History of Europe.* New York: Harper, 1948.

Heers, Jacques. "The 'Feudal' Economy and Capitalism: Words, Ideas and Reality." *Journal of European Economic History* 3 (1974): 609–653.

Helleiner, Karl F. "Moral Conditions of Economic Growth," *Journal of Economic History* 11 (1951): 97–116.

Hill, Christopher. *The Century of Revolution, 1603–1714.* Edinburgh: Nelson, 1963.

———. *Intellectual Origins of the English Revolution.* Oxford: Clarendon Press, 1965.

———. "Puritanism, Capitalism and the Scientific Revolution." *Past and Present* 29 (1964): 88–97.

———. *Reformation to Industrial Revolution: A Social and Economic History of Britain, 1530–1780*. London: Weidenfeld and Nicolson, 1969.

Hilton, R. H. *The English Peasantry in the Later Middle Ages: The Ford Lectures for 1973*. Oxford: Clarendon Press, 1975.

———. *A Medieval Society: The West Midlands at the End of the Thirteenth Century*. London: John Wiley, 1966.

Hobsbawm, Eric. "The General Crisis of the European Economy in the 17th Century," *Past and Present* 5 and 6 (1954): 33–53, 44–65.

Hodgett, Gerald. *A Social and Economic History of Medieval Europe*. London: Methuen, 1972.

Holderness, B. A. *Pre–Industrial England: Economy and Society, 1500–1750*. Totowa, N.J.: Rowman and Littlefield, 1976.

Howard, Michael. *War in European History*. Oxford: Oxford University Press, 1976.

Israel, Jonathan I. "A Conflict of Empires: Spain and the Netherlands 1618–1648." *Past and Present* 76 (1977): 34–74.

———. *The Dutch Republic and the Hispanic World, 1606–1661*. Oxford: Clarendon Press, 1982.

Jones, E. L. *Agriculture and Economic Growth in England, 1650–1815*. London: Methuen, 1967.

———. *Agriculture and the Industrial Revolution*. Oxford: Blackwell, 1974.

———. "English and European Agricultural Development 1650–1750." In R. M. Hartwell, ed., *The Industrial Revolution*. Oxford: Blackwell, 1970.

Jones, Richard Foster. *Ancients and Moderns: A Study of the Rise of the Scientific Movement in Seventeenth-Century England*. St. Louis, Mo.: Washington University Press, 1961.

Kaeuper, Richard W. *War, Justice, and Public Order: England and France in the Later Middle Ages*. New York: Oxford University Press, 1988.

Kamen, Henry. "The Decline of Spain: A Historical Myth." *Past and Present* 81 (1978): 24–50.

———. *The Iron Century: Social Change in Europe 1550–1660*. New York: Praeger, 1961.

———. *Spain 1469–1714: A Society of Conflict*. New York: Longman, 1983.

Kellenbenz, Hermann. *The Rise of the European Economy: An Economic History of Continental Europe from the Fifteenth to the Eighteenth Century*. New York: Holmes & Meier Publishers, 1976.

———. "Technology in the Age of the Scientific Revolution, 1500–1700." In Carlo M. Cipolla, ed., *The Fontana Economic History of Europe*: vol. 2, *The Sixteenth and Seventeenth Centuries*. London: Fontana/Collins, 1974.

Keller, Albert G., ed. *Earth Hunger and Other Essays*. New Haven: Yale University Press, 1913.

Kemp, Tom. *Economic Forces in French History*. London: Longman, 1971.

Kerridge, Eric. *The Agricultural Revolution*. New York: A. M. Kelley, 1968.

Kershaw, Ian. "The Great Famine and Agrarian Crisis in England, 1315–1322." *Past and Present* 59 (1973): 3–50.

Kjaergaard, T. "Origins of Economic Growth in European Societies since the Sixteenth Century: The Case of Agriculture." *Journal of European Economic History* 15 (1986): 591–598.

Lach, Donald. *Asia in the Making of Europe*, 2 vols. Chicago: University of Chicago Press, 1965, 1970.

Lambert, Audrey M. *The Making of the Dutch Landscape: An Historical Geography of the Netherlands*. London and New York: Seminar Press, 1971.

Landes, David S. *Revolution in Time: Clocks and the Making of the Modern World*. Cambridge, Mass.: Belknap Press of Harvard University Press, 1983.

Leff, Gordon. *The Dissolution of the Medieval Outlook: An Essay on Intellectual and Spiritual Change in the Fourteenth Century*. New York: New York University Press, 1976.

Le Goff, Jacques. *Time, Work, and Culture in the Middle Ages*. Chicago: University of Chicago Press, 1980.

Levy, Jack S. *War in the Modern Great Power System, 1495–1975*. Lexington: University of Kentucky Press, 1983.

Lewis, Archibald. *Nomads and Crusaders, A.D. 1000–1368*. Bloomington: University of Indiana Press, 1988.

———. *The Sea and Medieval Civilizations: Collected Essays*. London: Variorium Reprints, 1978.

Lewis, P. S. *The Recovery of France in the Fifteenth Century*. New York: Harper and Row, 1972.

Long, W. Harwood. "The Low Yields of Corn in Medieval England." *Economic History Review*, 2d ser., 32 (1979): 459–469.

Lynch, John. *Spain under the Hapsburgs*, 2 vols. Oxford: Blackwell, 1964.

Macfarlane, Alan. *The Origins of English Individualism: The Family Property and Social Transition*. Oxford: Blackwell, 1978.

MacKay, Angus. *Spain in the Middle Ages: From Frontier to Empire, 1000–1500*. London: Macmillan, 1977.

MacLeod, Murdo J. *Spanish Central America: A Socioeconomic History, 1520–1720*. Berkeley: University of California Press, 1973.

Mate, Mavis. "Medieval Agrarian Practices: The Determining Factors?" *Agricultural History Review* 33 (1985): 22–31.

Mauro, Frédéric. *Le XVIe Siècle Européen: Aspects Economiques*. Paris: Presses Universitaires de France, 1970.

McKay, Derek, and H. M. Scott. *The Rise of the Great Powers, 1648–1815*. New York: Longman, 1983.

McNeill, William H. "The Eccentricity of Wheels, or Eurasian Transportation in Historical Perspective." *American Historical Review* 92 (1987): 1111–1126.

———. *Europe's Steppe Frontier*. Chicago: University of Chicago Press, 1964.

———. *The Pursuit of Power: Technology, Armed Force, and Society since A.D. 1000*. Chicago: University of Chicago Press, 1982.

———. *The Rise of the West: A History of the Human Community*. Chicago: University of Chicago Press, 1963.

———. *The Shape of European History*. New York: Oxford, 1974.

Metcalf, D. M. "The Prosperity of North-Western Europe in the Eighth and Ninth Centuries." *Economic History Review*, 2d ser., 20 (1967): 344–357.

Meuvret, Jean. *Le Problème des subsistances à l'époque Louis XIV*. Paris: Mouton, 1977.

Michelet, Jules. *Histoire de France*, 16 vols. Paris: E. Flammarion, rev. ed., 1893–1899.

Miller, Edward, and John Hatcher. *Medieval England: Rural Society and Economic Change, 1086–1348*. London: Longman, 1978.

Miskimin, H. A. *The Economy of Early Renaissance Europe, 1300–1460*. London: Cambridge University Press, 1975.

Molenda, D. "Technological Innovations in Central Europe between the XIVth and XVIIth Centuries." *Journal of European Economic History* 17 (1988): 63–85.

Morris, Colin. *The Discovery of the Individual, 1050–1200*. London: S.P.C.K. for the Church Historical Society, 1972.

Mousnier, Roland. *Social Hierarchies: 1450 to the Present*, trans. Peter Evens, ed. Margaret Clarke. New York: Schocken Books, 1973.

Mundy, John H. *Europe in the High Middle Ages 1150–1309*. New York: Longman, 1973.

Musson, A. E. "Industrial Motive Power in the United Kingdom, 1800–1870." *Economic History Review* 29 (1976): 415–439.

Needham, Joseph. *Science and Civilisation in China*: vol. 2, *History of Scientific Thought*. Cambridge: Cambridge University Press, 1956.

Nef, J. U. *War and Human Progress*. New York: Norton, 1968.

Nelson, Benjamin. *The Idea of Usury*. Princeton: Princeton University Press, 1949.

Neuschel, Kristen B. *Word of Honor: Interpreting Noble Culture in Sixteenth-Century France*. Ithaca: Cornell University Press, 1989.

Oakley, Francis. *The Medieval Experience: Foundations of Western Cultural Singularity*. New York: Scribners, 1974.

O'Callaghan, Joseph F. *A History of Medieval Spain*. Ithaca: Cornell University Press, 1975.

O'Connell, Robert L. *Of Arms and Men: A History of War, Weapons, and Aggression*. New York: Oxford University Press, 1989.

Oliveira Margues, A. H. de. *History of Portugal*, 2 vols. New York: Columbia University Press, 1971–1972.

Olsh, John Lindsay. "The Growth of English Agricultural Productivity in the Seventeenth Century." *Social Science History* 1 (1977): 460–485.

Ortiz, Antonio Dominquez. *The Golden Age of Spain 1516–1659*. London and New York: Basic Books, 1971.

Outhwaite, R. B. "Progress and Backwardness in English Agriculture, 1500–1650." *Economic History Review*, 2d ser., 39 (1986): 1–18.

Ozment, Steven E. *The Age of Reform, 1250–1500*. New Haven: Yale University Press, 1980.

Parker, Geoffrey. *The Military Revolution: Military Innovation and the Rise of the West, 1500–1800*. New York: Cambridge University Press, 1988.

———. "The 'Military Revolution,' 1560–1660—A Myth?" *Journal of Modern History* 48 (1976): 195–214.

———. *The Thirty Years' War*. New York: Routledge and Kegan Paul, 1987.

Parker, Geoffrey, and Lesley M. Smith, eds. *The General Crisis of the Seventeenth Century*. London: Routledge and Kegan Paul, 1978.

Parker, William N., and E. L. Jones, eds. *European Peasants and Their Markets: Essays in Agrarian Economic History*. Princeton: Princeton University Press, 1975.

Phillips, Carla Rahn. "Time and Duration: A Model for the Economy of Early Modern Spain." *American Historical Review* 92 (1987): 531–562.

Pirenne, Henri. *Economic and Social History of Medieval Europe*. London: K. Paul, Trench, Trubner & Co., 1937.

Pocock, J. G. A., ed. *Three British Revolutions: 1641, 1688, 1776*. Princeton: Princeton University Press, 1980.

Polanyi, Karl. *The Great Transformation*. New York: Rinehart, 1944.

———. *The Livelihood of Man*. New York: Academic Press, 1977.

Postan, M. M. "The Chronology of Labour Services." In M. M. Postan, *Essays in Medieval Agriculture and General Problems of the Medieval Economy*. Cambridge: Cambridge University Press, 1973.

———. "England." In Chapter 7, "Medieval Agrarian Society in its Prime," in M. M. Postan, ed., *The Cambridge Economic History of Europe*, vol. 1, 2d ed. Cambridge: Cambridge University Press, 1966.

———. *Essays on Medieval Agriculture and General Problems of the Medieval Economy*. Cambridge: Cambridge University Press, 1973.

———. "Investment in Medieval Agriculture." *Journal of Economic History* 27 (1967): 576–587.

———. *The Medieval Economy and Society: An Economic History of Britain 1100–1500*. Berkeley and Los Angeles: University of California Press, 1972.

———. *Medieval Trade and Finance*. Cambridge: Cambridge University Press, 1973.

Pounds, N. J. G. *An Historical Geography of Europe 455 B.C.–A.D. 1330*. Cambridge: Cambridge University Press, 1973.

Pryor, John H. *Geography, Technology and War: Studies in the Maritime History of the Mediterranean, 649–1571*. New York: Cambridge University Press, 1988.

Rabb, T. K. "The Effects of the Thirty Years' War on the German Economy." *Journal of Modern History* 34 (1962): 40–51.

———. *The Struggle for Stability in Early Modern Europe*. New York: Oxford University Press, 1975.

Radding, Charles M. *A World Made by Man: Cognition and Society, 400–1200*. Chapel Hill: University of North Carolina Press, 1985.

Reynolds, Susan. *Kingdoms and Communities in Western Europe, 900–1300*. Oxford: Clarendon Press, 1984.

Richard, Guy. *Noblesse d'affaires au XVIIIe siècle*. Paris: A. Colin, 1974.

Richardson, R. C. *The Debate on the English Revolution*. New York: St. Martin's Press, 1977.

Riley, J. C. "The Dutch Economy after 1650: Decline or Growth?" *Journal of European Economic History* 13 (1984): 521–570.

Rosenberg, Nathan, and L. E. Birdzell. *How the West Grew Rich: The Economic Transformation of the Industrial World*. New York: Basic Books, 1986.

Russell, Conrad, ed. *The Origins of the English Civil War*. London: Macmillan, 1973.

Salmon, J. H. M. *Society in Crisis: France in the Sixteenth Century*. New York: St. Martin's Press, 1975.

Schalk, Ellergy. *From Valor to Pedigree: Ideas of Nobility in France in the Sixteenth and Seventeenth Centuries*. Princeton: Princeton University Press, 1986.

Schama, Simon. *The Embarrassment of Riches: An Interpretation of Dutch Culture in the Golden Age*. New York: Knopf, 1987.

Schwarzmann, Maurice. "Background Factors in Spanish Economic Decline." *Explorations in Entrepreneurial History* 3 (1951): 221–247.

Scoville, W. C. *The Persecution of Huguenots and French Economic Development 1680–1720*. Berkeley and Los Angeles: University of California Press, 1960.

Scribner, R. W. *The German Reformation*. Atlantic Highlands, N.J.: Humanities Press, 1986.

Shapre, J. A. *Early-Modern England: A Social History 1550–1760*. New York: Edward Arnold, 1988.

Simone, Franco. *The French Renaissance: Medieval Tradition and Italian Influence in Shaping the Renaissance in France*, trans. H. Gaston Hall. London: Macmillan, 1969.

Slicher van Bath, B. H. *The Agrarian History of Western Europe 500–1850*. New York: St. Martin's Press, 1963.

Solow, Barbara. "Caribbean Slavery and British Growth: The Eric Williams Hypothesis." *Journal of Development Economics* 17 (1985): 99–115.

Sombart, Werner. *A New Social Philosophy*, trans. Karl F. Geiser. Princeton: Princeton University Press, 1937.

Southern, R. W. *The Making of the Middle Ages*. New York: Penguin Books, 1970.

Spitz, Lewis W. *The Protestant Reformation, 1517–1559*. New York: Harper and Row, 1985.

Stavrianos, L. S. *A Global History of Man*. Boston: Allyn & Bacon, 1962.

Stone, Lawrence. *The Causes of the English Revolution, 1529–1642*. New York: Harper Torchbooks, 1972.

———. *The Crisis of the Aristocracy, 1558–1641*. New York: Oxford University Press, 1967.

———, ed. *Social Change and Revolution in England, 1540–1640*. London: Longman, 1965.

Stone, Lawrence, and J. C. Fawtier Stone. *An Open Elite? England 1540–1880*. Oxford: Clarendon Press, 1984.

Strayer, Joseph R. *On the Medieval Origins of the Modern State*. Princeton: Princeton University Press, 1970.

Tate, W. E. *The English Village Community and the Enclosure Movements*. London: Gollancz, 1967.

Thirsk, Joan. "The Common Fields." *Past and Present* 29 (1964): 3–25.

———. *English Peasant Farming: The Agrarian History of England and Wales*: vol. 4, *1500–1640*. London: Cambridge University Press, 1967.

Thompson, James Westfall. *Economic and Social History of Europe in the Later Middle Ages (1300–1530)*. New York: Frederick Ungar, 1960.

Tilly, Charles. *The Contentious French*. Cambridge: Belknap Press, 1986.

———, ed. *The Formation of National States in Western Europe*. Princeton: Princeton University Press, 1975.

Titow, J. Z. *English Rural Society, 1200–1350*. London: Allen & Unwin, 1969.

———. *Winchester Yields: A Study in Medieval Agriculture Productivity*. Cambridge: Cambridge University Press, 1972.

Trevor-Roper, Hugh. *The Rise of Christian Europe*. London: Thames and Hudson, 1965.

Van der Wee, Herman, and Eddy van Cauwenburghe, eds. *Productivity of Land and Agricultural Innovation in the Low Countries 1250–1800*. Leuven: Leuven University Press, 1977.

van Houtte, J. A. *An Economic History of the Low Countries, 800–1800*. New York: St. Martin's Press, 1977.

Vigarello, Georges. *Concepts of Cleanliness: Changing Attitudes in France since the Middle Ages*, trans. Jean Birrell. New York: Cambridge University Press, 1988 .

Vives, Jaime Vincens. *An Economic History of Spain*. Princeton: Princeton University Press, 1969.

Wallace-Hadrill, J. M. *The Barbarian West, 400–1000*, 3d ed. Oxford: Blackwell, 1989.

Watson, A. M. "The Arab Agricultural Revolution and Its Diffusion, 700–1100." *Journal of Economic History* 34 (1974): 8–35.

Watson, Alan. *The Evolution of Law*. Baltimore: Johns Hopkins University Press, 1985.

Weber, Max. *General Economic History*. New York: Free Press, 1927.

White, Lynn, Jr. "The Expansion of Technology 500–1500." In Carlo M. Cipolla, ed., *The Fontana Economic History of Europe*: vol. 1, *The Middle Ages*. London: Collins/Fontana, 1972.

———. *Medieval Technology and Social Change*. Oxford: Oxford University Press, 1962.

Whitrow, G. J. *Time in History: The Evolution of Our General Awareness of Time and Temporal Perspective*. New York: Oxford University Press, 1988.

Williams, Eric. *Capitalism and Slavery*. Chapel Hill: University of North Carolina Press, 1944.

Wilson, Charles. *England's Apprenticeship, 1603–1763*. New York: St. Martin's Press, 1965.

———. *The Transformation of Europe, 1558–1684*. Berkeley: University of California Press, 1976.

Winter, J. M., ed. *War and Economic Development*. Cambridge: Cambridge University Press, 1975.

Wittfogel, Karl A. *Oriental Despotism: A Comparative Study of Total Power*. New Haven: Yale University Press, 1957.

Wolf, Eric R. *Europe and the People Without History*. Berkeley: University of California Press, 1982.

Wolf, John B. *The Emergence of the Great Powers 1685–1715*. New York: Harper and Row, 1962.

Wrightson, Keith. *English Society, 1580–1680*. New Brunswick, N.J.: Rutgers University Press, 1982.

Wrigley, E. A. *People, Cities and Wealth: The Transformation of Traditional Society*. New York: Blackwell, 1989.

Wyman, W. D., and C. B. Kroeber, eds. *The Frontier in Perspective*. Madison: University of Wisconsin Press, 1965.

Yelling, J. A. *Common Field and Enclosure in England, 1450–1850*. Hamden, Conn.: Archon Books, 1977.

Zinkin, Maurice. *Asia and the West*. London: Chatto and Windus, 1951.

COMMERCE, CAPITALISM, AND EXPANSION

Andrews, Kenneth. *Trade, Plunder, and Settlement*. Cambridge: Cambridge University Press, 1984.

Ashton, T. S. "The Treatment of Capitalism by Historians." In F. A. Hayek, ed., *Capitalism and the Historians*. London: Routledge and Kegan Paul, 1954.

Ashtor, Eliyah. *Levant Trade in the Later Middle Ages*. Princeton: Princeton University Press, 1983.

Attman, Artur. *American Bullion in the European World Trade 1600–1800*, trans. Eva Green and Allan Green. Goteborg: Kungl, 1986.

———. *The Bullion Flow between Europe and the East, 1000–1750*, trans. Eva Green and Allan Green. Goteborg: Kungl, 1981.

———. *Dutch Enterprise in the World Bullion Trade, 1550–1800*, trans. Eva Green and Allan Green. Goteborg: Kungl, 1983.

Baechler, Jean. *The Origins of Capitalism*. Oxford: Blackwell, 1975.

Baechler, Jean, J. Hall, and M. Mann, eds. *Europe and the Rise of Capitalism*. Oxford: Blackwell, 1988.

Ball, J. N. *Merchants and Merchandise: The Expansion of Trade in Europe, 1500–1630*. London: Croom Helm, 1977.

Barbour, Violet. *Capitalism in Amsterdam in the Seventeenth Century*. Ann Arbor: University of Michigan Press, 1966.

Beaud, M. *A History of Capitalism*. London: Macmillan, 1984.

Beresford, M. W. *New Towns of the Middle Ages*. London: Lutterworth Press, 1967.

Berger, Peter. *The Capitalist Revolution*. New York: Basic Books, 1986.

Bergier, J-F. "The Industrial Bourgeoisie and the Rise of the Working Class 1700–1914." In Carlo M. Cipolla, ed., *The Fontana Economic History of Europe*: vol. 3, *The Industrial Revolution*. Glasgow: Fontana/Collins, 1973.

Bernard, Jacques. "Trade and Finance in the Middle Ages 900–1500." In Carlo M. Cipolla, ed., *Fontana Economic History of Europe*: vol. 1, *The Middle Ages*. London: Fontana/Collins, 1972.

Bogucka, Maria. "The Role of Baltic Trade in European Development from the XVIth to the XVIIIth Centuries." *Journal of European Economic History* 9 (1980): 5–20.

Boxer, C. R. *The Portuguese Seaborne Empire: 1415–1825*. New York: Knopf, 1969.

Boyajian, James C. *Portuguese Bankers at the Court of Spain, 1626–1650*. New Brunswick, N.J.: Rutgers University Press, 1983.

Braudel, Fernand. *Afterthoughts on Material Civilization and Capitalism*, trans. Patricia Ranum. Baltimore: Johns Hopkins University Press, 1977.

———. *Capitalism and Material Life 1400–1800*, trans. Miriam Kochan. New York: Harper, 1975.

———. *Civilization and Capitalism, 15th–18th Century*: vol. 1, *The Structures of Everyday Life*: vol. 2, *The Wheels of Commerce*: vol. 3, *The Perspective of the World*, trans. Sian Reynolds. New York: Harper and Row, 1981, 1982, 1984.

Brinley, Thomas. *Migration and Economic Growth: A Study of Great Britain and the Atlantic Economy*, 2d ed. Cambridge: Cambridge University Press, 1973.

Britnell, R. H. "Minor Landlords in England and Medieval Agrarian Capitalism." *Past and Present* 88 (1980): 3–22.

———. "The Proliferation of Markets in England, 1200–1349." *Economic History Review*, 2d ser., 34 (1981): 209–221

Burke, Peter. *Venice and Amsterdam: A Study of Seventeenth-Century Elites*. London: Temple-Smith, 1974.

Carus-Wilson, E. M. *Medieval Merchant Venturers: Collected Studies*. London: Methuen, 1967.

Chapman, Stanley D. "British Marketing Enterprise: The Changing Roles of Merchants, Manufacturers, and Financiers, 1700–1860." *Business History Review* 53 (1979): 205–234.

Chaunu, Pierre. *European Expansion in the Later Middle Ages*. Amsterdam: North-Holland Publishing, 1979.

Childs, Wendy R. *Anglo-Castilian Trade in the Later Middle Ages*. Manchester: Manchester University Press, 1978.

Cipolla, Carlo. *Guns, Sails and Empires: Technological Innovation and the Early Phases of European Expansion, 1400–1700*. New York: Pantheon, 1965.

———. *Money, Prices, and Civilization in the Mediterranean World: Fifth to Seventeenth Century*. Princeton: Published for University of Cincinnati by Princeton University Press, 1956.

Clark, Peter, and Paul Slack. *English Towns in Transition, 1500–1700*. London: Oxford University Press, 1976.

Coelho, Philip. "The Profitability of Imperialism: The British Experience in the West Indies, 1768–1772." *Explorations in Economic History* 10 (1973): 253–280.

Cohen, Jere. "Rational Capitalism in Renaissance Italy." *American Journal of Sociology* 85 (1980): 1340–1355.

Collins, J. B. "The Role of Atlantic France in the Baltic Trade: Dutch Traders and Polish Grain at Nantes, 1625–1675." *Journal of European Economic History* 13 (1984): 239–291.

Coornaert, E. L. J. "European Economic Institutions and the New World: The Chartered Companies." In E. E. Rich and C. H. Wilson, eds., *The Cambridge Economic History of Europe*, vol. 4. Cambridge: Cambridge University Press, 1967.

Cunningham, William. "Economic Change." In A. W. Ward, G. W. Prothero, and Stanley Leathes, eds., *The Cambridge Modern History: vol. 1, The Renaissance*. Cambridge: Cambridge University, 1902.

Curtin, Philip D. *Cross-Cultural Trade in World History*. Cambridge: Cambridge University Press, 1984.

Davies, K. G. *The North Atlantic World in the Seventeenth Century*. Minneapolis: University of Minnesota Press, 1974.

———. *The Royal African Company*. London: Longman, 1957.

Davis, Ralph. *English Merchant Shipping and Anglo-Dutch Rivalry in the Seventeenth Century*. London: H.M.S.O., 1975.

———. *English Overseas Trade 1500–1700*. London: Macmillan, 1973.

Debien, Gabriel. *Les engages pour les Antilles (1634–1715)*. Paris: Société de l'histoire des colonies françaises, 1952.

de Roover, Raymond. *Business, Banking and Economic Thought in Late Medieval and Early Modern Europe*. Chicago: University of Chicago Press, 1974.

———. "A Florentine Firm of Cloth Manufacturers: Management and Organization of a Sixteenth-Century Business." *Speculum* 16 (1941): 3–33.

———. *Money, Banking and Credit in Medieval Bruges.* Cambridge, Mass.: Mediaeval Academy of America, 1948.

———. *The Rise and Decline of the Medici Bank, 1397–1494.* Cambridge, Mass.: Harvard University Press, 1963.

de Vries, Jan. *European Urbanization, 1500–1800.* London: Methuen, 1984.

di Corcia, Joseph. "Bourg, Bourgeois, Bourgeois de Paris from the Eleventh to the Eighteenth Century." *Journal of Modern History* 50 (1978): 207–233.

Diffie, Bailey W., and George D. Winius. *Foundations of the Portuguese Empire, 1415–1580.* Minneapolis: University of Minnesota Press, 1977.

———. *Prelude to Empire: Portugal Overseas before Henry the Navigator.* Lincoln: University of Nebraska Press, 1960 .

Ehrenberg, Richard. *Capital and Finance in the Age of the Renaissance,* trans. H. M. Lucas. New York: Harcourt, Brace, 1928.

Einzig, Paul. *The History of Foreign Exchange.* New York: St. Martin's Press, 1962.

Engerman, Stanley L. "The Slave Trade and British Capital Formation in the Eighteenth Century: A Comment on the Williams Thesis." *Business History Review* 46 (1972): 430–443.

Faroqhi, S. "The Venetian Presence in the Ottoman Empire, (1600–1630)." *Journal of European Economic History* 15 (1986): 345–384.

Goitein, S. D. *Letters of Medieval Jewish Traders.* Princeton: Princeton University Press, 1973.

Goldthwaite, R. A. "Local Banking in Renaissance Florence." *Journal of European Economic History* 14 (1985): 5–56.

Goodman, J. "Financing Pre-Modern European Industry: An Example from Florence 1580–1660." *Journal of European Economic History* 10 (1981): 415–436.

Gough, J. W. *The Rise of the Entrepreneur.* London: Batsford, 1969.

Grassby, Richard. "English Merchant Capitalism in the Late Seventeenth Century: The Composition of Business Fortunes." *Past and Present* 46 (1970): 87–107.

———. "The Personal Wealth of the Business Community in Seventeenth Century England." *Economic History Review,* 2d ser., 23 (1970): 220–234.

Hamilton, Earl, Jr. "Prices and Progress: Prices as a Factor in Business Growth." *Journal of Economic History* 12 (1952): 325–349.

Heers, Jacques. *Société et économie à Gênes (XIVe–XVe siècles).* London: Variorum Reprints, 1969.

Herlihy, David. "Treasure Hoards in the Italian Economy, 960–1139." *Economic History Review,* 2d ser., 10 (1957): 1–14.

Jeannin, Pierre. *Merchants of the Sixteenth Century.* New York: Harper, 1972.

———. "The Sea-Borne and the Overland Trade Routes of Northern Europe in the Sixteenth and Seventeenth Centuries." *Journal of European Economic History* 11 (1982): 5–59.

Kedar, Benjamin Z. *Merchants in Crisis: Genoese and Venetian Men of Affairs and the Fourteenth Century Depression.* New Haven and London: Yale University Press, 1976.

Keynes, John Maynard. *A Treatise on Money,* 2 vols. New York: Harcourt Brace, 1930.

Kindleberger, Charles P. *A Financial History of Western Europe*. London: Allen & Unwin, 1984.

Konetzke, Richard. "Entrepreneurial Activities of Spanish and Portuguese Noblemen in Medieval Times." *Explorations in Entrepreneurial History* 6 (1953): 115–120.

Landes, David, ed. *The Rise of Capitalism*. New York: Macmillan, 1966.

Lane, Frederic C. "The Mediterranean Spice Trade: Further Evidence of Its Revival in the Sixteenth Century." *American Historical Review* 45 (1939–40): 581–590.

———. *Venice. A Maritime Republic*. Baltimore: Johns Hopkins University Press, 1973.

Lane, Frederic C., and Reinhold C. Meuller. *Money and Banking in Medieval and Renaissance Venice:* vol. 1, *Coins and Moneys of Account*. Baltimore: Johns Hopkins University Press, 1985.

Lewis, A. R. *The Northern Seas: Shipping and Commerce in Northern Europe, A.D. 300–1100*. Princeton: Princeton University Press, 1958.

Liss, Peggy K. *Atlantic Empires: The Network of Trade and Revolution 1713–1826*. Baltimore: Johns Hopkins University Press, 1982.

Lloyd, T. H. *Alien Merchants in England in the High Middle Ages*. New York: St. Martin's Press, 1982.

———. *The English Wool Trade in the Middle Ages*. Cambridge: Cambridge University Press, 1977.

Lopez, Robert. *The Commercial Revolution of the Middle Ages, 950–1350*. Englewood Cliffs, N.J.: Prentice Hall, 1971.

———. "The Evolution of Land Transport in the Middle Ages." *Past and Present* 9 (1956): 17–29.

———. "The Market Expansion: The Case of Genoa." *Journal of Economic History* 24 (1964): 445–464.

Maddison, Angus. *Phases of Capitalist Development*. Oxford: Oxford University Press, 1982.

Malowist, Marian. "The Economic and Social Development of the Baltic Countries from the Fifteenth to the Seventeenth Centuries." *Economic History Review* 2d ser., 12 (1959): 177–189.

———. "Poland, Russia and Western Trade in the Fifteenth and Sixteenth Centuries." *Past and Present* 13 (1958): 26–39.

———. "The Problem of the Inequality of Economic Development in Europe in the Later Middle Ages." *Economic History Review*, 2d ser., 19 (1966): 15–28.

Marchant, Alexander. *From Barter to Slavery: The Economic Relations of Portuguese and Indians in the Settlement of Brazil, 1550–1580*. Baltimore: Johns Hopkins University Press, 1942.

Mauro, F. *Le Portugal et L'Atlantique au XVIIe Siècle 1570–1670*. Paris: S.E.V.P.E.N., 1960.

McKendrick, Niel, John Brewer, and J. H. Plumb. *The Birth of a Consumer Society: The Commercialization of Eighteenth-Century England*. Bloomington: Indiana University Press, 1982.

McNally, David. *Political Economy and the Rise of Capitalism: A Reinterpretation*. Berkeley: University of California Press, 1989.

McNeill, William H. *Venice, the Hinge of Europe, 1081–1797*. Chicago and London: University of Chicago Press, 1974.

Miskimin, Harry A. *Money and Power in Fifteenth-Century France*. New Haven: Yale University Press, 1984.

———. *Money, Prices and Foreign Exchange in Fourteenth Century France*. New Haven: Yale University Press, 1963.

Moore, Ellen Wedemeyer. *Alien Merchants in England in the High Middle Ages*. Brighton: Harvester Press, 1982.

———. *The Fairs of Medieval England: An Introductory Study*. Toronto: Pontifical Institute of Medieval Studies, 1985.

Mundy, John H., and Peter Riesenberg. *The Medieval Town*. Princeton: D. Van Nostrand, 1958.

Nef, John. *The Conquest of the Material World*. Chicago: University of Chicago Press, 1964.

Newman, K. "Hamburg in the European Economy, 1660–1750." *Journal of European Economic History* 14 (1985): 57–94.

Ormrod, D. *English Grain Exports and the Structure of Agrarian Capitalism, 1700–1760*. Hull: Hull University Press, 1985.

Palliser, D. M. "A Crisis of English Towns? The Case of York, 1460–1640." *Northern History* 14 (1978): 108–125.

Parker, William N. *Europe, America, and the Wider World: Essays on the Economic History of Western Capitalism:* vol. 1, *Europe and the World Economy*. Cambridge: Cambridge University Press, 1984.

Parry, J. H. *The Age of Reconnaissance*. New York: Menton, 1964.

———. *The Discovery of the Sea*. Berkeley and Los Angeles: University of California Press, 1981.

Penrose, Boies. *Travel and Discovery in the Renaissance 1420–1620*. Cambridge, Mass.: Harvard University Press, 1952.

Phillips, J. R. S. *The Medieval Expansion of Europe*. New York: Oxford University Press, 1988.

Phythian-Adams, C. *Desolation of a City: Coventry and the Urban Crisis of the Late Middle Ages*. Cambridge: Cambridge University Press, 1979.

Pike, Ruth. *Aristocrats and Traders: Sevellian Society in the Sixteenth Century*. Ithaca: Cornell University Press, 1972.

———. *Enterprise and Adventure: The Genoese in Seville and the Opening of the New World*. Ithaca: Cornell University Press, 1966.

Pirenne, Henri. *Medieval Cities: Their Origins and the Revival of Trade*. Princeton: Princeton University Press, 1925.

———. "The Stages in the Social History of Capitalism." *American Historical Review* 19 (1913–1914): 494–515.

Power, Eileen. *The Wool Trade in English Medieval History*. London: Oxford University Press, 1941.

Prawer, Joshua. *Crusaders' Kingdom: European Colonialism in the Middle Ages*. New York: Praeger, 1972.

Pryor, John H. "Commenda: The Operation of the Contract in Long Distance Commerce at Marseilles during the Thirteenth Century." *Journal of European Economic History* 12 (1984): 397–440.

———. "The Origins of the *Commenda* Contract." *Speculum* 52 (1977): 5–37.

Pullen, Brian, ed. *Crisis and Change in the Venetian Economy in the Sixteenth and Seventeenth Centuries.* London: Methuen, 1968.

Rabb, Theodore K. *Enterprise and Empire: Merchant and Gentry Investment in the Expansion of England 1575–1630.* Cambridge, Mass.: Harvard University Press, 1967.

———. "The Expansion of Europe and the Spirit of Capitalism." *Historical Journal* 17 (1974): 675–689.

———. "Investment in English Overseas Enterprise, 1575–1630." *Economic History Review,* 2d ser., 19 (1966): 70–81.

Rapp, R. T. "The Unmaking of the Mediterranean Trade Hegemony." *Journal of Economic History* 35 (1975): 499–525.

Raynal, Abbé (Guillaume-Thomas). *Histoire philosophique et politique des établissemens et du commerce des Européens dans les deux Indes.* Geneva: Jean-Leonard Pellet, 1782.

Reynolds, Robert L. "In Search of a Business Class in Thirteenth-Century Genoa." *Journal of Economic History* 5 (supplement) (1945): 1–19.

Reynolds, Susan. *An Introduction to the History of English Medieval Towns.* Oxford: Clarendon Press, 1977.

Rodinson, Maxime. *Islam and Capitalism.* Austin: University of Texas Press, 1978.

Rorig, Fritz. *The Medieval Town.* London: Batsford, 1967.

Scammell, G. V. *The First Imperial Age: European Overseas Expansion 1400–1715.* Winchester: Unwin Hyman, 1989.

———. *The World Encompassed: The First European Maritime Empires, c. 800–1650.* Berkeley and Los Angeles: University of California Press, 1981.

See, Henri. *Modern Capitalism: Its Origins and Evolution.* London: Noel Douglas, 1928.

Sheridan, R. B. "The Plantation Revolution and the Industrial Revolution, 1625–1775." *Caribbean Studies* 9 (1969): 5–25.

———. "Planters and Merchants: The Oliver Family of Antigua and London, 1716–1784." *Business History* 13 (1971): 104–116.

———. "Simon Taylor, Sugar Tycoon of Jamaica, 1740–1813." *Agricultural History* 45 (1971): 285–296.

———. *Sugar and Slavery: An Economic History of the British West Indies, 1623–1775.* Baltimore: Johns Hopkins University Press, 1974.

———. "The Wealth of Jamaica in the Eighteenth Century." *Economic History Review,* 2d ser., 18 (1965): 292–311.

———. "The Wealth of Jamaica in the Eighteenth Century: A Rejoinder." *Economic History Review,* 2d ser., 21 (1968): 46–61.

Smith, Woodruff D. "The Function of Commercial Centers in the Modernization of European Capitalism: Amsterdam as an Information Exchange in the Seventeenth Century." *Journal of Economic History* 54 (1984): 985–1006.

Solow, Barbara L., and Stanley L. Engerman, eds. *British Capitalism and Caribbean Slavery: The Legacy of Eric Williams.* Cambridge: Cambridge University Press, 1987.

Sombart, Werner. *Der Moderne Kapitalismus,* 2 vols. Leipzig: Duncker and Humblot, 1902.

———. *The Jews and Modern Capitalism.* Glencoe: Free Press, 1951 (first published 1911).

————. *Luxury and Capitalism*. Ann Arbor: University of Michigan Press, 1967 (first published 1913).

————. *The Quintessence of Capitalism*. New York: Howard Fertig, 1967 (first published 1915).

Spufford, Peter. *Money and Its Use in Medieval Europe*. New York: Cambridge University Press, 1987.

Supple, B. E. *Commercial Crisis and Change in England, 1600–1642*. Cambridge: Cambridge University Press, 1959.

Sweezy, Paul M. *The Theory of Capitalist Development*. New York: Oxford University Press, 1942.

Thirsk, Joan. *Economic Policy and Projects: The Development of a Consumer Society in Early Modern England*. Oxford: Clarendon Press, 1978.

Thomas, Robert Paul. "Sugar Colonies of the Old Empire: Profit or Loss for Great Britain?" *Economic History Review*, 2d ser., 21 (1968): 30–45.

Tribe, Keith. *Geneologies of Capitalism*. Atlantic Highlands, N.J.: Humanities Press, 1981.

Unger, Richard. *The Ship in the Medieval Economy, 600–1600*. Montreal: Croom Helm, 1980.

Usher, A. P. *The Early History of Deposit Banking in Mediterranean Europe*. Cambridge, Mass.: Harvard University Press, 1943.

van der Wee, Herman. *The Growth of the Antwerp Market and the European Economy, Fourteenth–Sixteenth Centuries*, 3 vols. The Hague: Nijhoff, 1963.

van Houtte, J. A. "The Rise and Decline of the Market of Bruges." *Economic History Review*, 2d ser., 19 (1966): 29–47.

van Stuijvenberg, J. H. *The Interactions of Amsterdam and Antwerp with the Baltic Region, 1400–1800*. Leiden: Martinus Nijhoff, 1983.

Verlinden, Charles. *The Beginning of Modern Colonization. Eleven Essays with Introduction*, trans. Yvonne Freccero. Ithaca: Cornell University Press, 1970.

————. "From the Mediterranean to the Atlantic: Aspects of an Economic Shift (12th–18th Century)." *Journal of European Economic History* 1 (1972): 625–646.

————. "Italian Influence on Iberian Colonization." *Hispanic American Historical Review* 33 (1953): 199–211.

Vilar, Pierre. "Problems of the Formation of Capitalism." *Past and Present* 10 (1956): 15–38.

Weatherill, Lorna. *Consumer Behavior and Material Culture in Britain, 1660–1760*. New York: Routledge, 1988.

Webb, Walter Prescott. *The Great Plains*. Boston: Ginn, 1931.

Willan, T. S. *Studies in Elizabethan Foreign Trade*. Manchester: Manchester University Press, 1959.

Zins, Henryk. *England and the Baltic in the Elizabethan Era*, trans. H. C. Stevens. Manchester: Manchester University Press, 1972.

POPULATION HISTORY AND THE DEMOGRAPHIC IMPERATIVE

Anderson, Michael. "Historical Demography after *The Population History of England*." In Robert I. Rotberg and Theodore K. Rabb, eds., *Population and Economy:*

Population History from the Traditional to the Modern World. Cambridge: Cambridge University Press, 1986.

Appleby, Andrew. "Grain Prices and Subsistence Crises in England and France, 1590–1740." *Journal of Economic History* 39 (1979): 865–887.

Bois, Guy. *Crise du Féodalisme.* Paris: Editions de la Maison des sciences de l'homme, 1976.

Borah, Woodrow, and Shelburne F. Cook. *The Aboriginal Population of Central Mexico on the Eve of the Spanish Conquest.* Berkeley: University of California Press, 1963.

———. *Essays in Population History: Mexico and the Caribbean.* Berkeley: University of California Press, 1971 .

Boserup, Ester. *Population and Technological Change: A Study of Long-Term Trends.* Chicago: University of Chicago Press, 1981.

Bridbury, A. R. "The Farming Out of Manors." *Economic History Review,* 2d ser., 31 (1978): 503–520.

Campbell, Bruce M. S. "Agricultural Progress in Medieval England: Some Evidence from Eastern Norfolk." *Economic History Review,* 2d ser., 36 (1983): 25–46.

———. "Population Change and the Genesis of Commonfields on a Norfolk Manor." *Economic History Review,* 2d ser., 33 (1980): 174–192.

Chambers, J. D. *Population, Economy, and Society in Pre-Industrial England.* London: Oxford University Press, 1972.

Cipolla, Carlo M. *The Economic History of World Population.* Baltimore: Penguin Books, 1962.

Cowgill, George. "On Causes and Consequences of Ancient and Modern Population Change." *American Anthropologist* 77 (1975): 505–525.

Denevan, William M., ed. *The Native Population of the Americas in 1492.* Madison: University of Wisconsin Press, 1976.

Fleury, Michel, and Louis Henry. *Des registres paroissiaux à l'histoire de la population: Manuel de dépouillement et d'exploitation de l'état civil ancien.* Paris: Editions de l'Institut national d'études demographiques, 1956.

Flinn, M. W. *The European Demographic System.* Baltimore: Johns Hopkins University Press, 1981.

Freeman, Ronald, ed. *Population: The Vital Revolution.* New York: Anchor Books, 1964.

Gardner, Richard. "Bush, the U.N., and Too Many People." *New York Times,* 22 September 1989.

Glass, C. V., and D. E. C. Eversley, eds. *Population in History.* London: Edward Arnold, 1965.

Glass, C. V., and Roger Revelle, eds. *Population and Social Change.* London: Edward Arnold, 1972.

Goody, Jack. *The Development of the Family and Marriage in Europe.* Cambridge: Cambridge University Press, 1983.

Goody, Jack, Joan Thirsk, and E. P. Thompson, eds. *Family and Inheritance: Rural Society in Western Europe, 1200–1800.* London: Cambridge University Press, 1976.

Gottfried, Robert S. "Bury St. Edmunds and the Populations of Late Medieval Towns, 1270–1530." *Journal of British Studies* 20 (1980): 1–31.

Grigg, D. B. *Population Growth and Agrarian Change: An Alternative Perspective.* Cambridge: Cambridge University Press, 1980.

Habakkuk, H. J. *Population Growth and Economic Development since 1750.* Leicester: Leicester University Press, 1972.

Hajnal, J. "European Marriage Patterns in Perspective." In David Glass and D. E. C. Eversley, eds. *Population in History.* London: Edward Arnold, 1965.

Hallam, H. E. *Rural England, 1066–1348.* Atlantic Highlands, N.J.: Humanities Press, 1981.

Hanawalt, Barbara A. *The Ties That Bound: Peasant Families in Medieval England.* New York: Oxford University Press, 1986.

Helleiner, Karl F. "The Population of Europe from the Black Death to the Eve of the Vital Revolution." In E. E. Rich and C. H. Wilson, eds., *The Cambridge Economic History of Europe,* vol. 4. Cambridge: Cambridge University Press, 1967.

Henige, David. "On the Contact Population of Hispaniola: History as High Mathematics." *Hispanic American Historical Review* 58 (1978): 217–237.

Ho, Ping-Ti. *Studies in the Population of China, 1368–1953.* Cambridge, Mass.: Harvard University Press, 1959.

Hollingsworth, T. H. *Historical Demography.* Ithaca: Cornell University Press, 1969.

Houlbrooke, Ralph. *The English Family, 1450–1700.* New York: Longman, 1984.

Ladurie, Emmanuel Le Roy. "Family Structure and Inheritance Customs in Sixteenth Century France." In Jack Goody, Joan Thirsk, and E. P. Thompson, eds., *Family and Inheritance: Rural Society in Western Europe 1200–1800.* Cambridge: Cambridge University Press, 1976.

———. *The Peasants of Languedoc.* Urbana: University of Illinois Press, 1974.

Langer, W. L. "American Foods and Europe's Population Growth, 1750–1850." *Journal of Social History* 8 (1975): 51–66.

———. "Checks on Population Growth: 1750–1850." *Scientific American* 226 (1972): 92–99.

———. "Europe's Initial Population Explosion." *American Historical Review* 69 (1963): 1–17.

Laslett, Peter. *Family Life and Illicit Love in Earlier Generations.* Cambridge: Cambridge University Press, 1977.

———. *The World We Have Lost.* New York: Scribner, 1966.

Laslett, Peter, and Richard Wall. *Household and Family in Past Time.* Cambridge: Cambridge University Press, 1972.

Lee, Ronald Demos. *Population Patterns in the Past.* New York: Academic Press, 1977.

Lee, W. R., ed. *European Demography and Economic Growth.* New York: St. Martin's Press, 1979.

Levine, David. *Family Formation in an Age of Nascent Capitalism.* New York: Academic Press, 1977.

———. *Reproducing Families: The Political Economy of English Population History.* Cambridge: Cambridge University Press, 1987.

———, ed. *Proletarianization and Family History.* New York: Cambridge University Press, 1984.

Macfarlane, Alan. *Marriage and Love in England: Modes of Reproduction, 1300–1840.* Oxford: Blackwell, 1986.

Mate, Mavis. "Agrarian Economy after the Black Death: The Manors of Canterbury Cathedral Priory, 1348–91." *Economic History Review*, 2d ser., 37 (1984): 341–354.

McEvedy, Colin, and Richard Jones. *Atlas of World Population History*. Harmondsworth: Penguin Books, 1978.

McKeown, Thomas. *The Modern Rise of Population*. New York: Academic Press, 1976.

Meuvret, J. "Demographic Crisis in France from the Sixteenth to the Eighteenth Century." In David Glass and D. E. C. Eversley, eds., *Population in History*. Chicago: Aldine, 1965.

Miller, Edward. "The English Economy in the Thirteenth Century: Implications of Recent Research." *Past and Present* 28 (1964): 21–40.

Mols, Roger, S. J. "Population in Europe 1500–1700." In Carlo M. Cipolla, ed., *The Fontana Economic History of Europe:* vol. 2, *The Sixteenth and Seventeenth Centuries*. London: Fontana/Collins, 1974.

Palliser, D. M. "Tawney's Century: Brave New World or Malthusian Trap?" *Economic History Review*, 2d ser., 35 (1982): 339–353.

Poos, L. R. "The Rural Population of Essex in the Later Middle Ages." *Economic History Review*, 2d ser., 38 (1985): 515–530.

Postan, M. M. "The Chronology of Labour Services." In M. M. Postan, *Essays in Medieval Agriculture and General Problems of the Medieval Economy*. Cambridge: Cambridge University Press, 1973.

Pounds, N. J. C. "Overpopulation in France and the Low Countries in the Later Middle Ages." *Journal of Social History* 3 (1970): 225–247.

Razi, Zvi. *Life, Marriage and Death in a Medieval Parish. Economy, Society and Demography in Halesowen, 1270–1400*. Cambridge: Cambridge University Press, 1980.

Rotberg, Robert I., and Theodore K. Rabb, eds. *Hunger and History: The Impact of Changing Food Production and Consumption Patterns on Society*. Cambridge: Cambridge University Press, 1985.

———. *Population and Economy: Population and History from the Traditional to the Modern World*. Cambridge: Cambridge University Press, 1986.

Russell, Josiah Cox. *British Medieval Population*. Albuquerque: University of New Mexico, 1948.

———. *Late Ancient and Medieval Population Control*. Philadelphia: American Philosophical Society, 1985.

———. "Population in Europe 500–1500." In Carlo M. Cipolla, ed., *The Fontana Economic History of Europe:* vol. 1, *The Middle Ages*. London: Fontana/Collins, 1972.

———. "The Pre-Plague Population of England." *Journal of British Studies* 5 (1966): 1–21.

Schofield, Roger S. "Through a Glass Darkly: *The Population History of England* as an Experiment in History." In Robert I. Rotberg and Theodore K. Rabb, eds., *Population and Economy: Population and History from the Traditional to the Modern World*. Cambridge: Cambridge University Press, 1986.

Silver, Morris. "A Non-Neo Malthusian Model of English Land Values, Wages and Grain Yield before the Black Death." *Journal of European Economic History* 12 (1984): 631–650.

Thompson, John A. *The Transformation of Medieval England 1370–1529*. New York: Longman, 1983.

Thrupp, Sylvia L. "The Problem of Replacement-Rates in Late Medieval English Population." *Economic History Review*, 2d ser., 18 (1965): 101–119.

Tranter, N. L. *Population and Society, 1750–1940: Contrasts in Population Growth*. London: Longman, 1985.

Wrigley, E. A. "Family Limitation in Pre-Industrial England." *Economic History Review*, 2d ser., 19 (1966): 82–109.

———. *Population and History*. New York: McGraw-Hill, 1969.

Wrigley, E. A., and R. S. Schofield. *The Population History of England, 1541–1871: A Reconstruction*. Cambridge, Mass: Harvard University Press, 1981.

Zambardino, R. A. "Critique of David Henige's 'On the Contact Population of Hispaniola,' " *Hispanic American Historical Review* 58 (1978): 700–708.

MARXISM AND HISTORY

Adamson, Walter L. *Marx and the Disillusionment of Marxism*. Berkeley and Los Angeles: University of California Press, 1985.

Althusser, Louis. *For Marx*. London: New Left Books, 1977.

Althusser, Louis, and Etienne Balibar. *Reading Capital*. London: New Left Books, 1977.

Anderson, Perry. *Arguments within English Marxism*. London: Verso, 1980.

———. *Considerations on Western Marxism*. London: New Left Books, 1976.

———. *Lineages of the Absolutist State*. London: New Left Books, 1974.

———. *Passages from Antiquity to Feudalism*. New York: Schocken, 1978.

Aston, T. H., and C. H. E. Philpin, eds. *The Brenner Debate: Agrarian Class Structure and Economic Development in Pre-Industrial Europe*. Cambridge: Cambridge University Press, 1985.

Avineri, Schlomo. *The Social and Political Thought of Karl Marx*. Cambridge: Cambridge University Press, 1972.

Bober, M. M. *Karl Marx's Interpretation of History*. New York: Norton, 1965.

Bottomore, Tom, ed. *A Dictionary of Marxist Thought*. Cambridge, Mass.: Harvard University Press, 1983.

Brenner, Robert. "Agrarian Class Structure and Economic Development in Pre-Industrial Europe." *Past and Present* 70 (1976): 30–75.

Carver, Terrell. *A Marx Dictionary*. Totowa, N.J.: Barnes & Noble Books, 1987.

Cobban, Alfred. *The Social Interpretation of the French Revolution*. Cambridge: Cambridge University Press, 1964.

Cohen, G. A. *Karl Marx's Theory of History: A Defence*. Princeton: Princeton University Press, 1978.

Cohen, Jon S. "The Achievement of Economic History: The Marxist School." *Journal of Economic History* 38 (1978): 29–57.

Comninel, George C. *Rethinking the French Revolution: Marxism and the Revisionist Challenge*. New York: Verso, 1987.

Daniels, Robert V. "Marxian Theories of Historical Dynamics." In Werner J. Cahnman and Alvin Boskoff, eds., *Sociology and History: Theory and Research*. Glencoe: Free Press, 1964.

Dobb, Maurice. *Studies in the Development of Capitalism.* New York: International Publishers, 1984 (first published 1947).

Doyle, William. *Origins of the French Revolution.* New York: Oxford University Press, 1980.

Ellis, G. "The 'Marxist Interpretation' of the French Revolution." *English Historical Review* 93 (1978): 353–376.

Elster, Jon. *Making Sense of Marx.* Cambridge: Cambridge University Press, 1985.

Engels, Friedrich. *The Origin of the Family, Private Property and the State.* Chicago: Kerr, 1902.

Foster-Carter, Aidan. "The Modes of Production Controversy." *New Left Review* 107 (1978): 47–77.

Giddens, Anthony. *A Contemporary Critique of Historical Materialism.* Berkeley: University of California Press, 1981.

Goodman, David, and Michael Redcliffe. *From Peasant to Proletarian: Capitalist Development and Agrarian Transitions.* New York: St. Martin's Press, 1982.

Gottlieb, Roger S. "Feudalism and Historical Materialism: A Critique and a Synthesis." *Science and Society* 48 (1984): 1–37.

Greenlaw, Ralph W., ed. *The Social Origins of the French Revolution: The Debate on the Role of the Middle Classes.* Lexington: D. C. Heath, 1975.

Heller, Henry. "The Transition Debate in Historical Perspective." *Science and Society* 49 (1985): 208–213.

Hill, Christopher. *The English Revolution, 1640.* London: Lawrence & Wishart, 1955.

———. *Intellectual Origins of the English Revolution.* Oxford: Clarendon Press, 1965.

Hilton, R. H. *Bond Men Made Free: Medieval Peasant Movements and the English Rising of 1381.* London: Methuen, 1973.

———. "Capitalism—What's in a Name?" *Past and Present* 1 (1952): 32–43.

———. "A Crisis of Feudalism." *Past and Present* 80 (1978): 3–19.

———. *The English Peasantry in the Later Middle Ages.* Oxford: Clarendon Press, 1975.

Hilton, R. H., and T. H. Aston, eds. *The English Rising of 1381.* New York: Cambridge University Press, 1984.

Hilton, R. H., et al. *The Transition from Feudalism to Capitalism.* London: Verso, 1978.

Hindess, Barry, and Paul Q. Hirst. *Pre-Capitalist Modes of Production.* London: Routledge and Kegan Paul, 1975.

Johnson, Richard. "Edward Thompson, Eugene Genovese, and Socialist-Humanist History." *History Workshop* 6 (1978): 79–100.

Kaye, Harvey J. *The British Marxist Historians: An Introductory Analysis.* New York: Polity Press, 1984.

Kosminsky, E. "The Evolution of Feudal Rent in England from the XIth to the XVth Centuries." *Past and Present* 7 (1955): 13–36.

Kula, Witold. *An Economic Theory of the Feudal System: Towards a Model of the Polish Economy, 1500–1800.* London: New Left Books, 1976.

Laski, Harold J. *Harold J. Laski on the Communist Manifesto: An Introduction.* New York: Pantheon, 1967.

Lefebvre, Georges. *The Coming of the French Revolution, 1789,* trans. R. R. Palmer. Princeton: Princeton University Press, 1947.

Lichtheim, George. *Marxism.* London: Routledge and Kegan Paul, 1971.

Martin, John E. *Feudalism to Capitalism: Peasant and Landlord in English Agrarian Development.* Atlantic Highlands, N.J.: Humanities Press, 1983.

Marx, Karl. *Capital: A Critique of Political Economy,* 3 vols. Trans. Samuel Moore and Edward Areling, ed. Friedrich Engels. Chicago: Kerr, 1906–1909.

———. *A Contribution to the Critique of Political Economy,* trans. N. I. Stone. New York: International Library, 1904.

McLellan, David. *Karl Marx: His Life and Thought.* New York: Harper and Row, 1973.

Merrington, J. "Town and Country in the Transition to Capitalism." *New Left Review* 93 (1975): 71–92.

Richardson, R. C. *The Debate on the English Revolution.* London: Methuen, 1977.

Stone, Lawrence. "The Bourgeois Revolution of Seventeenth-Century England Revisited." *Past and Present* 109 (1985): 44–54.

Taylor, George V. "Non-Capitalist Wealth and the French Revolution," *American Historical Review* 72 (1967): 486–496.

Therborn, Goran. *Science, Class and Society: On the Formation of Sociology and Historical Materialism.* London: New Left Books, 1976.

Thompson, E. P. *The Making of the English Working Class.* New York: Vintage, 1966.

Trevor-Roper, H. R. "The General Crisis of the Seventeenth Century." *Past and Present* 16 (1959): 31–64.

Williams, Raymond. "Base and Superstructure in Marxist Cultural Theory." *New Left Review* 82 (1973): 3–16.

Willigan, Denis J. "Marxist Methodologies of History." *Historical Methods* 17 (1984): 219–228.

Wright, Erik Olin, et al. "The American Class Structure." *American Sociological Review* 47 (1982): 709–726.

Zagorin, Perez. "The Social Interpretation of the English Revolution." *Journal of Economic History* 19 (1959): 376–401.

Zaller, Robert. "What Does the English Revolution Mean? Recent Historiographical Interpretations of Mid-Seventeenth Century England." *Albion* 18 (1987): 617–636.

THE WEBER THESIS, RELIGION, AND HISTORY

Andreski, Stanislav. "Method and Substantive Theory in Max Weber." *British Journal of Sociology* 15 (1964): 1–18.

Ball, Donald W. "Catholics, Calvinists, and Rational Control: Further Explorations in the Weberian Thesis." *Sociological Analysis* 26 (1965): 181–188.

Bendix, Reinhard. *Max Weber: An Intellectual Portrait.* New York: Doubleday, 1960.

Bendix, Reinhard, and Guenther Roth. *Scholarship and Partisanship: Essays on Max Weber.* Berkeley and Los Angeles: University of California Press, 1971.

Bossy, John. *Christianity in the West, 1400–1700.* New York: Oxford University Press, 1985.

Burger, Thomas. *Max Weber's Theory of Concept Formation: History, Laws, and Ideal Types.* Durham: Duke University Press, 1976.

Cahnman, Werner J. "Max Weber and the Methodological Controversy in the Social Sciences." In Werner J. Cahnman and Alvin Boskoff, eds., *Sociology and History: Theory and Research.* Glencoe: Free Press, 1964.

Collins, Randall. *Max Weber: A Skeleton Key.* Beverly Hills: Sage, 1985.

————. *Weberian Sociological Theory.* New York: Cambridge University Press, 1986.

Eisenstadt, S. N. "The Implications of Weber's Sociology of Religion for Understanding Processes of Change in Contemporary Non-European Societies and Civilizations." In C. Y. Glock and P. E. Hammond, eds., *Beyond the Classics? Essays in the Scientific Study of Religion.* New York: Harper and Row, 1973.

————. "Some Reflections on the Significance of Max Weber's Sociology of Religions for the Analysis of Non-European Modernity." *Archives de Sociologie des Religions* 32 (1971): 29–52.

————, ed. *The Protestant Ethic and Modernization: A Comparative View.* New York: Basic Books, 1968.

Fischoff, Ephraim. "The Protestant Ethic and the Spirit of Capitalism—The History of a Controversy." *Social Research* 2 (1944): 53–77.

George, Charles H. "English Calvinist Opinion on Usury, 1600–1640." *Journal of the History of Ideas* 18 (1957): 455–474.

George, Charles H., and Katherine George. *The Protestant Mind of the English Reformation, 1570–1640.* Princeton: Princeton University Press, 1961.

————. "Protestantism and Capitalism in Pre-Revolutionary England." *Church History* 27 (1958): 351–371.

Gerth, H. H., and C. W. Mills. "Introduction: The Man and His Work." In H. H. Gerth and C. W. Mills, eds., *From Max Weber: Essays in Sociology.* London: Routledge and Kegan Paul, 1970.

Giddens, Anthony. *Politics and Sociology in the Thought of Max Weber.* London: Macmillan, 1972.

Green, Robert W., ed. *Protestantism and Capitalism: The Weber Thesis and Its Critics.* Lexington, Mass.: D. C. Heath, 1973.

Hansen, Niles. "The Protestant Ethic as a General Precondition for Economic Development." *Canadian Journal of Economics and Political Science* 29 (1963): 462–474.

Headley, John M. *Luther's View of Church History.* New Haven: Yale University Press, 1963.

Hennis, Wilhelm, ed. *Max Weber, Essays in Reconstruction,* trans. Keith Tribe. Winchester: Unwin Hyman, 1987.

Hill, Christopher. "Protestantism and the Rise of Capitalism." In F. J. Fisher, ed., *Essays in the Economic and Social History of Tudor and Stuart England in Honour of R. H. Tawney.* Cambridge: Cambridge University Press, 1961.

————. "Science, Religion and Society in the Sixteenth and Seventeenth Centuries." *Past and Present* 32 (1965): 110–112.

Hyma, Albert. "Calvinism and Capitalism in the Netherlands, 1555–1700." *Journal of Modern History* 10 (1938): 321–343.

Jedin, Hubert, et al. *History of the Church,* vol. 5, *Reformation and Counter Reformation.* New York: Seabury Press, 1980.

Kalberg, Stephen. "Max Weber's Types of Rationality." *American Journal of Sociology* 85 (1980): 1145–1179.

Kearney, H. F. "Puritanism, Capitalism and the Scientific Revolution." *Past and Present* 28 (1964): 81–101.

Kitch, M. J., ed. *Capitalism and the Reformation*. London: Longman, 1967.

Lachmann, L. M. *The Legacy of Max Weber*. London: Heinemann, 1970.

Little, Lester K. *Religious Poverty and the Profit Economy in Medieval Europe*. Ithaca: Cornell University Press, 1978.

Love, John. "Max Weber and the Theory of Ancient Capitalism." *History and Theory* 25 (1986): 152–172.

Luethy, Herbert. "Once Again: Calvinism and Capitalism." *Encounter* 22 (1964): 26–38.

Mandrou, Robert. "Capitalisme et protestantisme: La science et le mythe." *Revue Historique* 235 (1966): 101–106.

Marshall, Gordon. "The Dark Side of the Weber Thesis: The Case of Scotland." *British Journal of Sociology* 21 (1980): 419–440.

———. *In Search of the Spirit of Capitalism: An Essay on Max Weber's Protestant Ethic Thesis*. New York: Columbia University Press, 1982.

———. *Presbyteries and Profits: Calvinism and the Development of Capitalism in Scotland, 1560–1707*. Oxford: Clarendon Press, 1980.

———. "The Weber Thesis and the Development of Capitalism in Scotland." *Scottish Journal of Sociology* 3 (1979): 173–211.

Mason, S. F. "Science and Religion in Seventeenth Century England." *Past and Present* 3 (1953): 28–44.

McCormack, Thelma. "The Protestant Ethic and the Spirit of Socialism." *British Journal of Sociology* 20 (1969): 266–276.

McNeill, John T. *The History and Character of Calvinism*. New York: Oxford University Press, 1967.

Mitzman, Arthur. *The Iron Cage*. New York: Knopf, 1970.

———. *Sociology and Estrangement: Three Sociologists of Imperial Germany*. New York: Knopf, 1973.

Mommsen, Wolfgang J. "Max Weber as a Critic of Marxism." *Canadian Journal of Sociology* 2 (1977): 373–398.

———. "Max Weber's Political Sociology and His Philosophy of World History." *International Social Science Journal* 17 (1965): 23–45.

Moore, Robert. "History, Economics and Religion: A Review of 'The Max Weber Thesis.' " In Arun Sahay, ed., *Max Weber and Modern Sociology*. London: Routledge and Kegan Paul, 1971.

Nussbaum, Frederick L. *A History of the Economic Institutions of Modern Europe: An Introduction to Der Moderne Kapitalismus of Werner Sombart*. New York: Crofts, 1935.

Otsuka, Hisao. *The Spirit of Capitalism: The Max Weber Thesis in an Economic Historical Perspective*, trans. Masaomi Kondo. Tokyo: Iwanami Shoten, 1982.

Prades, J. A. *La Sociologie de la Religion chez Max Weber*. Louvain: Editions Nauwelaerts, 1969.

Prestwich, Menna, ed. *International Calvinism 1541–1715*. New York: Oxford University Press, 1985.

Rabb, Theodore K. "Puritanism and the Rise of Experimental Science in England." *Cahiers d'Histoire Mondiale* 7 (1962): 46–67.

————. "Religion and the Rise of Modern Science." *Past and Present* 31 (1965): 111–126.

Razzell, Peter. "The Protestant Ethic and the Spirit of Capitalism: A Natural Scientific Critique." *British Journal of Sociology* 28 (1977): 17–37.

Riemersma, J. C. *Religious Factors in Early Dutch Capitalism, 1550–1650.* The Hague: Mouton, 1967.

Rotenberg, Mordechai. *Damnation and Deviance: The Protestant Ethic and the Spirit of Failure.* New York: Free Press, 1978.

Roth, Guenther, and Wolfgang Schluchter. *Max Weber's Vision of History.* Berkeley and Los Angeles: University of California Press, 1979.

Samuelsson, Kurt. *Religion and Economic Action.* London: Heinemann, 1961.

Schluchter, Wolfgang. "The Paradox of Rationalization: On the Relation of Ethics and the World." In G. Roth and W. Schluchter, eds., *Max Weber's Vision of History: Ethics and Methods.* Berkeley and Los Angeles: University of California Press, 1979.

————. *The Rise of Western Rationalism: Max Weber's Developmental History,* trans. with introduction by Guenther Roth. Berkeley and Los Angeles: University of California Press, 1981.

See, Henri. "Dans quelle mesure Puritains et Juifs ont-ils contribué aux progrès du capitalisme moderne?" *Revue Historique* 155 (1927): 57–68.

Sprinzak, Ehud. "Weber's Thesis as an Historical Explanation." *History and Theory* 11 (1972): 294–320.

Strauss, Gerald. *Luther's House of Learning: Indoctrination of the Young in the German Reformation.* Baltimore: Johns Hopkins University Press, 1978.

Sutton, F. X. "The Social and Economic Philosophy of Werner Sombart: The Sociology of Capitalism." In Harry Elmer Barnes, ed., *An Introduction to the History of Sociology.* Chicago: University of Chicago Press, 1965.

Tawney, R. H. *Religion and the Rise of Capitalism.* Harmondsworth: Penguin, 1972 (first published 1926).

Tenbruck, Friedrich H. "The Problem of Thematic Unity in the Works of Max Weber." *British Journal of Sociology* 31 (1980): 316–351.

Turner, Bryan S. *Weber and Islam.* London: Routledge and Kegan Paul, 1974.

van der Sprenkel, Otto B. "Max Weber on China." *History and Theory* 3 (1963): 348–370.

Wagner, Helmut. "The Protestant Ethic: A Mid-Twentieth Century View." *Sociological Analysis* 25 (1964): 34–40.

Warner, R. Stephen. "The Role of Religious Ideas and the Use of Models in Max Weber's Comparative Studies of Non-Capitalist Societies." *Journal of Economic History* 30 (1970): 74–99.

Weber, Marianne. *Max Weber: A Biography.* London: John Wiley, 1975 (first published 1926).

Weber, Max. *Ancient Judaism,* trans. Hans H. Gerth and Don Martindale. Glencoe: Free Press, 1952 (originally published in *Archiv für Sozialwissenschaft und Sozialforschung,* 1917–1918).

————. "Anticritical Last Word on 'The Spirit of Capitalism,' by Max Weber." *American Journal of Sociology* 83 (1978): 1105–1131 (first published 1910).

———. *Economy and Society*, 3 vols., trans. Ephraim Fischoff and others, eds. Guenter Roth and Claus Wittich. New York: Bedminster Press, 1968 (first published 1922).

———. *The Methodology of the Social Sciences*, trans. Edward A. Shils and Henry A. Finch. New York: Free Press, 1969 (previously published 1904, 1906, 1917–1918).

———. *The Protestant Ethic and the Spirit of Capitalism*, trans. Talcott Parsons. New York: Scribner, 1958 (first published 1904–1905).

———. *The Religion of China: Confucianism and Taoism*, trans. Hans H. Gerth. New York: Free Press, 1951 (originally published in *Archiv für Sozialwissenschaft und Sozialforschung*, 1916).

———. *The Religion of India: The Sociology of Hinduism and Buddhism*, trans. Hans H. Gerth and Don Martindale. Glencoe: Free Press, 1958 (originally published in *Archiv für Sozialwissenschaft und Sozialforschung*, 1916–1917).

DEPENDENCY AND WORLD-SYSTEMS

Abu-Lughod, Janet L. *Before European Hegemony: The World System, A.D. 1250–1350*. New York: Oxford University Press, 1989.

Amin, Samir. *Unequal Development: An Essay on the Social Formation of Peripheral Capitalism*. New York: Monthly Review Press, 1976.

Arrighi, G., Terence Hopkins, and Immanuel Wallerstein. "Rethinking the Concepts of Class and Status-Group in a World-System Perspective." *Review* 6 (1983): 283–304.

Blomstrom, Magnus, and Bjorn Hettne. *Development Theory in Transition: The Dependency Debate and Beyond—Third World Responses*. London: Zed, 1984.

Bousquet, Nicole. "Esquisse d'une théorie de l'altérnance de périodes de concurrence et d'hégémonie au centre de l'économie-monde capitaliste." *Review* 2 (1979): 501–517.

Brenner, Robert. "The Origins of Capitalist Development: A Critique of Neo-Smithian Marxism." *New Left Review* 104 (1977): 25–92.

Cardoso, Fernando H. "The Consumption of Dependency Theory in the United States." *Latin American Research Review* 12 (1977): 7–24.

Cardoso, Fernando H., and Enzo Faletto. *Dependency and Development in Latin America*. Berkeley: University of California Press, 1979.

Chase-Dunn, C. *Global Formation: Structures of the World-Economy*. Oxford: Blackwell, 1989.

Chilcote, Roland H. "Dependency: A Critical Synthesis of the Literature." *Latin American Perspectives* 1 (1974): 3–29.

———, ed. *Dependency and Marxism: Toward a Resolution of the Debate*. Boulder: Westview, 1982.

Chirot, Daniel, and Thomas D. Hall. "World-System Theory." *Annual Review of Sociology* 8 (1982): 81–106.

Dodgshon, Robert A. "The Modern World-System: A Spatial Perspective." *Peasant Studies* 6 (1977): 8–19.

DuPlessis, Robert S. "The Partial Transition to World-Systems Analysis in Early Modern European History." *Radical History Review* 39 (1987): 22–27.

Flynn, Dennis. "Early Capitalism Despite New World Bullion: An Anti-Wallerstein Interpretation of Imperial Spain." Paper presented at meeting of Social Science Historical Association, Washington, D.C. 1983.

Foster-Carter, Aiden. "Neo-Marxist Approaches to Development and Underdevelopment." *Journal of Contemporary Asia* 3 (1973): 7–33.

Frank, André Gunder. *Capitalism and Underdevelopment in Latin America: Historical Studies of Chili and Brazil.* New York: Monthly Review Press, 1967.

―――. "Dependence is Dead, Long Live Dependence and the Class Struggle." *Latin American Perspectives* 1 (1974): 87–106.

―――. *Dependent Accumulation and Underdevelopment.* London: Macmillan, 1978.

―――. *Latin America: Underdevelopment or Revolution.* New York and London: Monthly Review Press, 1969.

―――. *Lumpenbourgeoisie: Lumpendevelopment, Dependence, Class and Politics in Latin America.* New York: Monthly Review Press, 1972.

―――. *Sociology of Development and Underdevelopment of Sociology.* London: Pluto Press, 1971.

―――. *World Accumulation, 1492–1789.* London: Macmillan, 1978.

Garst, Daniel. "Wallerstein and His Critics." *Theory and Society* 14 (1985): 445–468.

Goldfrank, Walter L., ed. *The World-System of Capitalism: Past and Present.* Beverly Hills: Sage, 1979.

Gulap, Haldun. "Frank and Wallerstein Revisited: A Contribution to Brenner's Critique." *Journal of Contemporary Asia* 11 (1981): 169–188.

Hopkins, Terence, and Immanuel Wallerstein, eds. *Process of the World-System.* Beverly Hills: Sage, 1980.

―――. *World-System Analysis.* Beverly Hills: Sage, 1982.

Inikori, Joseph. *Forced Migration: The Impact of the Export Slave Trade on African Societies.* New York: Africana, 1982.

Jewsiewicki, Bogumil. "The African Prism of Immanuel Wallerstein." *Radical History Review* 39 (1987): 50–68.

Kaplan, Barbara H. *Social Change in the Capitalist World-Economy.* Beverly Hills: Sage, 1978.

Kay, Geoffrey. *Development and Underdevelopment: A Marxist Analysis.* London: Macmillan, 1975.

Leys, Colin. "Underdevelopment and Dependency: Critical Notes." *Journal of Contemporary Asia* 7 (1977): 92–107.

Palma, Gabriel. "Dependency: A Formal Theory of Underdevelopment or a Methodology for the Analysis of Concrete Situations of Underdevelopment." *World Development* 6 (1978): 881–894.

Petras, James. "Dependency and World-System Theory: A Critique and New Directions." In Ronald H. Chilcote, ed., *Dependency and Marxism: Toward a Resolution of the Debate.* Boulder: Westview, 1982.

Prebisch, R. *The Economic Development of Latin America and Its Principal Problems.* New York: United Nations, 1950.

Ragin, Charles, and Daniel Chirot. "The World System of Immanuel Wallerstein: Sociology and Politics as History." In Theda Skocpol, ed., *Vision and*

Method in Historical Sociology. Cambridge: Cambridge University Press, 1984.

Rodney, Walter. *How Europe Underdeveloped Africa.* London and Dar es Salaam: Bogle-L'Ouverture Publications, 1972.

Seers, Dudley. *Dependency Theory: A Critical Reassessment.* London: Frances Printer, 1981.

Skocpol, Theda. "Wallerstein's World Capitalist System: A Theoretical and Historical Critique." *American Journal of Sociology* 82 (1977): 1075–1090.

Smith, Alan. "Where Was the Periphery? The Wider World and the Core of the World-Economy." *Radical History Review* 39 (1987): 28–49.

So, Alvin Y. *Social Change and Development: Modernization, Dependency, and World-System Theories.* Newbury Park, Calif.: Sage, 1990.

Stern, Steve J. "Feudalism, Capitalism, and the World-System in the Perspective of Latin America and the Caribbean." *American Historical Review* 93 (1988): 829–872.

Taylor, John G. *From Modernization to Modes of Production: A Critique of the Sociologies of Development and Underdevelopment.* Atlantic Highlands, N.J.: Humanities Press, 1979.

Thompson, William R. *Contending Approaches to World-System Analysis.* Beverly Hills: Sage, 1983.

Trimberger, Ellen Kay. "World Systems Analysis: The Problem of Unequal Development." *Theory and Society* 8 (1979): 101–126.

Wallerstein, Immanuel. *The Capitalist World-Economy.* New York: Cambridge University Press, 1979.

———. *The Modern World-System I: Capitalist Agriculture and the Origins of the European World-Economy in the Sixteenth Century.* New York: Academic Press, 1974.

———. *The Modern World-System II: Mercantilism and the Consolidation of the European World-Economy, 1600–1750.* New York: Academic Press, 1980.

———. *The Modern World-System III: The Second Era of Great Expansion of the Capitalist World-Economy, 1730–1840s.* New York: Academic Press, 1989.

———. *The Politics of the Capitalist World-Economy.* Cambridge: Cambridge University Press, 1984.

———. "Underdevelopment Phase-B: Effect of the Seventeenth-Century Stagnation on Core and Periphery of the European World-Economy." In Walter L. Goldfrank, ed. *The World-System of Capitalism: Past and Present.* Beverly Hills: Sage, 1979.

———. "World-System Analysis." In Anthony Giddens and Jonathan H. Turner, eds., *Social Theory Today.* Stanford: Stanford University Press, 1987.

Weaver, James, and Marguerite Berger. "The Marxist Critique of Dependency Theory: An Introduction." In Charles K. Wilber, ed., *The Political Economy of Development and Underdevelopment.* New York: Random House, 1984.

Worsley, Peter. "One World or Three? A Critique of the World-System Theory of Immanuel Wallerstein." In David Held, ed., *State and Societies.* New York: New York University Press, 1982.

ENVIRONMENTAL HISTORY

Bailes, Kendall E., ed. *Environmental History: Critical Issues in Comparative Perspective*. Lanham, Md.: University Press of America, 1985.

Bennett, John W. *The Ecological Transition: Cultural Anthropology and Human Adaptation*. Elmsford, N.Y.: Pergamon, 1976.

Bertrand, Georges. "Pour une histoire écologique de la France rurale." In Georges Duby, ed., *Histoire de la France rurale*. Paris: Seuil, 1975.

Bilsky, Lester J., ed. *Historical Ecology: Essays on Environment and Social Change*. Port Washington, N.Y.: Kennikat Press, 1980.

Blouet, Brian, and Frederick C. Luebke, eds. *The Great Plains: Environment and Culture*. Lincoln: University of Nebraska Press, 1979.

Bolton, Geoffrey. *Spoils and Spoilers: Australians and Their Environment, 1788–1980*. Sydney: Allen & Unwin, 1981.

Burton, Ian, Robert W. Kates, and Gilbert F. White. *The Environment as Hazard*. New York: Oxford University Press, 1978.

Cantor, Leonard. *The Changing English Countryside 1400–1700*. New York: Routledge, 1987.

Carson, Rachel. *Silent Spring*. Boston: Houghton Mifflin, 1962.

Clark, Andrew H. *The Invasion of New Zealand by People, Plants, and Animals: The South Island*. New Brunswick, N.J.: Rutgers University Press, 1949.

Cronon, William. *Changes in the Land: Indians, Colonists, and the Ecology of New England*. New York: Hill & Wang, 1983.

Crosby, Alfred W. *The Columbian Exchange: Biological and Cultural Consequences of 1492*. Westport, Conn.: Greenwood, 1972.

————. *Ecological Imperialism: The Biological Expansion of Europe, 900–1900*. New York: Cambridge University Press, 1986.

————. "Virgin Soil Epidemics as a Factor in the Aboriginal Depopulation in America." *William and Mary Quarterly* 33 (1976): 289–299.

Ekirch, Arthur A., Jr. *Man and Nature in America*. New York: Columbia University Press, 1963.

Ellen, Roy F. *Environment, Subsistence and System: The Ecology of Small-Scale Social Formations*. Cambridge: Cambridge University Press, 1982.

Elton, Charles. *The Ecology of Invasions by Animals and Plants*. London: Methuen, 1958.

Fleure, H. J., and Margaret Davies. *A Natural History of Man in Britain: Conceived as a Study of Changing Relations between Men and Environments*. London: Collins, 1970.

Geertz, Clifford. *Agricultural Involution: The Process of Ecological Change in Indonesia*. Berkeley and Los Angeles: University of California Press, 1971.

Glacken, Clarence. *Traces on the Rhodian Shore: Nature and Culture in Western Thought from Ancient Times to the End of the Eighteenth Century*. Berkeley and Los Angeles: University of California Press, 1967.

Goudie, Andrew. *The Human Impact on the Natural Environment*, 2d ed. Cambridge, Mass.: MIT Press, 1986.

Hancock, William Keith. *Discovering Monaro: A Study of Man's Impact on His Environment*. Cambridge: Cambridge University Press, 1972.

Harris, Marvin. *Cultural Materialism: The Struggle for a Science of Culture.* New York: Random House, 1979.

Herlihy, David. "Ecological Conditions and Demographic Change." In Richard L. De Molen, ed., *One Thousand Years: Western Europe in the Middle Ages.* Boston: Houghton Mifflin, 1974.

Hoskins, W. G. *The Making of the English Landscape.* London: Hodder and Stoughton, 1977.

Hughes, J. Donald. *Ecology in Ancient Civilizations.* Albuquerque: University of New Mexico Press, 1975.

Jacobs, Wilbur. "The Great Despoliation: Environmental Themes in American Frontier History." *Pacific Historical Review* 47 (1978): 1–26.

Jones, E. L. "Disasters and Economic Differentiation across Eurasia: A Reply." *Journal of Economic History* 45 (1985): 675–682.

———. "Environment, Agriculture, and Industrialization in Europe." *Agricultural History* 51 (1977): 491–502.

———. "The Environment and the Economy." In Peter Burke, ed., *The New Cambridge Modern History:* vol. 13, *Companion Volume.* Cambridge: Cambridge University Press, 1979.

———. *The European Miracle: Environments, Economies, and Geopolitics in the History of Europe and Asia.* Cambridge: Cambridge University Press, 1981.

Kjekshus, Helge. *Ecology Control and Economic Development in East African History: The Case of Tanganyika, 1850–1950.* Berkeley and Los Angeles: University of California Press, 1977.

Lauwerys, J. A. *Man's Impact on Nature.* London: Aldus Books, 1969.

Leeds, Anthony, and Andrew P. Vayda, eds. *Man, Culture, and Animals: The Role of Animals in Human Ecological Adjustments.* Washington, D.C.: American Association for the Advancement of Science, 1965.

Levins, Richard. *Evolution in Changing Environments.* Princeton: Princeton University Press, 1968.

Loomis, R. S. "Ecological Dimensions of Medieval Agrarian Systems: An Ecologist Responds." *Agricultural History* 52 (1978): 478–483.

Lovelock, J. E. *Gaia: A New Look at Life on Earth.* New York: Oxford University Press, 1979.

McNeill, William H. *The Human Condition: An Ecological Perspective.* Princeton: Princeton University Press, 1980.

Meinig, D. W. *The Shaping of America: A Geographical Perspective on 500 Years of History:* vol. 1, *Atlantic America: 1492–1800.* New Haven: Yale University Press, 1986.

Moran, Emilio F. *Human Adaptability: An Introduction to Ecological Anthropology.* North Scituate, Mass.: Duxbury Press, 1979.

Nash, Roderick. "Environmental History." In Herbert J. Bass, ed., *The State of American History.* Chicago: Quadrangle Press, 1970.

Opie, John. "Frontier History in Environmental Perspective." In Jerome O. Steffen, ed., *The American West: New Perspectives, New Dimensions.* Norman: University of Oklahoma Press, 1979.

———. *Wilderness and the American Mind,* 3d ed. New Haven: Yale University Press, 1982.

Osborn, Fairfield. *Our Plundered Planet.* Boston: Little, Brown, 1948.

Parsons, Howard L., ed. *Marx and Engels on Ecology*. Westport, Conn.: Greenwood, 1977.

Passmore, John. *Man's Responsibility for Nature: Ecological Problems and Western Traditions*. New York: Charles Scribners' Sons, 1974.

Petulla, Joseph. *American Environmental History: The Exploitation and Conservation of Natural Resources*. San Francisco: Boyd & Fraser, 1977.

Post, J. D. *Food Shortage, Climatic Variability, and Epidemic Disease in Preindustrial Europe: The Mortality Peak in the Early 1740s*. Ithaca: Cornell University Press, 1985.

————. *The Last Great Subsistence Crisis in the Western World*. Baltimore: Johns Hopkins University Press, 1977.

Richards, John F. "World Environmental History and Economic Development." In William C. Clark and R. E. Munn, eds., *Sustainable Development of the Biosphere*. Cambridge: Cambridge University Press, 1986.

Roll, Eric C. *They All Ran Wild: The Story of Pests on the Land in Australia*. Sydney: Angus & Robertson, 1969.

Russell, W. M. S. *Man, Nature and History: Controlling the Environment*. Garden City: Natural History Press, 1967.

Salaman, Redliffe (with revisions and new introduction by J. G. Hawkins). *The History and Social Influence of the Potato*. New York: Cambridge University Press, 1985.

Sauer, Carl O. *Seventeenth-Century North America*. Berkeley: Turtle Island, 1980.

————. *Sixteenth-Century North America: The Land and People as Seen by the Europeans*. Berkeley and Los Angeles: University of California Press, 1971.

Seymour, John, and Herbert Girandet. *Far from Paradise: The Story of Man's Impact on the Environment*. London: British Broadcasting Corporation, 1986.

Steward, Julian. *The Theory of Culture Change: The Methodology of Multilinear Evolution*. Urbana: University of Illinois, 1955.

Stretton, Hugh. *Capitalism, Socialism, and the Environment*. Cambridge: Cambridge University Press, 1976.

TeBrake, William R. "Air Pollution and Fuel Crises in Preindustrial London, 1250–1650." *Technology and Culture* 16 (1975): 337–359.

————. *Medieval Frontier: Culture and Ecology in Rijnland*. College Station: Texas A & M University Press, 1985.

Viola, Herman J., and Carolyn Margolis, eds. *Seeds of Change: A Quincentennial Commemoration*. Washington, D.C.: Smithsonian Institution, 1991.

Vogt, William. *Road to Survival*. New York: Sloane Associates, 1948.

Walters, A. Harry. *Ecology, Food and Civilisation: An Ecological History of Human Society*. London: Charles Knight, 1973.

Ward, Barbara, and René Dubos. *Only One Earth: The Care and Maintenance of a Small Planet*. New York: Norton, 1972.

Weiner, Douglas R. *Models of Nature: Conservation, Ecology, and Cultural Revolution*. Bloomington: Indiana University Press, 1988.

White, Lynn, Jr. "The Historic Roots of Our Ecologic Crisis." *Science* 155 (1967): 1202–1207.

White, Richard. "American Environmental History: The Development of a New Historical Field." *Pacific Historical Review* 54 (1985): 297–335.

Wilkinson, Richard G. *Poverty and Progress: An Ecological Perspective on Economic Development.* New York: Praeger, 1973.

Worster, Donald. *Dust Bowl: The Southern Plains in the 1930s.* New York: Oxford University Press, 1977.

———. *Nature's Economy: A History of Ecological Ideas,* 2d ed. New York: Cambridge University Press, 1985.

———, ed. *The Ends of the Earth: Perspectives on Modern Environmental History.* New York: Cambridge University Press, 1988.

CLIMATE

Anderson, J. L. "Climatic Change in European Economic History." *Research in Economic History* 6 (1981): 1–34.

Bryson, Reid A., and Christine Padoch. "On the Climates of History." *Journal of Interdisciplinary History* 10 (1980): 583–597.

Bryson, Reid A., and Thomas J. Murray. *Climates of Hunger: Mankind and the World's Changing Weather.* Madison: University of Wisconsin Press, 1977.

Claxton, Robert H. "Climate and History: From Speculation to Systematic Study." *The Historian* 45 (1985): 220–236.

———. "Climatic and Human History in Europe and Latin America: An Opportunity for Comparative Study." *Climatic Change* 1 (1978): 195–203.

de Vries, Jan. "Measuring the Impact of Climate on History: The Search for Appropriate Methodologies." *Journal of Interdisciplinary History* 10 (1980): 599–630.

Herlihy, David. "Climate and Documentary Sources: A Comment." *Journal of Interdisciplinary History* 10 (1980): 713–717.

Huntington, E. *Civilisation and Climate.* New Haven: Yale University Press, 1915.

Jones, E. L. *Seasons and Prices: The Role of the Weather in English Agricultural History.* London: Allen & Unwin, 1964.

Kates, Robert W., Jesse H. Ausubel, and Mimi Berberian, eds. *Climate Impact Assessment: Studies of the Interaction of Climate and Society.* New York: John Wiley and Sons, 1985.

Ladurie, Emmanuel Le Roy. "Histoire et climat." *Annales, E.S.C.* 14 (1959): 3–34, translated as "History and Climate." In Peter Burke, ed., *Economy and Society in Early Modern Europe.* New York: Harper and Row, 1972.

———. *Times of Feast, Times of Famine: A History of Climate since the Year 1000,* trans. Barbara Bray. Garden City: Doubleday, 1971.

Lamb, H. H. *Climate, History and the Modern World.* London: Methuen, 1982.

Lamb, H. H., and M. J. Ingram. "Climate and History." *Past and Present* 89 (1980): 136–141.

———. *Climate Present, Past and Future:* vol. 2, *Climatic History and the Future.* London: Methuen, 1977.

Lambert, L. Don. "The Role of Climate in the Economic Development of Nations." *Land Economics* 47 (1971): 339–344.

Parry, M. L. *Climatic Change, Agriculture and Settlement.* Folkestone: William Dawson & Sons, 1978.

Pfister, C. "Climate and Economy in Eighteenth Century Switzerland." *Journal of Interdisciplinary History* 9 (1978): 223–243.

————. "The Little Ice Age: Thermal and Wetness Indices for Central Europe." *Journal of Interdisciplinary History* 10 (1980): 665–696.

Post, John D. "Climatic Change and Historical Discontinuity." *Journal of Interdisciplinary History* 14 (1983): 153–160.

————. "The Impact of Climate on Political, Social and Economic Change: A Comment." *Journal of Interdisciplinary History* 10 (1980): 719–723.

————. "Meteorological Historiography." *Journal of Interdisciplinary History* 3 (1973): 721–732.

Rabb, Theodore K., and Robert I. Rotberg, eds. *Climate and History: Studies in Interdisciplinary History.* Princeton: Princeton University Press, 1981.

Titow, J. Z. "Evidence of Weather in the Account Rolls of the Bishopric of Winchester, 1209–1350." *Economic History Review,* 2d ser., 12 (1960): 360–407.

Utterström, Gustaf. "Climatic Fluctuations and Population in Early Modern History." *Scandinavian Economic History Review* 3 (1955): 3–47.

Wrigley, T. M. L., M. J. Ingram, and G. Farmer, eds. *Climate and History: Studies in Past Climates and Their Impact on Man.* Cambridge: Cambridge University Press, 1981.

DISEASE

Alexander, John T. *Bubonic Plague in Early Modern Russia: Public Health and Urban Disaster.* Baltimore: Johns Hopkins University Press, 1980.

Appleby, Andrew B. "The Disappearance of Plague: A Continuing Puzzle." *Economic History Review,* 2d ser., 33 (1980): 161–173.

————. "Epidemics and Famine in the Little Ice Age." *Journal of Interdisciplinary History* 10 (1980): 643–663.

————. "Famine, Mortality, and Epidemic Disease: A Comment." *Economic History Review,* 2d ser., 30 (1977): 508–512.

Bean, J. M. W. "The Black Death: The Crisis and its Social and Economic Consequences." In Daniel Williman, ed., *The Black Death: The Impact of the Fourteenth Century Plague.* Binghamton: Center for Medieval and Early Renaissance Studies, 1982.

Biraben, J. N. "Current Medical and Epidemiological Views of Plague." In *The Plague Reconsidered: A New Look at Its Origins and Effects in Sixteenth and Seventeenth Century England.* Cambridge: Cambridge Group for the History of Population and Social Structure, 1977.

————. *Les Hommes et la peste en France et dans les pays européens et méditerranéens,* 2 vols. Paris: Mouton, 1975.

Biraben, J. N., and J. Le Goff. "La Peste du haut moyen age." *Annales E.S.C.* 24 (1969): 1484–1510.

————. "The Plague in the Early Middle Ages." In R. Foster and O. Ranum, eds., *Biology of Man in History.* Baltimore: Johns Hopkins University Press, 1975.

Bridbury, A. R. "The Black Death." *Economic History Review,* 2d ser., 26 (1973): 577–592.

Cipolla, C. M. *Public Health and the Medical Profession in the Renaissance*. Cambridge: Cambridge University Press, 1976.

Clarkson, Leslie. *Death, Disease and Famine in Pre-Industrial England*. Dublin: Gill & Macmillan, 1975.

Courtenay, William J. "The Effect of the Black Death on English Higher Education." *Speculum* 60 (1980): 696–714.

Dols, Michael W. "Al-Manbijti's 'Report of the Plague': A Treatise on the Plague of 764–65/1362–64 in the Middle East." In Daniel Williman, ed., *The Black Death: The Impact of the Fourteenth-Century Plague*. Binghamton: Center for Medieval and Early Renaissance Studies, 1982.

———. *The Black Death in the Middle East*. Princeton: Princeton University Press, 1977.

Evans, Richard J. "Epidemics and Revolutions: Cholera in Nineteenth Century Europe." *Past and Present* 120 (1988): 123–147.

Flinn, M. W. "Plague in Europe and the Mediteranean Countries." *Journal of European Economic History* 8 (1979): 131–148.

Gottfried, Robert S. *The Black Death: Natural and Human Disaster in Medieval Europe*. New York: Free Press, 1983.

———. *Epidemic Disease in Fifteenth Century England: The Medical Response and the Demographic Consequences*. New Brunswick, N.J.: Rutgers University Press, 1978.

———. "Population, Plague, and the Sweating Sickness: Demographic Movements in Late Fifteenth Century England." *Journal of British Studies* 15 (1977): 12–37.

Hackett, L. W. *Malaria in Europe: An Ecological Study*. Oxford: Oxford University Press, 1937.

Hirst, L. Fabian. *The Conquest of Plague: A Study in the Development of Epidemiology*. Oxford: Clarendon Press, 1953.

Hopkins, Donald. *Princes and Peasants: Smallpox in History*. Chicago: University of Chicago Press, 1983.

Howe, George Melvyn. *Man, Environment and Disease in Britain: A Medical Geography of Britain through the Ages*. Newton Abbot: David & Charles, 1972.

Kahan, Arcadius. "Social Aspects of the Plague Epidemics in Eighteenth-Century Russia." *Economic Development and Cultural Change* 27 (1979): 255–266.

McNeill, W. H. *Plagues and Peoples*. Garden City: Anchor Press/Doubleday, 1976.

Mullett, Charles Frederic. *The Bubonic Plague in England: An Essay in the History of Preventive Medicine*. Lexington: University of Kentucky Press, 1956.

Norris, John. "East or West? The Geographic Origins of the Black Death." *Bulletin of the History of Medicine* 51 (1977): 1–24.

Patterson, K. David. *Pandemic Influenza 1700–1900: A Study in Historical Epidemiology*. Totowa, N.J.: Rowan and Littlefield, 1986.

Post, J. D. "Famine, Mortality, and Epidemic Disease in the Process of Modernization." *Economic History Review*, 2d ser., 29 (1976): 14–37.

Riley, James C. "Insects and the European Mortality Decline." *American Historical Review* 91 (1986): 833–858.

Shrewsbury, J. F. D. *History of Bubonic Plague in the British Isles*. Cambridge: Cambridge University Press, 1970.

Slack, Paul. "The Disappearance of the Plague: An Alternative View." *Economic History Review,* 2d ser., 34 (1981): 469–476.

Twigg, Graham. *The Black Death: A Biological Re-Appraisal.* New York: Schocken, 1984.

Zinsser, Hans. *Rats, Lice, and History.* Boston: Little, Brown, 1935.

Index

D 16 .G78 1993

Green, William A., 1935-

History, historians, and tl
dynamics of change

D 16 .G78 1993

Green, William A., 1935-

History, historians, and tl
dynamics of change

DEC 16 1993   DEMCO